Enjoy this "Tour" of God's Land - Israel.

Let's go there!

In Christ,

Bob C. Ross

Phil 1:21

DISCOVER ISRAEL

AN ILLUSTRATED GUIDE

An Overview of Israel's Geographical Areas,
Mountains, Rivers, Valleys, Cities,
Biblical, Historical and Archaeological Sites

Extensive Historical and Biblical Details,
Scripture References for each Location, Study Maps,
Including Bible Prophecies Pointing to God's Faithfulness

A Foundation for Understanding Israeli/Arab
Conflicts and Israel's Relationships with her Neighbors.

DISCOVER ISRAEL MINISTRIES
DALLAS TEXAS • USA

Discover Israel, First Edition.
Questions about usage should be directed to Bob Ross at
www.discoverisraelministries.com

ISBN 978-0-9905109-0-1

PRINTED IN THE UNITED STATES OF AMERICA

Dedicated to my Wonderful Wife

Barbara Craig Ross

Barbara has journeyed with me as we grew in our love for God,
His Land, Israel and His People.
Our six decades together have been thrilling and never dull.
Without her, ***Discover Israel*** would not have come to fruition.
She has been an incredible help-meet, challenging me to new heights.
My Love, you are worthy!

"An excellent wife...her worth is far above jewels...
The heart of her husband trusts in her,
She does him good...all the days of her life.
Many daughters have done nobly, but you excel them all...
A woman who fears the Lord, she shall be praised..."
(Proverbs 31:10-12, 29,30)

Also
Dedicated to our Incredible Children -
Randall, Michael, Sherri and Terri

CONTENTS

DIVISION OF ISRAEL BY GEOGRAPHICAL AREAS

JERUSALEM

GEOGRAPHICAL AREAS CONTINUED

PROPHECY AND ISRAEL

GOD'S PROMISES AND PROPHECIES CONCERNING ISRAEL

JOSHUA II • WHOSE LAND TODAY? THE JEWS OR THE ARABS? AN HISTORICAL STUDY OF PROMISES, CLAIMS, AND RECENT WARS

MAPS PLUS

ENDORSEMENTS

"I grew-up in Nazareth, Israel, and lived and served in the Middle East for over twenty-five years. My assessment is this; Bob Ross' ***Discover Israel*** *is the best guidebook to the Holy Land, no equal!*

Dr. Ross' work draws on five decades of in-country experience and expertise. He was a first-hand witness to the rebirth of the Jewish people and the in-gathering of the exiles to their Promised Land. The New Israel was but a decade old when he arrived to travel, observe, and study God's Land.

Discover Israel's *presentation is a unique blend of the Biblical, socio-cultural and political-military factors in the region as well as a comprehensive guide to understanding the Land of The Bible. It leaves no stone unturned. If I were to recommend only one book for experiencing and understanding the Land of Israel, this would be the one."*

William (Bill) G. Baker
Lt. Colonel, USAF (Ret.)
Senior Lecturer in Arabic and Middle East Studies
Assistant Director of Middle East Studies
Baylor, University

"With ***Discover Israel*** *you will experience her past, present and future on every page. The phrase, 'a picture is worth a thousand words' is especially true of this beautifully illustrated volume.*

For any Israeli guide, tour-host, fellow traveler, or 'arm chair' student (who can never go to Israel), this book sets the stage and greatly enhances the study of God's Land and His Word.

Thanks to my good friend, Bob Ross, you can gain Biblical, historical, and cultural perspective on the promises God made to Abraham and his descendants."

Dr. Gene A. Getz
Professor, Pastor, Author
President, **Center for Church Renewal**

*"****Discover Israel*** *is absolutely the best publication for a Holy Land traveler I have seen. It is a personal "guide" for anyone who wants to take a "virtual reality tour" of Israel, whether at home or in a classroom.*

The Biblical, historical, and archaeological narrative is accurately and masterfully woven into each geographical region and site. It is a seminary class in a book with breathtaking photography.

I will make this book a requirement for all my future tour groups to Israel. I know of nothing comparable!"

Jim Henry
Author, Pastor-Teacher, past president of the **Southern Baptist Convention**
Pastor Emeritus – **First Baptist Church of Orlando, FL**

ENDORSEMENTS

"Passion and knowledge are essential in creating value. Bob Ross possesses an abundance of both and it flows from every page of ***Discover Israel****.*

Combining beautiful photography with insightful commentary, this rare glimpse of 'The Land of Promise' will leave readers longing for more. Leveraging a lifetime of study and his personal pilgrimages, Bob captures the history, the beauty and the blessing of the most fascinating place on earth.

You will find no better guide through The Land, the Scriptures or through life. I know first hand … I am his son."

Dr. Randy Ross
Speaker, Consultant, Coach and Author of ***Remarkable!***

"Having lived in Israel for a total of 30 years, I am profoundly impressed by Bob Ross' deep grasp of the land of Israel's profile. What he has accomplished in this volume has never been as well presented in any other overview that I have seen. It is an absolute must read for anyone who loves the Word and the Land."

Merv Watson
Conceiver and co founder of the **International Christian Embassy**, Jerusalem.
Founder of Jerusalem's Christian ***Feast of Tabernacles Celebration***

"Bob Ross has truly captured the essence of the Holy Land in ***Discover Israel****. All who love Israel will cherish this book."*

Randall Christy
Founder – **The Gospel Station Network**
Chairman of the Board & CEO – ***The Great Passion Play***, Eureka Springs, Arkansas

"Bob Ross' ***Discover Israel*** *is a gem and a wonderful resource for those who visit or revisit their trip to the Holy Land.*

It is everything you would want in a tour manual; great pictures, comprehensive text, helpful descriptions, colorful maps and graphics. With this book you can visit Israel again and again and never leave home!"

Doug Greenwold
Senior Teaching Fellow – ***Preserving Bible Times***

Mt. Moreh rises from the Valley of Jezreel near Nazareth.

INTRODUCTION

THINKING ABOUT OUR HERITAGE

Question...Can you name your great-great grandparents? What can you tell us about them? Many of us know very little about our direct bloodline and heritage beyond our grandparents. At the most you have gleaned a few scattered insights from your family tree. Maybe you had the privilege of hearing about some of your grandparents' experiences, but like most folks you recall very little. It is sad that in our culture our bloodline and heritage means little to most of us.

On the other hand, let's consider together our spiritual heritage. What does this mean to you? Can you name those who have influenced you spiritually? What do you know about them? Let's focus instead on our spiritual heritage.

Who taught you about God? Who shared with you how you could have a personal relationship with the Lord? Who paved the way for you to experience your new life in Christ? Begin with the person who shared Jesus with you; likely you will remember that person. But when you attempt to trace any lineage to a person who shared Christ with them, most likely you are stuck. Beyond that second generation we usually know nothing.

Now let's go deeper. Take a leap back to the Hebrew Scripture of the Old Testament and New Testament. Now, who has influenced you spiritually? The following may come to mind: Abraham, Isaac, Jacob, Moses, Joshua, Ruth, Samuel, David, Solomon, Jonah, Jeremiah, Isaiah, Amos, and Micah, to name only a few.

Now, add the New Testament personalities of Joseph, Mary, Matthew, Mark, Luke, John, Peter, Andrew, Mary Magdalene, Paul, John Mark, Barnabas and dozens of others. What a list!

These are your spiritual ancestors in the faith. We could sit for hours discussing their lives, their experiences with God, where they lived, what they did and what we have learned from them.

JESUS' HERITAGE

These spiritual ancestors are the heritage of every Jew and Christian. As Christians we are told in God's Word that we have been *"grafted into the olive tree of Israel"* (Romans 9-11). Our spiritual roots are totally Jewish.

Our Lord was born into a Jewish home. He faithfully observed the Jewish law. He studied the Jewish Scriptures (which were all faithfully recorded by Jewish writers). He worshiped in Jewish synagogues. He observed Jewish festivals and taught all Jewish disciples, with one exception. (Sidelight) For the first 15 years after Jesus' resurrection all the followers of Jesus, Rabbi of Nazareth, were Jews.

At Pentecost *3,000* received Jesus as *Messiah;* later *5,000* followed Him. Then, that early movement of *Messiakim / Believers* began to *"multiply"* in Jerusalem, Judea and all the Land of Israel. All was according to God's plan. God chose to place his "*only begotten Son*" in the spiritual lineage of Judaism in His land of Israel. And now, Christians have been *"grafted into"* that same heritage (Rom 11:11-24).

Sidelight

Proposal: Judas was from Kerioth in Moab-Edom, and not from Kerioth in Judah.

Judas *"Ish Kerioth"* gives this indication, as *"ish"* means *"from the suburbs"*. If he had been from Judah, his name would have been *"Judah Mi - Kerioth"*. I believe that Judas was Jesus' only non-Jewish disciple.

EVERY CHRISTIAN HAS THESE SPIRITUAL ROOTS.
PRAISE GOD FOR THIS ADOPTION THROUGH JESUS!

Southern end of the Sea of Galilee

Summer view from Lower Galilee toward Mt. Arabel and the Sea of Galilee

The Golan Heights are in the background.

Welcome To Israel!

When visiting the Land of Israel you "return" to your true ancestral home. A visit to Israel will be the single most exciting journey of your lifetime. You are *coming home* to your roots! You will walk where Abraham, Joshua, Jesus and Paul walked and taught. Every few miles you will come to another important Biblical site. You will sail on the Sea of Galilee where Jesus quieted the storm and walked on the water. You will pray in the synagogue where He taught and healed. You will see Calvary where He died and stand in the Garden Tomb where He arose from the dead. You will traverse the rolling hills covered in the springtime with the *"lilies of the fields"* and see shepherds with their flocks, just as they were in Jesus' day. You will eat the foods He enjoyed.

You will fall in love with God's Land and the Israelis as you grow in your love for Jesus. The words of your Bible will turn to living color in your heart. This experience is more than a vacation, more than a pilgrimage, more than you can possibly imagine or anticipate. It is more, so much more! As your flight crosses the white sands of Israel's Mediterranean shore, you know in your heart that you are ***coming home***.

When your plane lands at David ben Gurion Airport, your adventure begins. Welcome to Eretz Israel! You are in the Land of the Book. If you love the Author and the Book, you will surely love His Land!

Hebrew (the language the Old Testament) is the language of Israel today.

Hebrew was the language spoken in Israel in Jesus' time, and it was the original written language of Matthew, Mark, Luke and the first 15 chapters of Acts. Over 85% of the Bible was written originally in Hebrew.

Jeremiah promised that Hebrew would be revived and spoken again in the land (Jer. 31:23). After 1900 years, it is so. Even though most Israelis know English, and many other languages, Hebrew is the language of the nation. Since God is the same yesterday, today, and always, I contend that Hebrew was God's choice when He spoke the world into existence, and that would make Hebrew the language of Heaven.

MARK TWAIN'S COMMENT ON THE JEWS:

"The Egyptian, the Babylonian, and the Persian rose, filled the planet with sound and splendor, then faded to dream-stuff and passed away; the Greek and the Roman followed; and made a vast noise, but they are gone; other people have sprung up and held their torch high for a time, but it burned out, and they sit in twilight now, or have vanished. The Jew saw them all, beat them all, and is now what he always was, exhibiting no decadence, no infirmities of age, no weakening of his parts, no slowing of his energies, no dulling of his alert and aggressive mind. All things are mortal but the Jew; all other forces pass, but he remains. What is the secret of his immortality?"

THE LAND OF ISRAEL IS GOD'S "FIFTH GOSPEL"

"In Israel, in order to be a realist, you must believe in miracles."
David Ben Gurion

Israel is described as the "Miracle on the Mediterranean". The Land was chosen by God, a Land like no other. God gave the Land to His people, Israel, *"all the Land of Canaan"* (Gen. 17:8).

In Exodus 3:8 God told Moses, *"I have come down to deliver them (Israel) from the power of the Egyptians, and bring them up to that land to a good and spacious Land, to a Land flowing with milk and honey, to the place of the Canaanite and the Hittite and the Amorite and the Perizzite and the Hivite and the Jebusite."* This passage describes Israel of today, plus parts of western Jordan, western Syria and the eastern part of Lebanon.

The term *"milk and honey"* likely describes a wild and fruitful land that sustained milk producing cattle and fruit-producing trees. *Honey* describes a jam made from fruit. The *honey* in the Land was wild and a rare delicacy.

In Ezek. 20:6, God promised that Israel would be *"the glory of all the lands"* (principal among the nations in God's eyes). Israel was the nation intended to reflect His love to all nations of the world.

Israel is very small but is greatly blessed with location, climate, and terrain. Israel sustains vegetation and animal life from four different ecological zones: African, Asian, Mediterranean, and Euro-Siberian. These ecological zones criss-cross Israel at their extremities. In God's Land we find tropical zones, mountainous regions, deserts and swamps.

Often Israel raises apples and oranges in the same field. Israelis raise a variety of produce including bananas, pineapples and strawberries. Israel has over 3,000 plant species, while her neighbor Egypt, with her fertile Nile, has less than 1500.

Jesus referred to the Scarlet Anemone as the *"Lilies of the Fields"* (Matt. 6:25-34)

Wild ducks welcome the breaking day as they play and feed in the shallows at the southern end of the Sea of Galilee

White storks migrating between Africa and Poland, take a *"rest stop"* in the friendly Huleh Basin, in northern Israel.

Israel is a bird sanctuary and supports over 460 species, some from as far away as South Africa and Greenland. Birds from neighboring continents know Israel is a safe haven for them when they migrate. Diverse animals include the Siberian wolf and the African leopard. Israel has lofty mountains (Mt. Hermon is the highest at 9,232') and the lowest place on the surface of the planet (the Dead Sea at 1,312' below sea level). You can snow ski on the Alpine-like slopes of Mt. Hermon and two hours later swim in the warm Sea of Galilee. All this is crammed into a nation about the size of the state of New Jersey.

The Land belongs to God. Lev. 25:23 *"The Land, moreover shall not be sold permanently, for the Land is Mine; for you are but aliens and sojourners with Me."* God holds the title. To this Land He called His servant Abraham in Genesis 12:1-3, and promised The Land to Abraham and his descendants through Isaac and Jacob. That covenant is *everlasting* and not conditional. In Genesis 17:7-8 we read, *"I will establish My covenant between Me and you and your descendants after you throughout the generations for an everlasting covenant, to be God to you and to your descendants after you. I will give to you and to your descendants after you, the Land of your sojourns, all the land of Canaan, for an everlasting possession, and I will be their God."*

The surrounding Muslim nations also claim to be the sons of Abraham through *Ishmael.* The Qur'an says that *Ishmael,* not *Isaac (*contrary to the Biblical account), received Abraham's blessing. Muslim's believe they are entitled to possess the Land. Hagar, the mother of Ishmael, was an Egyptian and not an Arab. Egypt would not be Islamized for another 2300 years after Abraham. Thus, Abraham's son, Ishmael, was half Mesopotamian (Abraham's ethnic background), and half Egyptian (through Hagar) - neither were Arab. After Hagar and Ishmael left Abraham's camp, they dwelt in lands to the east later inhabited by nomadic Arab tribes.

The Word of God in Genesis 17:15-21 unequivocally states that the Land belongs to *Isaac, Jacob,* and *his descendants.* If we believe the Bible, as opposed to Muhammad's teachings, God chose *Isaac* instead of *Ishmael.* However, He promised to bless *Ishmael* and make him fruitful, *"the father of 12 princes...a great nation"* (Gen. 17:20).

Wild donkeys in the Arabah Valley

The Land of Promise (according to God) was given to *Isaac, Jacob and their descendants.* God's angel promised Ishmael that, *"He will be a wild donkey of a man, his hand will be against everyone, and everyone's hand will be against him; and he will live to the east of all his brothers"* (Gen. 16:11-12).

God specifically said, *"My Covenant will I establish with Isaac"* (Gen. 17:21). Later, Esau (Isaac's son, who sold his birthright to his brother) took his family and moved out of The Land (away from his brother Jacob). He moved to the land of Edom on the Eastern side of the Dead Sea (today's Southern Jordan).

The Covenants of God regarding The Land are *everlasting* and unconditional. Scripturally and historically the Land of Israel was given to the descendants of Abraham, Isaac and Jacob; the Jews. Since the late 1800's, when they began their return to their Land, the Jews purchased much of the Land from the Turks and Arabs. They have won every war the Arabs have started, and have increased their borders each time toward that limit which God has promised in the "end times". Israel belongs to the Jews from every possible legal consideration.

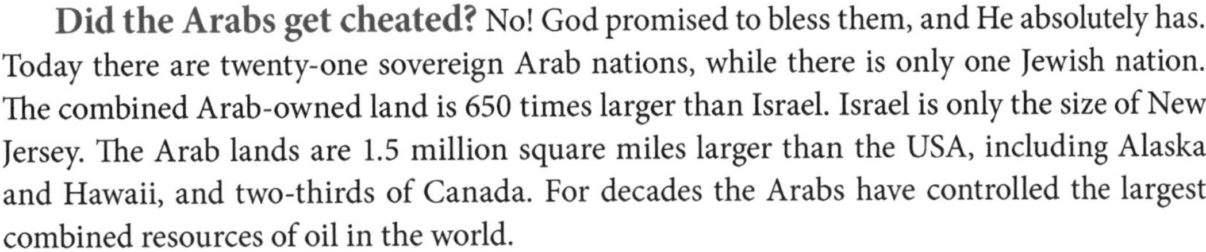

Did the Arabs get cheated? No! God promised to bless them, and He absolutely has. Today there are twenty-one sovereign Arab nations, while there is only one Jewish nation. The combined Arab-owned land is 650 times larger than Israel. Israel is only the size of New Jersey. The Arab lands are 1.5 million square miles larger than the USA, including Alaska and Hawaii, and two-thirds of Canada. For decades the Arabs have controlled the largest combined resources of oil in the world.

The return of the Jews to their homeland in the last 100 years is truly a miracle. Read again what the prophets said about this return (Ezek. 39:25, 27-28; Amos 9:14-15; Ezek. 36:23-24). God is bringing Israel back to prove the integrity of His Holy Name and to show that He is a God who keeps His promises. God is the Great Promise Keeper!

Israel is today returning from exile among the nations of the world, and is being restored to the Land God has promised His People. In God's final plans, Israel's redemption and spiritual renewal will take place in His Land. Rabbis and the spiritual leaders of Israel refer to these "end days" as the "Messianic Days". Truly, God has not forgotten His People, nor failed in his love for them. The Land and the returning Jews become one, as God prospers them and moves them toward His plans for their future.

Israel, under God's blessings, has been transformed from a forgotten Turkish dust-bowl into the lush, green agricultural wonder of the Middle East. Since the State of Israel was founded in 1948, there has been a renaissance in the Jewish world. Jews everywhere have focused on the Land of Israel, and reaffirmed the Biblical claims of their ancestral homeland.

The Land of Israel is like no other nation on earth. God called the nation of Israel to His divine purpose. The constant interplay between the sacred and the secular moves Israel toward God's Messianic goal. With the return of God's people to His Land, the growth of Israel, and her leadership in our world today. This is truly God's miracle! Only God could accomplish these things.

Randy Ross and his wife Lu Anne view the Temple Mount from the Mount of Olives.

Only six decades ago Israel was struggling to survive. Today, Israel has developed the only democratic system of government in the Middle East, an incredibly strong economy, and one of the most powerful defense systems in the world. Israel has built a self-sufficient agricultural system which helps feed the Middle East and Europe. The infrastructure of electricity and power is enough to support the entire Middle East. Israel has provided water resources and constructed new homes for her immigrants. The young Nation has developed a comprehensive social, educational, welfare and medical system which provides for all of her citizens, Jews and Arabs alike.

Israel is a miracle in progress. Her government, like all others, has plenty of flaws. But, under God's leadership, it has survived against all odds. Our Faithful God is in charge, both spiritually and physically. Watch for His signs that shout – God at Work!

LINKING SCENES TO YOUR STUDY

Since 1959, I have taken 60,000 photographs related to Israel. Knowing that "a picture is worth a thousand words", I decided to include my favorites in this book. Some of these photographs are half a century old. Frankly, when I made the decision to add these photographs to *Discover Israel*, I did not understand the time, cost and labor of adding these 400 carefully chosen photographs to the publication. It has been a major task. I hope that this effort will greatly bless your study of the Land of Israel.

Savor the beautiful scenes, illustrations and maps that complement the text. As you move from one geographical section to another, take time to study the historical and archaeological information related to each site. Most important, take time to read the related Scriptures for each location.

From the beginning, my goal has been to share God's Land with Bible students everywhere. May the beauty of His Land cause you to fall more in love with our Lord Jesus, His people and Israel.

**God's Land will come alive in your heart.
Enjoy this study to the fullest. Bon Voyage!**

Mt. Hermon in the summer with bee hives in the foreground.
"But I said to you, 'You will possess their land; I will give it to you as an inheritance, a land flowing with milk and honey.' I am the Lord your God, who has set you apart from the nations".
(Lev. 20:24)

Historical Overview of God's Land and God's People

Modern Israel was "born" on May 14, 1948. Chaim Weizmann was President and David Ben Gurion was Prime Minister. Jerusalem was declared the capital. God restored Israel as a Jewish Nation after 2,000 years. Arab Nations surrounded her for war; the combatants being Lebanon to her north, Syria and Jordan to the east, and Egypt to her south. After winning the War of Independence, Israel's boundaries encompassed some 8,000 sq. miles. After the after the Six Day War, in June of 1967, Israel's size increased to 26,000 sq. miles.

PRE-BIBLICAL PERIOD (9000-2000 BC)

The oldest communities on earth were located in this area of the Middle East and Israel.

CHALCOLITHIC AGE (4000-3100 BC)

EARLY BRONZE AGE (3150-1850 BC)

BIBLICAL PERIOD of the PATRIARCHS (2000-1700 BC)

Abram was born in **Ur** of the **Chaldees**, also known as Southern Mesopotamia (Iraq today). He migrated along the **Fertile Crescent** to **Haran,** and **God** directed him to **Canaan.**

1877* BC **Abraham** arrived in **The Land** of **Canaan,** and there he fathered two sons, **Ishmael** by **Hagar** and **Isaac** by **Sara. Isaac** fathered **Esau** and **Jacob.**

MIDDLE BRONZE AGE (1850-1550 BC)

1662* BC **Jacob** led his family to **Egypt,** and then their **Sojourn** in **Egypt** began. **Josephus** says it lasted **215 yrs. (Antiq. XV:2);** however, some believe the period lasted five centuries.

LATE BRONZE AGE (1550-1200 BC)

1527* BC **Moses** was born in **Egypt.**

1447* BC The **Exodus** began as **Moses** left **Egypt** under **Pharoah Dudimose.** *He led some two million ex-slaves into the **Sinai Wilderness. God** led and cared for **Israel** in **His Desert School** for 40 years. **God** gave them the **Law,** and dwelt in their midst in the **Tabernacle. Moses** viewed the **Promised Land,** and then died on **Mt. Nebo.**

1410* BC **Joshua** entered the **Promised Land** of **Canaan** and **God** led in the **Conquest. The Land** was divided among the **Twelve Tribes** of **Israel,** and they possessed it for 1,340 years.

1420 BC The **Philistines** came from **Crete,** invaded **Canaan/Israel's Coast,** and occupied much of **The Land** by **1050.**

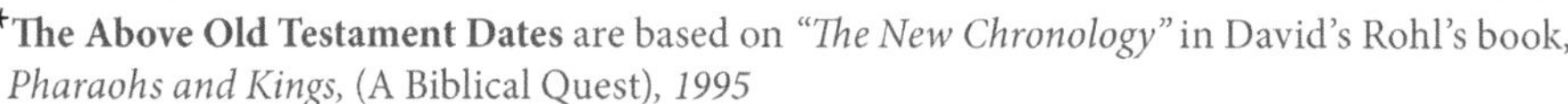
***The Above Old Testament Dates** are based on *"The New Chronology"* in David's Rohl's book, *Pharaohs and Kings,* (A Biblical Quest), *1995*

IRON AGE I (1200-930 BC)

1030* BC **Saul** was crowned first King over **Israel** and reigned 20 years while **Pharoah Akhenaten*** reigned in **Egypt.** The **Tel-Amarna Letters** contain communication between the **"Habiru" (most probably refers to the Hebrew Nation)** and **Egypt.**

1010* BC **King David** ruled from **Hebron** for seven years.
1004* BC **Jerusalem** became **David's** capital for 33 years (I Chron. 29:27).
970* BC **Solomon** began his reign following **David's** death.
966* BC In **Solomon's** *"4th year"* he began construction of the Temple (I Kings 6:1).

IRON AGE II (931-586 BC)

931* BC **Israel's Kingdom** is divided between **Judah** and **Israel.**
722 BC **Assyrians** captured **Samaria** and took most of **Israel** into **Captivity,** beginning the dispersion of **Israel's** "10 lost tribes".

BABYLONIAN PERIOD (612-538 BC)

612 BC **Babylon** conquered **Assyria** and captured **Ninevah.**
586 BC **Nebuchadnezzar** destroyed **Jerusalem** and **Solomon's Temple.** Most of **Judea** was taken into **captivity** in **Babylon.**

PERSIAN PERIOD (538-323 BC)

538 BC **Cyrus** permitted the **Jews** to return to **Jerusalem** under **Ezra** and **Nehemiah.**
512 BC The **Second Temple and Jerusalem's walls** were **rebuilt.**

GREEK PERIOD (332-167 BC)

334 BC **Alexander the Great** conquered **Persia** and **Israel.** After his death, control was passed to the **Ptolemies** of **Egypt.**
197 BC **Antiochus III** defeated **Egypt's Ptolmies, Israel** controlled by **Syrian Seleucid Empire.**
175 BC **Seleucid King, Antiochus Epiphanes,** desecrated **God's Temple** by sacrificing a hog on the altar.

HASMONEAN PERIOD (167 BC-63 BC)

167 BC **Jewish** revolt against the **Seleucids. Jewish** control of **Israel** under the **Maccabees** brought 100 years of **Jewish Independence.**

ROMAN PERIOD (63 BC -313 AD)

63 BC **Pompey** conquered **Israel** for the **Roman Empire.**
40 BC **Parthians** surprised **Romans** and took **The Land of Israel,** led by **Antigonus. Herod the Great,** half **Jew** and half **Arab,** conquered the **Parthians** for Rome and served as King of the Jews until **4 BC.**
5 BC Spring Herod became ill. (In the Roman Calendar the new year started on Sept. 1st).
See Diagram of the Herodian Dynasty of Jesus' Day, page 183.

***The Above Old Testament Dates** are based on *"The New Chronology"* in David's Rohl's book, *Pharaohs and Kings,* (A Biblical Quest), *1995*

HISTORY OF THE GOSPELS (4 BC-29AD)

4 BC mid-Sept	**JESUS CHRIST was born in Bethlehem of Judea.**
BC Sept. 4	According to Josephus, Herod the Great died before the end of Sept. (This was obviously after his decree to kill all the babies of Bethlehem under *"two years"*).
AD 8 or 9	At age 12 **Jesus** went to the **Temple** in **Jerusalem** to prepare for **bar mitzvah.**
26 Fall AD	**Jesus** was **baptized** by **John the Baptist** in the **Jordan River** on the eve of **Yom Kippur.** **At age 30**, **Jesus** entered *"His full vigor"* and His **3 1/2 years** earthly **ministry.**
26-32 AD	**Pontius Pilate** served as Procurator for **Rome** over **Judea.**
29 AD Spring	**Jesus was crucified at Calvary. He arose from the Garden Tomb!**

NEW TESTAMENT HISTORY CONTINUED
Suggested dates for Paul's Letters

29 AD	**Jerusalem Pentecost** (all Jews), (Acts 2). **Apostles'** ministry in **Jerusalem,** and persecution (Acts 8:1-3).
36 AD	**Phillip's** ministry in **Samaria,** ***"the Samaritan Pentecost"*** for half Jews (Acts 8:4-24).
36 AD	**Saul met Jesus** on the **Damascus Road.** He spent the next 3 years in **Arabia (36-38).**
36 AD	**Peter's** roof-top vision in **Joppa** led him to minister to **Cornelius** in **Caesarea Maritina.** **Paul** went to **Jerusalem,** and from there, to **Tarsus,** his hometown. **Paul** and **Barnabas - First Missionary Journey.**
50 AD	**Jerusalem Conference** - Q. "What to do with *Gentile/Goy* converts?"
49-56 AD	**Second Missionary Journey** (I and II Thessalonians). **Third Missionary Journey** (**56 A.D.** - I and II Corinthians, Romans, Galatians). **Paul** was imprisoned and tried at **Caesarea.** **Paul** journeyed to **Rome** and was imprisoned there. He wrote Colossians, Philemon, Ephesians, and Philippians. After **Paul's** acquittal in **Rome,** he wrote Timothy and Titus.
64 AD	**Paul** arrested and put to death outside of **Rome.**
66 AD	**First Jewish Revolt** against **Rome** led by the **Zealots,** started at **Caesarea.**
70 AD	**Jerusalem/Herod's Temple** was destroyed by **Titus. Jews** scattered in the **Diaspora.**
73 AD	Last **Jewish** stronghold, **Masada,** fell to **Rome.**
90 AD	At **Yavne,** Jewish leaders tried to save **Judaism** and separate **Jews** from the **Messianists,** or the **Followers of Jesus.**
96 AD	**John** wrote **Revelation** on the **Isle of Patmos.**
132-135 AD	**Second Jewish Revolt** under **Bar Kokhba. Hadrian** rebuilt **Jerusalem** (but, no **Jews** were allowed). **Jerusalem** was renamed **Aelia Capitolina.** The **Romans** named **the Land** "**Palestina**" after **Jerusalem** was defeated in 66-70 AD. This was a degrading term used to indicate that **the Land** had belonged to the **Philistines** instead of **Israel** or **Judah.**

BYZANTINE EMPIRE (325-636 AD)

325 AD	**Constantine converted to Christianity and made it the religion of the Empire. Constantinople/Byzantium** became the capital of the **Eastern Roman Empire.** Churches were built and Universal Christianity spread after Constantine's conversion.

MUHAMMAD'S LIFE (570-632)

570 AD **Muhammad** born in **Mecca.** At age 43 he received revelations, which became the **Qur'an.** He established **Islam** by uniting the scattered **Arab** tribes of **Arabia.** At his death the Sunni-Shiite dispute escalated, and they split over who would succeed Muhammad as Islam's spiritual head. In **Muslim** tradition, he was taken to heaven on his "white winged steed". **Muslims** claim **Jerusalem** as their third most sacred city after **Mecca** and **Medina.** (The city of Jerusalem is never mentioned in the Qur'an).

632 Ad **Muhammad** died. In only 19 years he had united the Arab tribes under a new religion.

ARAB PERIOD (636-1099 AD)

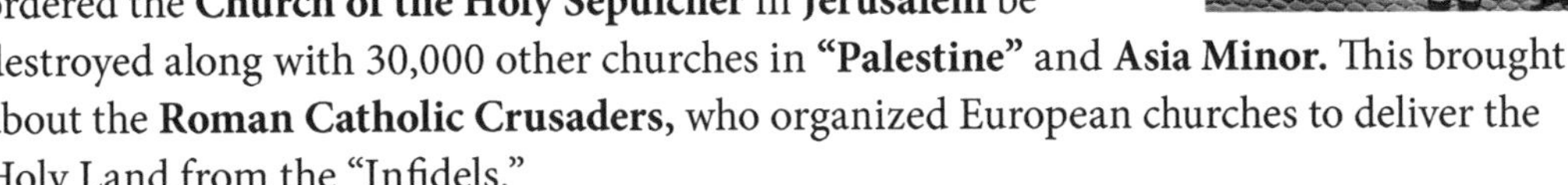

636 AD **Jerusalem** was taken by the **Persians,** who destroyed **Christian churches** over their 300 years of occupation. The Land of **"Palestine"** came under **Muslim** control. **Muslim** leadership ordered the **Church of the Holy Sepulcher** in **Jerusalem** be destroyed along with 30,000 other churches in **"Palestine"** and **Asia Minor.** This brought about the **Roman Catholic Crusaders,** who organized European churches to deliver the Holy Land from the "Infidels."

Note: The Arabs conquered God's Land 2513 years after Jews inhabited the Land.

691 AD The **Dome of the Rock** was built on the ruins of the Jewish Temple.

CRUSADER PERIOD (1099-1263 AD)

1098-99 AD The **First Crusade** was mustered to take Israel from the Muslims, who destroyed some 30,000 Christian churches in the Holy Land.

1099 AD **Jerusalem** was taken by the **Crusaders,** with their Latin capital based in **Jerusalem.** Many Jews were massacred.

1187 AD **Saladin,** the **Muslim** prince from **Egypt,** gained control of **Egypt, Syria, Mesopotamia** and **Palestine.** In the final battle, he defeated the **Crusaders** at the **Horns of Hattin** in **Galilee,** and invited all Jews to return to their land.

MAMELUKE PERIOD (1263-1516 AD)

1263 AD **Mameluke, Sultan Baybars** of **Egypt,** captured the remaining fortresses and secured **Muslim** control of the coastal cities of Israel for the next 250 years - Jews fled Jerusalem.

1400 AD The **Mongol** invasion, under **Tamerlane,** caused the fall of the **Mameluke Empire.**

1492 AD Jews were expelled from Spain (**Spanish Inquisition**). Many came to Safed and Jerusalem.

TURKISH PERIOD (1517-1917 AD)

1517 AD **Turkish Ottoman Empire** conquered the **Land.** During their 400 year reign The Land's resources were stripped and depleted. A Jewish state was created around Tiberias.

1799 AD **Napoleon Bonaparte** unsuccessfully tried to add **Palestine** to his **French Empire.** He captured **Joppa,** but failed to capture **Acre (Acco).** He encouraged Jews to reestablish Jerusalem.

1878 AD **Petach Tikvah** became the first **Jewish** agricultural village in Israel after their return to The Land promised by God.

1911 AD **Degania** became the first **Jewish** kibbutz, and was founded near the **Sea of Galilee.**

THE BRITISH MANDATE (1917-1948 AD)

1917 AD In **WWI General Allenby** and the **Allied Forces** took **Jerusalem** from **Turkey** on Christmas Day in a bloodless surrender. At that time **Britain** took control of **The Land** (populated by both **Jews** and **Arabs**). The **British Mandate** was confirmed by the **League of Nations** in **1922.** The **British Parliament** passed the **Balfour Declaration,** opening the way for a **"National Homeland in Palestine for the Jewish people".**

1922 AD **The League of Nations** took 77% of Palestine to establish Trans-Jordan. Arab leaders refused a Jewish homeland in the Middle East.

1939 AD **Holocaust** in Europe. **Jewish Brigade** joined Allies. Jerusalem's Mufti supported the Nazis.

1947 AD The **United Nations** adopted a Partition Plan to divide **Palestine** between **Israel** & **Jordan.** The Palestinians rejected the offer of an Arab state beside Israel.

May 14, 1948

The NEW NATION OF ISRAEL WAS BORN
"Can a nation be born in a day?" (Isaiah 66:8)

On May 14, 1948, the British high command withdrew from their headquarters at the King David Hotel in Jerusalem and raised the Red Cross flag in its place. The next day the Arab League attacked Israel.

The watching world believed that Israel would not survive. To the contrary, Israel not only survived but won independence. July 18, 1949 was the official end of the Jewish War of Liberation. Palestine was divided between Israel and Jordan by the UN. Jordan received the vast majority of the Land. David Ben Gurion became the first Prime Minister of Israel. He was a secular Zionist and unfortunately an agnostic.

For more details on Israel's wars, see "Joshua II" (pages 139-157).
For Israel's history since 1948, see pages 158-169.

Note: Many books have been written about God's intervention for Israel in our day. No book is adequate to describe God's miracles.

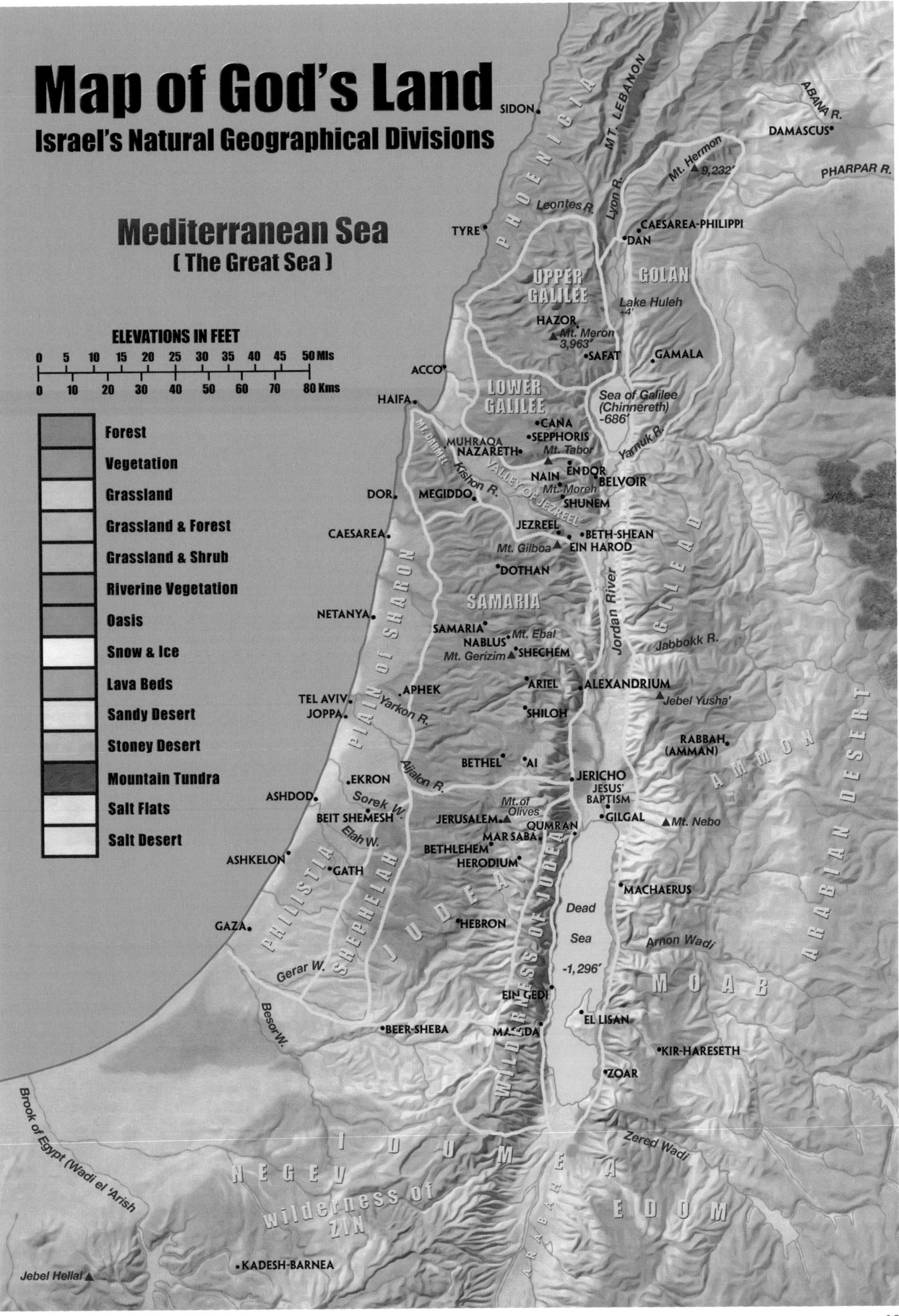

Map of God's Land
Israel's Natural Geographical Divisions
Mediterranean Sea
(The Great Sea)
ELEVATIONS IN FEET
0 5 10 15 20 25 30 35 40 45 50 Mls
0 10 20 30 40 50 60 70 80 Kms
Forest
Vegetation
Grassland
Grassland & Forest
Grassland & Shrub
Riverine Vegetation
Oasis
Snow & Ice
Lava Beds
Sandy Desert
Stoney Desert
Mountain Tundra
Salt Flats
Salt Desert
SIDON
PHOENICIA
MT. LEBANON
ABANA R.
DAMASCUS
Mt. Hermon
9,232'
PHARPAR R.
Leontes R.
Lyon R.
TYRE
CAESAREA-PHILIPPI
DAN
UPPER GALILEE
GOLAN
Lake Huleh
HAZOR
Mt. Meron
3,963'
SAFAT
GAMALA
ACCO
HAIFA
LOWER GALILEE
Sea of Galilee
(Chinnereth)
-686'
CANA
SEPPHORIS
MUHRAQA
NAZARETH
Mt. Tabor
Yarmuk R.
MT. CARMEL
Kishon R.
VALLEY OF JEZREEL
NAIN
ENDOR
BELVOIR
Mt. Moreh
DOR
MEGIDDO
SHUNEM
JEZREEL
BETH-SHEAN
CAESAREA
Mt. Gilboa
EIN HAROD
DOTHAN
Jordan River
GILEAD
SAMARIA
NETANYA
PLAIN of SHARON
SAMARIA
Mt. Ebal
NABLUS
Jabbokk R.
Mt. Gerizim
SHECHEM
ARIEL
ALEXANDRIUM
APHEK
Jebel Yusha'
TEL AVIV
JOPPA
Yarkon R.
SHILOH
RABBAH
(AMMAN)
AMMON
BETHEL
AI
JERICHO
Aijalon R.
EKRON
JESUS' BAPTISM
ASHDOD
Sorek W.
Mt. of Olives
GILGAL
BEIT SHEMESH
JERUSALEM
Mt. Nebo
Elah W.
QUMRAN
MAR SABA
BETHLEHEM
ASHKELON
HERODIUM
GATH
PHILISTIA
SHEPHELAH
JUDEA
MACHAERUS
Dead Sea
-1,296'
HEBRON
GAZA
Arnon Wadi
ARABIAN DESERT
Gerar W.
WILDERNESS OF JUDEA
MOAB
EIN GEDI
Besor W.
EL LISAN
BEER-SHEBA
KIR-HARESETH
ZOAR
Brook of Egypt (Wadi el 'Arish
IDUMEA
Zered Wadi
NEGEV
wilderness of ZIN
ARABAH
EDOM
KADESH-BARNEA
Jebel Hellal

The Golan Heights is the tableland south of Mount Hermon. The territory was allotted to Syria after WWI. Syria never populated or utilized the Golan Heights except for military purposes against Israel. In June of 1967, during the "Six Day War", Israel took control of the Golan. Since '67 they have developed lakes, agriculture, Israeli settlements, grasslands, ranch lands, tourist sites and areas for military training and maneuvers.
Israel gives protection to the Druze who inhabit the southern foothills of Mount Hermon. Kitzrim is the Israeli capital of the Golan.

Golan Heights

The Golan Heights is the tableland northeast of the Sea of Galilee. Syria received the Golon Heights under the French Mandate after WWI, but it corresponds to the Old Testament area of the tribe of Manasseh. Twenty years of Syrian shelling from these heights (1948-1967) led to the Six Day War. As a result, Israel regained its God-given possession of the Golan.

Full map on page 19

Mount Hermon (sacred mountain) is the southernmost peak of the Lebanon mountain range and is snow covered most of the year. In Abraham's day, it was inhabited by the Amorites, and the heights were called "the sanctified". It was held in veneration and awe by the Canaanites, and was believed to be the abode of their god, Baal-Hermon (I Chron. 5:23).

Hermon was the northernmost limit of Joshua's conquest, and was allotted to the tribe of Manasseh (Josh. 11:17, 12:1, 13:5; Deut. 3:8). Psalm 89:12 states, *"The north and the south, you have created them; Tabor and Hermon shout for joy at your name."* Mount Hermon was the northernmost limit of Jesus' travels (Matt. 16:13; Mk. 8:27). Many believe Hermon is the *"exceedingly high mountain"* where Jesus was transfigured (Matt. 4:8).

Mount Hermon is the granddaddy of all the mountains in Israel, 9200' altitude, and is snowcapped most of the year.

Caesarea Philippi is where Jesus retreated with His Disciples. Here He asked, *"Who do men say that I am?"* Peter responded, *"You are the Christ, the Son of the Living God."*

Caesarea Philippi was the cultic center of the land. Below - The ancients called the cave *the "Gates of Hades"* (Matt. 16:18).

Paneas/CaesareaPhilippi/Banias is located at the foot of Mt. Hermon. This area was dotted with Canaanite shrines to Baal-Hermon, and Roman shrines to the god Pan. When Caesar Augustus gave Paneas to Herod the Great, Herod erected a white marbled temple to Augustus and Pan. When Herod died in 4 BC, the city became part of Philip's Tetrarchy. He renamed the city in honor Caesar Tiberias and himself. Thus, the name, Caesarea Philippi.

This city was part of the Decapolis and lay 50 miles from Damascus. During the Jewish War (66-70 AD), the Roman armies, under Titus and Vespasian, gathered here at this center of Greco -Roman influence.

Jesus brought His disciples to Caesarea Philippi on a retreat, and asked them, *"Who do men say that I am?"* Peter responded with his great confession, *"Thou are the Christ, the Son of the Living God"* (Matt. 16:13-20, Mk. 8:27-30, Lk. 9:18-21). From this place Christ *"set his face toward Jerusalem"* and his coming death.

The so-called "Cyclop" city wall at ancient Laish / Dan

The Jordan River begins its flow at the springs of melting snow from Mt. Hermon. Arabs can't pronounce the "P" in Paneas and call it "Banias". These springs are the largest of Jordan's sources.

Druse villages dot the slopes of Mt. Hermon. The Golan tableland is lush and covered with lakes. The Damascus Road of Paul's day skirted Mt. Hermon en route. Today, as a result of the heightened tension between Israel and Syria, this road has been closed.

Dan (judge) is located on the northern limit of Israel. The Old Testament phrase *"from Dan to Beersheba..."* referred to the area of King David's reign

Altar where Israel sacrificed to the Golden Calf

and territory. Joshua allotted Dan an area located in the Philistine territory near the Mediterranean Sea coast. Life with the Philistines became very difficult after Samson's death. Scouts from the tribe of Dan were sent to investigate the possibilities of relocation. With only 600 men, they took the city of Laish. They relocated their tribe and renamed the city Dan (Josh. 18).

Jeroboam chose Dan as his second cultic site (after Bethel), and erected his Sanctuary of the Golden Calf (Josh. 21:5, 23, 24). The sanctuary survived Jehu's reform (II Kings 10:29), but the city was later taken by Ben-Hadad of Syria as recommended by King Asa of Judah (I Kings 15:20). Jeremiah describes the Assyrian invasion in Jer. 4:15 and 8:16.

A path through the Nature Preserve to the excavation of Dan takes one along the beautiful Dan tributary of the Jordan River. It crosses springs and streams on black basalt (volcanic rock) through a jungle-like area of lush growth. This is one of the most breathtakingly beautiful places in all of Israel.

Nimrod Castle was built as the Fortress for the Muslim Assassins. It was conquered by the Crusaders and later by the Mamelukes. The fortress in the Golan provides an incredible view of the Upper Jordan Valley, and protected the upper pass leading to Damascus.

Nimrod's Castle, a Muslim fortress

Banias Falls, an incredible double waterfall of about 40 feet in height, is the likely location where King David wrote Psalm 42:1-7.

Likely, David wrote Psalm 42 concerning Banias Falls.

Tel Hai Memorial (Hill of Life) commemorates the young Israelis who gave their lives by holding off the 1947 and 1948 Syrian attacks against the kibbutz. The Lion of Judah statue inscription reads, "It is good to die for our country." A small museum at this site helps us under-

Operational olive press at Katzrin, with crushed olives

stand the life of the Israeli settlers in the 1930's and 40's, prior to Israel's becoming a nation.

Abel-Beth Maacah (meadow of the house of oppression) was located in the tribal area of Naphtali. It was a fortified city at the intersection of the Damascus/Tyre Highway and the Via Maris. Here Sheba rebelled against David when Israel began to desert David. Joab, David's captain, besieged the city. A woman in the city threw Sheba's severed head over the wall to Joab, persuading him to spare the city (II Sam. 20).

Katzrin, the capital of the Golan, has a first century village that has been reconstructed as it was in the days of Jesus. It is replete with examples of Jewish life in a rural village, from homes to synagogue. In modern Katzrin, we will visit the museum and view a presentation of the Roman attack on Gamala, called "the Masada of Galilee".

The scripture says that Jesus taught in synagogues throughout Galilee. Only a few First Century synagogues have been discovered however. The Gamala synagogue would have been one of His teaching locations in Galilee.

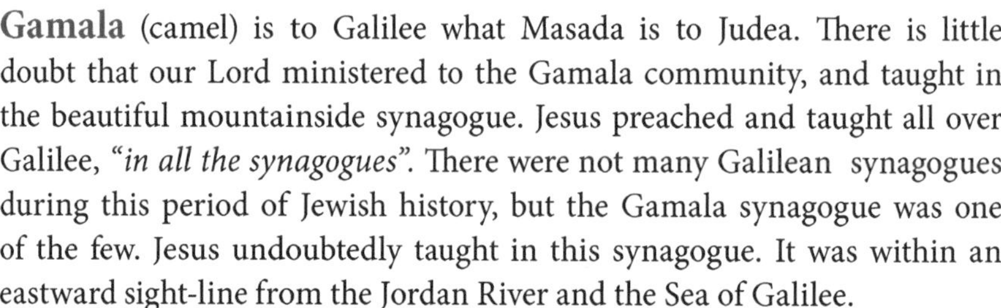

Gamala (camel) is to Galilee what Masada is to Judea. There is little doubt that our Lord ministered to the Gamala community, and taught in the beautiful mountainside synagogue. Jesus preached and taught all over Galilee, *"in all the synagogues"*. There were not many Galilean synagogues during this period of Jewish history, but the Gamala synagogue was one of the few. Jesus undoubtedly taught in this synagogue. It was within an eastward sight-line from the Jordan River and the Sea of Galilee.

Josephus' account of Gamala is a must read. The strenuous hike and tour of Gamala will take most of a day, but is well worth the effort. The excavations and the view from Gamala will be remembered for a lifetime.

At Gamala 10,000 Jews leapt to their death rather than being taken as slaves of Rome.
The synagogue is in the lower left of the picture.

Upper Galilee

Galilee means region or circle. Upper Galilee is made up of high terrain and rugged contours. Saul and David helped to establish Israel's reign over this area. Two New Testament rulers controlled Galilee – Herod the Great and Herod Antipas. The first reigned at the time of Jesus' birth and the second during His ministry. Jesus traveled and ministered throughout the entire region of Galilee (John 7:1).

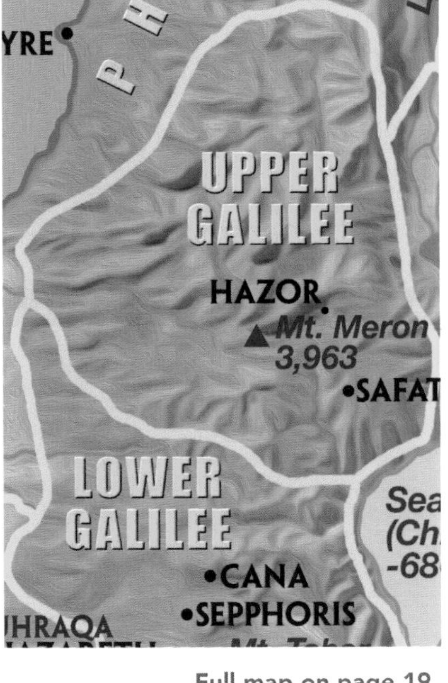

Full map on page 19

Lake Huleh/Waters of Merom (height or upper waters) was the smallest body of water in the Jordan River chain. Here the tributaries of the Jordan joined. The lake was called the Waters of Merom in the Hebrew scriptures of the Old Testament. Here Joshua made a lightning attack on a coalition of the Canaanite kings, and took Upper Galilee for Israel (Josh. 11:1-9).

Lake Huleh is 4 feet above sea level. From the Huleh Basin the Jordan River flows through steep gorges until it arrives at the Sea of Galilee (686 feet below sea level). Lake Huleh was once 4 miles long and 2 miles wide.

The lake was drained in 1957. The once malaria-stricken area is today beautiful, fertile farmland. However, salt is rising to the surface of the soil, and the farmers are presently allowing much of the ground to remain fallow. Also, the Sea of Galilee has recently grown algae which created many problems for Israel's fresh water supply. This was the first time in recorded history that such strange things happened to the Sea. It has been discovered that the Huleh swamp served as a filtration system for the Sea of Galilee across the years. Today, Israel has re-flooded some of the Huleh Basin to solve the problem, and a small portion of the basin has been preserved in its natural state for a wildlife and migratory bird sanctuary.

Here Joshua made a lightning attack on a coalition of the Canaanite kings, and took Upper Galilee for Israel (Josh. 11:1-9).

From the Huleh Basin the Jordan River flows through steep gorges until it reaches the Sea of Galilee (686′ below sea level).

Mt. Hermon's springs join the turbulent headwaters of the Jordan River near Dan.

The Jordan River (descender) flows through rocky gorges from the Lake Huleh Basin as it winds south toward the Sea of Galilee. The Jordan Valley is a part of the Great Rift Valley. On either side of the river, mountains rise to heights ranging from 2000 – 2500 feet. The Jordan is the only river in the world that runs nearly its entire course below sea level. When it leaves the Huleh Basin it dips below sea level, and when it reaches the Dead Sea it is 1292 feet lower. The Bridge of Jacob's Daughters crosses the Jordan between the Huleh Basin and the Sea of Galilee. It connects Lower Galilee with the Golan Heights.

Perhaps you have heard it said that Kabbalah, from the Jewish mystics, is just **"abracadabra"**. People believe it is simply gibberish. However, in Hebrew, **"abracadabra"** is literally translated ...**"(A-ba-ra) *Let it come to pass,* (ca) *as,* (da-ba-ra) *it is spoken*"**. The word is not an Aramaic word, but is Hebrew. That mistake has led to numerous conflicting folk etymologies, and has given Jewish Kabbalah a bad name.

Safat/Safed, Israel's highest city, sits atop her loftiest mountain range (3962 feet). This is probably the city Jesus pointed out from the Sea of Galilee: *"a city set on a hill cannot be hidden..."* (Matt. 5:14). Safat was a Jewish stronghold against the Romans, and later became one of the Jews' four holiest cities (along with Hebron, Jerusalem and Tiberias).

Sephardic Jews journeyed across the hot sands of North Africa and came here, escaping persecution in Spain (in 1492). They developed the mystical interpretation of the Old Testament called the "Kabbalah". It is the center of Jewish mysticism. Today one can visit the quaint artist colony, ancient synagogues and narrow streets. In 1948 the city had some 10,000 Arabs and 2200 Jewish inhabitants, but when war broke out the Arabs fled.

Hazor (enclosure for flocks of sheep) lies on the southern edge of Upper Galilee. The city/state sat astride the celebrated Via Maris that led from Egypt to Mesopotamia. Hazor was inhabited as early as 4,500 years ago, and many Scripture references point to her strategic importance. Joshua's victory at the Waters of Merom briefly secured Hazor for Israel.

Hazor's King, Jabin, led the northern Canaanite coalition of kings against Israel at Mt. Tabor. Barak of Kedesh-Naphtali (in Upper Galilee) and Deborah (from Bethel) led Israel to victory when Israel again controlled Hazor.

Solomon rebuilt Hazor and made her a royal city with a garrison of chariots (I Kings 9:15). The city remained in Israel's hands until it was captured by Tiglath-Pileser III of Assyria in 732 BC (II Kings 15:29).

At Hazor, 21 cities were built over each other forming the tel. (A tel is a mound of the remains from previous civilizations that occupied the site. It is not a natural hill). Excavations on Hazor's 25-acre tel reveals a story of her 3000 years of habitation. The city dates to 2500 BC.

North end of the Sea of Galilee looking toward Mt. Arabel

The Sea of Galilee

The Sea of Galilee is thirteen miles long, eight miles wide, and about 130-150 feet deep. The surface is 686 feet below sea level. In the Old Testament the sea was called Chinnereth or Kinneret, meaning "harp-shaped". In the New Testament it was called Gennesaret, and the Romans called it the Sea of Tiberias, at the request of Herod Antipas. The tribe of Gad settled on its shores (Deut. 3:17, Joshua 13:27).

Flowers in the beautiful Plain of Ginnosar

This beautiful sub-tropical lake has always been the center of Galilean life. In Jesus' day there were seven cities surrounding the Sea, each with a population of more than 15,000 inhabitants. Jesus made His headquarters on the northern shore at Capernaum. He ministered there for two and a half years. This is where Jesus called His disciples (Matt. 4:18-22; Mk. 1:16-20, 2:13-14; Lk. 5:1-11), calmed the storm (Matt. 8:23-27), walked on the water (Jn. 6:16-21) and healed many in the cities and surrounding area (Mk. 1:29-45). Beside the Sea, He taught, discipled the twelve, and performed many miracles (Matt. 13:1-52; Mk. 4:1-34; Lk. 8:4-18). In the hills beside the lake Jesus

The Sea of Galilee is a sub-tropical lake and has always been the center of Galilean life. In Jesus' day there were seven cities surrounding the Sea, each with a population of more than 15,000 residents.

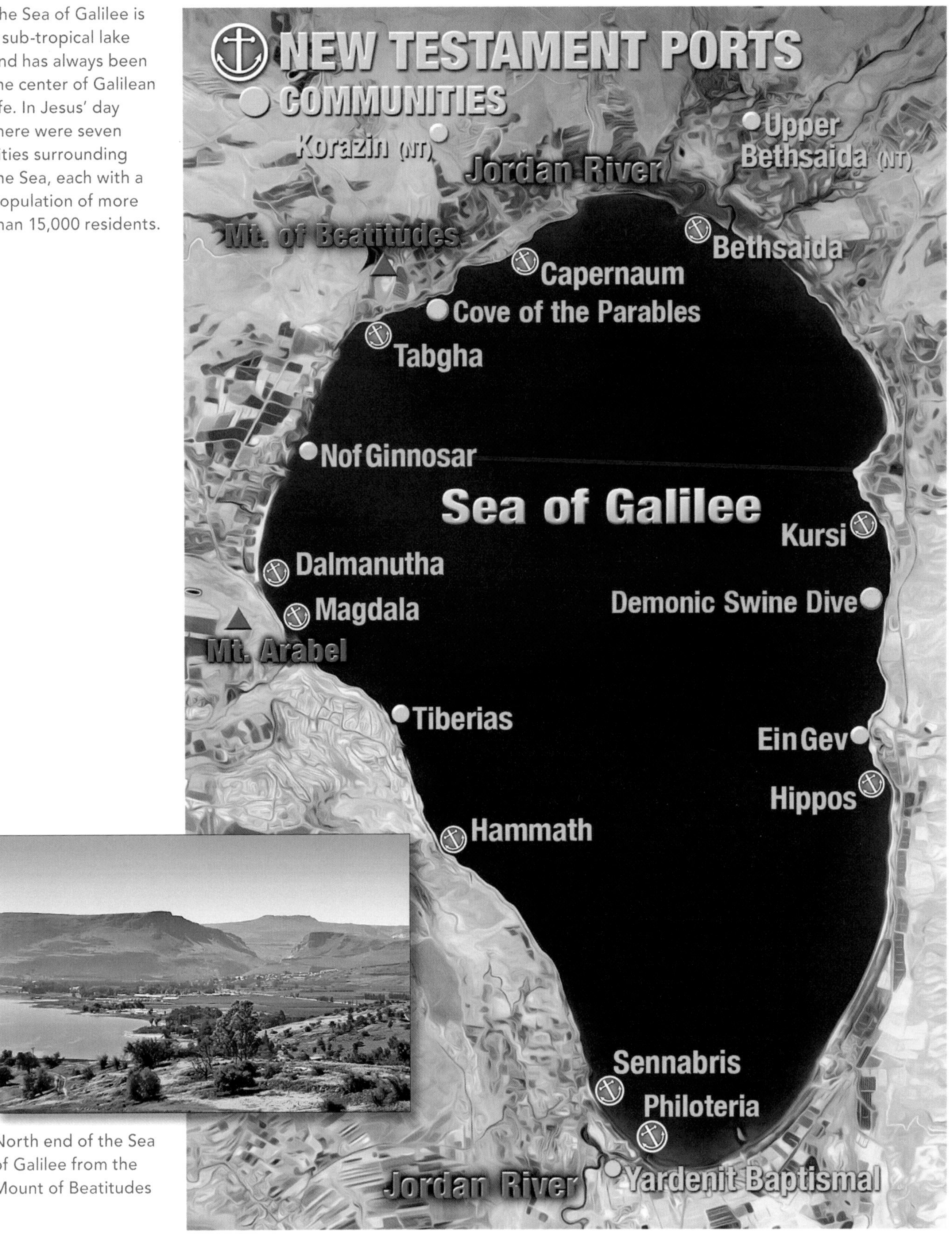

North end of the Sea of Galilee from the Mount of Beatitudes

multiplied the loaves and the fish and fed the 5,000 (Jn. 6:1-14). On the eastern shore Jesus cast the demons out of the Gadarene demoniac (Mk. 5:1-20). Near Bethseida He cleansed lepers. Jesus supplied a miraculous catch of fish on two different occasions (Lk. 5:4-11; Jn 21:6-8). He taught from Peter's boat at the unique natural amphitheater on the north shore at the base of the Mount of Beatitudes (Lk. 5:1-3).

Beautiful Ron Beach Hotel on the Sea of Galilee with Tiberias in the background

Tiberias became the capital of Galilee following Jesus' ministry. It was built by Herod Antipas in 26 AD and named for Caesar Tiberias. Soon all Galilean roads converged here. Jesus never ministered in Tiberias, but many came from the city in small boats to sit and witness His teaching (Jn. 6:23).

At first Jews refused to reside in Tiberias because the city was built over an ancient Jewish cemetery. Herod built a marvelous synagogue for the Jews, and then they came. Many Jews settled here after Jerusalem fell in 70 AD. Today's excavations reveal many hot springs and extensive Roman ruins. In Jesus' day the hot springs of Hamat were renowned throughout the world for healing powers.

The Jerusalem Talmud was compiled in Tiberias in 400 AD. The vowels for the Hebrew language were added by the scholars of Tiberias, and many Jewish sages are buried here.

The city fell to the Muslims in 637 AD. It later became a strategic Crusader city, and then was taken by the Turks. Ruins of fortresses from both periods are located near the sea. Today, Tiberias and Eilat are Israel's leading winter resorts. Tiberias is the only major city on the Sea of Galilee. In 1837 an earthquake destroyed the city. Today, a mix of the old and new makes Tiberias a most interesting city, and a great place for taking evening strolls and cappuccino breaks, or enjoying ice cream.

Many believe that Tiberias is the place where Herod Antipas beheaded John the Baptist.

Herod's banquet for his leaders in Galilee is mentioned in Mk. 6:21b, and in the Merged Gospels section 100. Herod *"gave a banquet for his lords and military commanders and the leading men of Galilee..."* (Mk. 6:21). This banquet surely would have taken place in Galilee, in Herod and Bernice's new palace and banquet facilities at Tiberias, and not at his isolated Dead Sea fortress of Machareus. That fortress was located 80 miles from Galilee on the barren eastern side of The Dead Sea.

The small amphitheater at Bernice's Palace was perhaps the place where Salome danced and John the Baptist's head was delivered on a platter. Herod had gathered his leaders of Galilee at his new palace. The palace has not been excavated, and it is difficult to know where the banquet room and John's prison was located.

Josephus records that John the Baptist had been in prison at Machareus, and many have assumed he died there. More than likely he was transferred to a prison in Tiberias before Herod's banquet and his subsequent death. The ruins of Bernice's palace can be visited today. They are located on the mountainside behind the modern city of Tiberias.

Josephus served in the Roman military, and was stationed at Migdal.

Magdala/Migdal (Watchtower) was located just north of Tiberias on the highway leading around the lake. Both towns were in the tribal area of Naphtali (Josh. 19:38). Migdal (guard tower-Heb.) had a fortress tower protecting the highway which converged at the Valley of Robbers, at the base of Mt. Arabel.

Migdal was the home of Mary Magdalene, (Lk. 8:2). It was the first city Jesus visited when He came to the Sea of Galilee. Later, He visited the city after feeding the 5,000 (Matt. 15:39). Here the Pharisees and Sadducees sought a sign from Jesus (Matt. 15:39-16:4).

The city was quite wealthy, and was a center of agriculture, fishing, fish curing, shipbuilding and trade. Rabbinical tradition says the city was known for its sexual sins. The Jewish historian Josephus, governor of Galilee, fortified the town. Despite these efforts, the city fell to Titus, and 6700 Jews were killed. Six thousand Jews were sent as slaves to build the Corinth Canal, while another 30,000 were auctioned off and scattered throughout the Empire.

Recently, Israeli architect and archaeologist Mattityahu Avshalomov excavated a beautiful synagogue, and a First Century yeshiva/seminary located there. This is the only yeshiva discovered at the Sea of Galilee, and likely Jesus taught here.

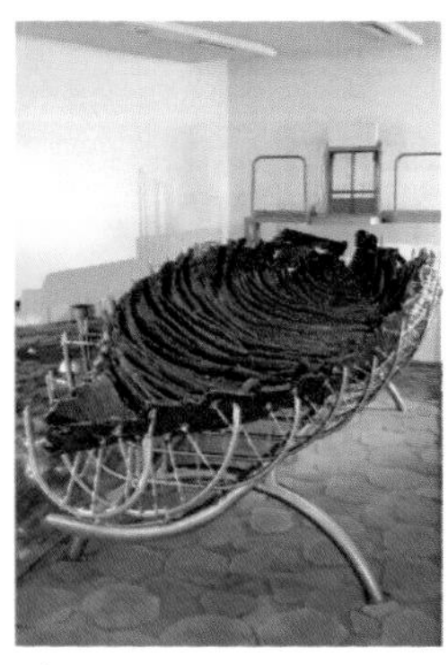

The "Jesus' Boat"

Dalmanutha (Gk.-gold or fountain), a New Testament city was recently excavated near Migdal.

Mt. Arabel rises abruptly to the west of these two cities. Some three decades before Jesus ministered in this area, Jewish rebels, living in the Arabel caves, threatened traffic on the main road between them and the lake. King Herod had his soldiers lowered over the cliffs to the caves below, and with poles and hooks, they flung the rebels to their death below. Josephus tells us that many threw their families down, rather than being killed by their enemies.

Jesus and His family came from Nazareth through the Arabel Valley to the Sea of Galilee to begin His 2 1/2 year ministry at Capernaum. Jewish tradition indicates that when the Messiah comes, He will be revealed to Israel from this valley.

Plain of Ginnosar/Gennesaret (garden of the minister) is perhaps the most beautiful agricultural plain in Israel. Jesus taught here and healed many; some simply *"touched the hem of His garment"* and were healed (Matt. 14:13-21, 15:32-39; Mk. 6:53-56). The city of Gennesaret was located on the northern edge of the Plain of Ginnosar.

Italian chapel at the top of the Mount of Beatitudes

The "Jesus' Boat" is an ancient fishing boat from the time of Jesus, discovered in 1986 at **Nof Ginnosar**, a fishing kibbutz, on the north-west shore of the Sea of Galilee. The remains of the 27′ fishing boat first appeared as the result of low lake levels during a drought. The "Jesus Boat" Museum and bookstore are well worth one's visit.

Tabgha/Heptapegon, (Gk.- seven springs) is the site of "Peter's Primacy". A Byzantine mosaic in the Church of the Multiplication depicts the loaves and the fishes (Mk. 6:31-44; Matt. 14:13-21). The Church of Peter's Primacy, located on the shore, is the oldest church in Galilee.

Overlooking the Sea of Galilee from the Mount of Beatitudes

Mount of Beatitudes rises just north of Tabgha. A chapel was built for the Italian Franciscan sisters by Mussolini. Many believe this was the site where Jesus preached His Sermon on the Mount. This sermon was a compilation of all that Jesus taught throughout His Galilean ministry. Read Matt. 5-7 before you visit the area.

In the Merged Gospels #53 *"Jesus went out to the mountain"* and *"up the mountain to pray"*. It is likely He prayed all night at "the Wilderness Cave/Erasmos Cave" on the lower edge of the Mount of Beatitudes. When morning came, He chose His *"12 apostles"*. This area is just up the mountain from the Cove of the Parables/Sower's Cove (where I believe He first called Peter, Andrew, James and John from their fishing boat and nets).

Many believe Jesus did not gather the multitude to the top of mountain for His message. More reasonably, after calling His disciples, He met the multitude on the lower edge of the mountainside at a beautiful *"level place"* (Lk. 6:17). Here He taught the Beatitudes.

There is an incredible view of the lake and the Plain of Ginnosar from this mountain. We believe this is the *"mountain in Galilee"* (Matt. 28:16) where the risen Lord appeared to His disciples.

From the *"Seat of Moses"*/Cathedra in Korazin Jesus unrolled the Scroll for His synagogue teaching.

Korazin was one of three synagogues assigned by the Galilean Sanhedrin to Jesus' as the "Teaching Rabbi".

Korazin/Chorazin (secret) is built of basalt stone, perched on the edge of Upper Galilee. It overlooks the Sea of Galilee, and is located just north of the Mount of Beatitudes. Here Jesus often taught in the village and synagogue. He placed a curse on the city because of their unbelief in His works (Matt. 11:20-24). Judgment came to Korazin when the city was destroyed in 70 AD. It was never rebuilt. Most of the population fled to the Golan Heights.

A Jewish cathedra, the honored seat in the synagogue, was used by the person unrolling the scroll. A First Century cathedra was discovered in the ruins. Likely, Jesus sat on this seat to open the scroll prior to reading the Scripture. Jesus was assigned the Korazin synagogue as "Teaching Rabbi".

Jesus often taught at the Capernaum Synagogue. He was a well educated Rabbi. I believe He was evidently assigned as the "Teaching Rabbi" to the cities of Capernaum, Bethsaida and Chorazin by the Galilean Sanhedrin. Jesus was often called *"Rabbi"* by his disciples and others, including the spiritual leaders of Israel who never would have used the term *"Rabbi"* loosely.

Capernaum / Kefar Nahum (Village of Nahum) is located on the north shore of the Sea. In Jesus' day it was an important customs station and fishing center. The Roman centurion stationed here helped to *"build the synagogue"*. It is the only synagogue I have seen in all Israel decorated with Roman eagles. Jesus relocated from His hometown of Nazareth and made Capernaum His home and headquarters (Matt. 4:13-17). It seems that Zebedee lived here with his family. James and John were partners in his fishing company, along with Simon Peter and Andrew from Bethsaida (Matt. 8:5, 14).

Capernaum is where Jesus healed Peter's mother-in-law (Matt. 8:14) and called His disciples to become *"fishers of men"* (Matt. 4:13, 18-22, 9:9-13). Jesus called Levi/Matthew from his tax collecting. He often preached in the Capernaum synagogue (Lk. 4:31-33). He cast out demons (Matt. 9:27-35, 12:22-45; Mk. 3:22-30; Luke 11:14-26) and healed many, even one let down through a roof. Jesus healed a nobleman's son (John 4:46-54) and raised Jairus' daughter to life. Jairus was the *"ruler of the synagogue"* and not the teaching Rabbi. (Lk. 8:40-56) At Capernaum Jesus sent Simon Peter to catch a fish and pay the temple tax with the shekel from the fish's mouth (Matt. 17:24-27). Jesus performed more miracles in Capernaum than any other city. The city came under Jesus' warning of doom because they refused to repent of their sins (Matt. 11:23, 24). Some of Jesus' greatest messages were delivered in the synagogue (Jn. 6:22- 71). Here He spoke on *"the Bread of Life"* and taught the little children who came to Him (Matt. 18:1-6; Mk. 9:33-37; Lk. 9:46-48).

Basalt village millstone at Capernaum

THE COVE OF THE PARABLES is one of the most important Biblical sites on the Sea of Galilee. It is a natural amphitheater located exactly one mile west of Capernaum.

It is the author's firm belief that this cove was the favorite teaching area of our Lord at the Sea of Galilee.

THE COVE OF THE PARABLES / SOWER'S COVE

The Cove of the Parables is one of the most important Biblical sites in all of Israel for Christians. It is a natural amphitheater located exactly one mile west of Capernaum. Extensive acoustical studies show how Jesus could have easily taught 8000 persons south of the road, and up to 14,000 in the entire "bowl". The acoustics are perfect, especially when one is speaking from a boat in the middle of the cove.

It was probably here that Zebedee (father of James and John) moored his fishing boats, locating them a mile closer to the warm springs during the spring fishing season. Jesus borrowed Peter's boat and taught the crowds who came. In the deeper waters of the cove, Peter and others dropped their nets for a large catch of fish (Matt. 4:18-22; Mk. 1:16-20; Lk. 5:1-11, 1:19-20; Merged Gospels #40).

I believe it was here, early in His Galilean ministry, that Jesus called several of His first disciples from mending their nets and fishing. In this cove Jesus taught many key parables, including the Parable of the Sower (Matt.13:1-9; Mk. 4:1-9; Lk. 8:4-8).

Here our risen Lord appeared to His disciples who had fished all night and caught nothing. On this rocky basalt shore, Jesus ate breakfast with His disciples and restored Simon Peter, who had openly denied Him during His trial in Jerusalem (Jn. 21:1-23).

The Cove of the Parables in the springtime, with mustard blooming in the foreground.

Bob Ross on the hillside at the Cove of the Parables pointing toward the area where Jesus likely taught. This is Bob's favorite spot on planet earth.

Today, beautiful olive and avocado trees grow above the cove, but the inner bowl near the water's edge is an unkempt agricultural refuse area. This has preserved its New Testament condition, leaving the cove much as it would have appeared in Jesus' day.

Bethsaida (house of fishing) was located near the place where the Jordan enters the Sea at the north end. Peter, Andrew and Philip lived and fished here (Jn. 1:44, 12:21-22). Here Jesus healed the blind man (Mk. 8:22-26). Nearby, He fed the multitudes the fish and loaves in the hills above the Sea, though many believe the miracle took place in a desolate location north of Bethsaida (Matt. 14:13-21; Mk. 6:31-44; Lk. 9:10-17; Jn. 6:1-14).

The Merged Gospels places the feeding of the 5,000 on the opposite side of the lake, south of Tiberias. Dr. Crossland bases his supposition on the Scripture that records Jesus coming to His disciples walking on the water in the *"middle of the lake"* (Merged Gospels # 102). The disciples had rowed most of the night, fighting the storm on the lake, but had only traveled about 4 miles. The boat was still in the *"middle of the lake"* when the disciples saw Jesus *"walking on the sea and drawing near to the boat"* (Jn. 6:19a).

Gadara, in Mark, means walls or fences. In the book of Matthew **Gergesa** likely refers to Gerasa, the capital of the Decapolis. Later Gerasa was named Jerash. Both are located on the eastern side of the Sea. In this area Jesus and His disciples encountered a man who lived in the tombs and was possessed by demons. Jesus sent the demons into a herd of swine, and they were drowned in the Sea (Lk. 8:26-39; Matt. 8:28-34).

A fourth century Byzantine church was discovered after the 1967 Six Day War. Road construction was delayed to complete the excavation near the eastern shore. Byzantine mosaics in the church depict Jesus' miraculous healing by casting out the demons from the demoniac. Some believe that the desolate area between Capernaum and Kursi is where Jesus fed the 4000.

The *"other side"* was sometimes a substitute phrase for the Gentile land of the Gadarenes.

The cave tombs, inhabited by the demoniac, are seen in the upper right.

From these cliffs the "deviled ham" rushed down into the Sea and were drowned.

FISHING ON THE SEA OF GALILEE

The late **Mendel Nun**, from **Kibbutz Ein Gev**, was an expert on fishing and the Sea of Galilee. He reported that there are 18 species of fish in the Sea, but only 10 of these have commercial value (Matt. 13:47-48).

Jesus' miraculous catches of fish took place at the Sea of Galilee.

The real name of "St Peter's Fish" is Musht, meaning "comb" in Arabic, and Annun meaning "to nurse" in Hebrew. The fish can reach 16 inches in length, and raises her young in her mouth. The mother protects the small fish until they are large enough to leave her care. After they are on their own, the mother fish then fills her mouth with a bright object such as a coin or rock from the bottom of the lake. This fish is unique only to this Sea. Peter found a Temple Shekel in this fish's mouth; thus, it is called "St. Peter's Fish". You will probably be offered this tasty fish for lunch while at the Sea of Galilee.

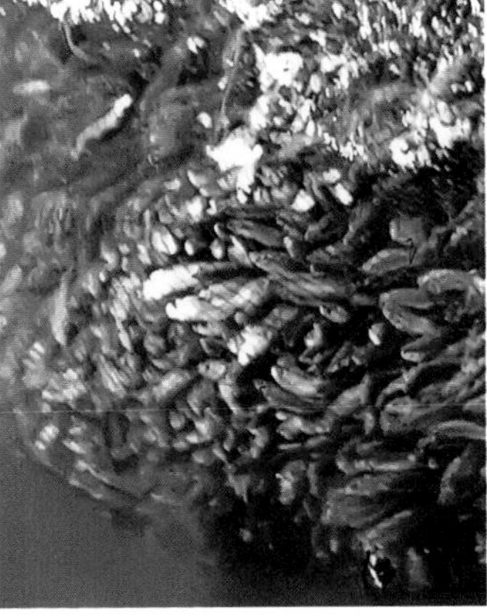

Nets filled with fish at the Sea of Galilee - Photos by Dr. Richard Cleave

Center picture from *The Sea of Galilee and Its Fishermen* by Mendel Nun

Horns of Hattin looking east - The last conflict between the Crusaders and the Muslims, under Saladin, took place on this battlefield. Saladin set the scrub brush on fire, causing the Crusaders, in their heavy body armor, to succumb to the smoke and heat.

Lower Galilee

Horns of Hattin is a hill shaped like two animal horns, which rise above the Sea on the western side. Here Saladin and his Muslim horsemen defeated the Crusaders on a hot July day in 1187 AD. This brought an end to Crusader control of the Holy Land. Some believe Jesus preached His Sermon on the Mount here (Matt. 5-7). If this is so, history presents a very interesting irony! Was this really the place where our Lord taught, "Blessed are the peace makers, for they shall be called the Sons of God"?

Gath-Hepher (winepress of digging) was the hometown of Jonah, the reluctant preacher who tried to escape God's call to preach in Nineveh. He caught a ship at Joppa on the Mediterranean Coast, but was swallowed by a huge fish in a storm. When the fish could not *stomach him* any longer, it vomited him onto the shore, and Jonah made a beeline for Nineveh. He preached repentance to the Gentiles there (II Kings 14:25; Jonah).

Turan is an Arab village today. Many believe it was in the fields near Turan that Jesus' disciples were criticized for picking grain, *"threshing"* it in their hands, and eating it on the Sabbath (Matt. 12:1; Lk. 6:1).

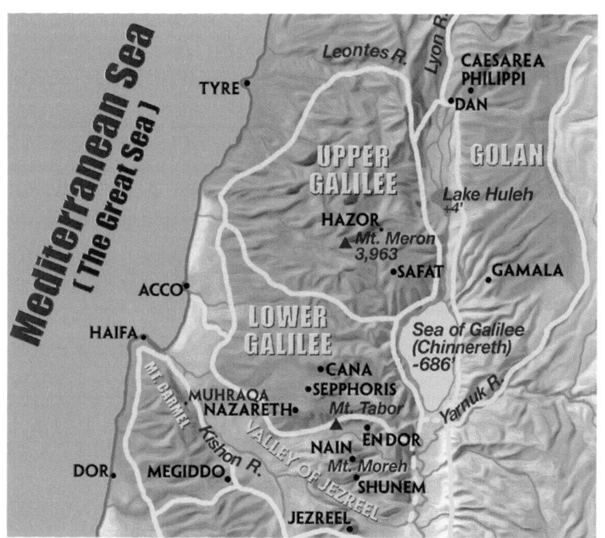

Cana (place of reeds) is the traditional site of Jesus' first miracle, when He changed the water into wine at the marriage feast (Jn. 2:1-11) and called Nathanael to become His disciple (Jn. 1:45-51). In route between Cana and Capernaum Jesus healed the centurion's son from a distance (Jn. 4:46-54).

Sepphoris /Tzippori (bird) was the Roman capital of Galilee under Herod Antipas from 4 BC to 39 AD. Thereafter, Tiberias became the capital. Sepphoris means "bird", and the city was perched on top of a hill. It was the hometown of Jesus' mother, Mary.

The excavations of today have proven it was one of the largest Roman cities in the Middle East. In Jesus' day it had a population of approximately 30,000. The author believes that Jesus received His formal rabbinical training at the Jewish yeshiva/seminary in Sepphoris (the closest yeshiva to Nazareth). The Sanhedrin of Galilee met here in Jesus' day. Every Jewish Sanhedrin had an accompanying yeshiva nearby. But in Sepphoris it has not yet been identified. In Jesus' day many yeshivas met in the local synagogues.

Nazareth was 5 kilometers from Sepphoris in those days. An insurrection in Sepphoris, when Jesus was about 10 years old, brought Rome's wrath. The road between Sepphoris and Nazareth was lined with thousands of crosses. Every carpenter/craftsman in the area was forced to construct these crosses. Joseph was likely included and if so, this would have been Jesus' first encounter with a Roman cross.

First century excavations at Sepphoris

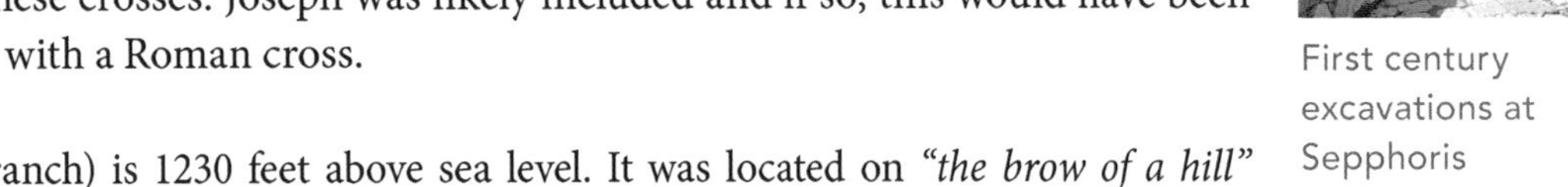

Nazareth (shoot/branch) is 1230 feet above sea level. It was located on *"the brow of a hill"* overlooking the Valley of Jezreel. This was Jesus' early boyhood home where He would have attended school and worshiped in the synagogue with His family (Lk. 2:39, 51-52). He was trained in the *"craftsman's"* shop by Joseph, until His adopted father died.

Women on the way to market in narrow Nazareth street, 1959

In Nazareth, Mary heard the angel Gabriel's announcement of Jesus' birth (Isa. 7:14; Lk. 1:26-38). The Church of Annunciation stands over the traditional site of this announcement. After Jesus' birth in Bethlehem and a brief stay in Egypt, Mary and Joseph brought Him back to Nazareth as a babe in arms (Matt. 2:21-23). At the age of 30 Jesus entered His ministry; no Jewish rabbi entered his ministry prior to age 30. Then, in God's timing, He went to the Jordan River where John the Baptist baptized Him (Mk. 1:9). This experience was His baptism, His ordination for ministry, and we believe the completion of His bar mitzvah.

In the Nazareth synagogue Jesus preached His first sermon, and was rejected by His own townspeople. He indicated that His message was for Jews and Gentiles (Lk. 4:16-31). This really upset them. Though born in Bethlehem, Jesus was called a *"Nazarene"*, since Nazareth was His home for about 27 years. Nathanael spoke unfavorably of Nazareth because it was a small and obscure village (Jn. 1:46).

A model of a Craftsman's Shop at Nazareth Village

Today the Baptist and evangelical work in Nazareth is quite strong. The Baptist Church and seminary is the center of Galilean outreach. The Paul Rowden High School is recognized as one of the finest in Israel for the preparation of university students. (The author and his wife's first son was born in Nazareth).

Tours often visit **Nazareth Village**, on the western edge of the city. The village is rebuilt reflecting archaeological evidence on how it would have appeared in Jesus' day. It gives a pretty accurate view of life in Nazareth. Many scenes from the movie *Nativity* were filmed at this location. You can find more details about the village, and reservations can be made at www.nazarethvillage.com

Looking south from Megiddo, one overlooks the Valley of Jezreel, with the mountains of Samaria in the distance.

Valley of Jezreel

ARMAGEDDON or ESDRAELON

The Valley of Jezreel (God sows or scatters) is the largest and most fertile valley in all Israel. The Valley separates the mountains of Galilee from those of Samaria. Jezreel or Armageddon, has been a battlefield for some of the world's most important generals.

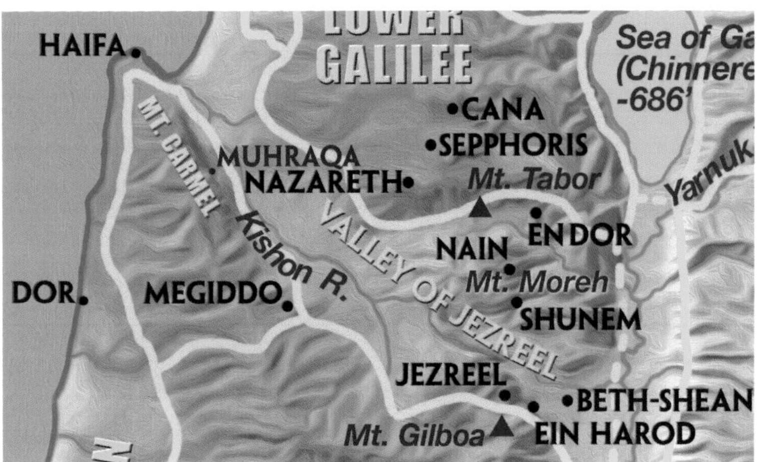

Twenty one battles of the Old Testament were fought in this valley. The Egyptians, Hittites, Israelites, Philistines, Assyrians, Syrians, Persians, Greeks, Romans, Crusaders, Muslims, Turks, French and British have fought here. While in exile on the Isle of Patmos, John experienced a vision revealing the final War of Armageddon, which he recorded in the book of Revelation.

That final battle of world history relates to this *"gathering place"* (Rev. 16:16, 18-21). However, according to the prophecies in *Zech. 12-14,* that final battle will take place in

Jerusalem. Perhaps Armageddon is the gathering place for the armies of the world in preparation for the final battle which will include Jerusalem.

The wide fertile valley was easy prey for the world's mightiest armies, making it the warpath and battlefield of the empires. There are five entrances to the valley. At each of the entrances a fortress city protected the pass. Esdraelon was in the tribal area of Issachar. While Deborah, Barak and Gideon were victorious in Jezreel, the kings Ahab, Josiah, and Saul, as well as his son, Jonathan, all died in this valley.

In Nazareth, on the north eastern edge of this historic plain, Jesus grew to manhood. We are reminded of the statement, *"Jesus was going throughout all Galilee teaching in the synagogues and proclaiming the Gospel of the Kingdom..."* (Matt. 4:23).

The statue of Elijah at Muhraka recalls God's victory over the prophets of Baal.

Mount Carmel (fruitful garden) is a wedge-shaped mountain of limestone 13 miles long. The **Plain of Acco** lies on the north-west, with the mountains of Jordan and the Jordan Valley to the east. Carmel's height is approximately 1600′. Ancients considered Carmel to be the "Garden of God", and it has been famous through history for its lush vegetation. The garden-like loveliness attracted the Egyptians and Canaanites to the worship of Baal of Carmel. Baal was the counterpart of the Greek god, Zeus and the Roman god, Jupiter.

Elijah's choice of this site for the contest with the Baal prophets was surely God led. Elijah confronted the very sanctuary of Baalism, and God led him to victory (I Kings 18:19-40).

The tribe of Asher inherited the Carmel range (Josh. 19:26). In Elijah and Elisha's time, they often retreated to Carmel to spend time with God. The drought during Ahab's reign was broken when Elijah and his servant spotted *"a cloud the size of man's hand"* over the Mediterranean Sea (I Kings 18:41-46). He then ran from Carmel, ahead of Ahab's chariot, to the entrance of the city of Jezreel.

Later the bereaved Shunemite woman found Elisha on Carmel, and he restored her son to life (II Kings 4:25-37). The prophets spoke of the fertility and lush growth of Carmel as a symbol of plenty (Isa. 35:2; Jer. 50:19; Mic. 7:14). When Carmel lost her foliage, there was drought and desolation in the whole Land (Isa. 33:9; Amos 1:2; Nah. 1:4).

Looking south from beautiful Mt. Carmel, the Valley of Jezreel, Armageddon unfolds.

Mukhraka (scorching) is the horn or peak of Mt. Carmel (1600' alt.). It is mentioned in the Hebrew Scriptures as the highest point of the mountain. It was the location for the confrontation between Elijah and the Baal prophets. Today, a Greek Catholic monastery stands at the horn of Carmel, and provides an incredible view toward the Mediterranean Sea to the West. The Southern view from Carmel presents the Valley of Jezreel in all her beauty.

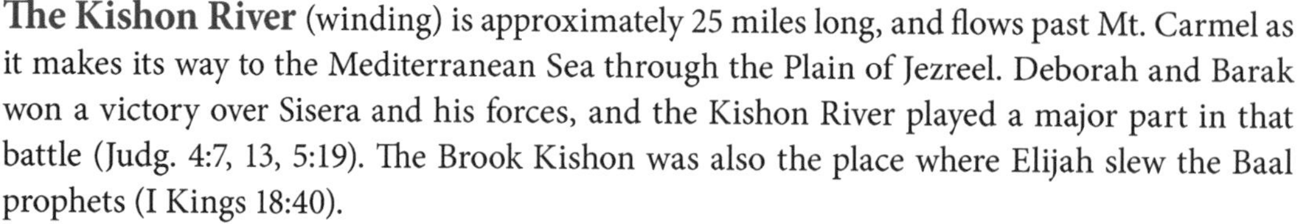

The Kishon River (winding) is approximately 25 miles long, and flows past Mt. Carmel as it makes its way to the Mediterranean Sea through the Plain of Jezreel. Deborah and Barak won a victory over Sisera and his forces, and the Kishon River played a major part in that battle (Judg. 4:7, 13, 5:19). The Brook Kishon was also the place where Elijah slew the Baal prophets (I Kings 18:40).

The Lion of Judah, the Seal of Megiddo, was stolen from the Orient Express en route to the Constantinople Museum.

Megiddo (place of troops) was a powerful Canaanite city-state. It was strategically located for war at the pass where the Via Maris entered the Valley of Jezreel. The city protected the greatest trade route in the Old Testament world. The narrow pass through the Carmel Mountain chain was the main artery of communication between Egypt, Assyria and Phoenicia. Under the shadow of the fortress passed the great armies of history. Many of their most decisive battles were fought in the plain below. Military leaders like Thutmoses, Ramses, Shishak, Necho, Sennacherib, Alexander the Great, Pompey, Titus, Saladin, Napoleon and British General Allenby fought here.

Valley of Jezreel from Megiddo, with Mt. Moreh to the left, and Mt. Gilboa to the right

Har Megiddo, the "mountain of war", and the plain below have become a symbol of the final war on planet earth (Rev. 16:13-16; Ezek. 38:39; Ezek. 39; Zech. 14:2-3). It seems this battle will be extended to include Jerusalem in that day. Armageddon simply means the Mount of Megiddo.

Megiddo was occupied as early as 4000 BC. The walls are 26 feet thick and over 13 feet high, and date from 2900-2600 BC. Megiddo was briefly taken by Joshua, but was not occupied by Israel due to the strength of the Canaanites. Megiddo was not truly conquered until David's time. Under Solomon, the fortress became the major defense city for Israel, and had great influence in politics, art, craftsmanship, war, literature, religion and science.

Solomon fortified Megiddo with casement walls. He built special gates and added this fortress to his other chariot cities of Hazor and Gezer (I Kings 9:15). The famous stables, however, belonged to King Ahab's period, along with his palace and the underground water system. Ahab had 2000 war chariots and 500 horses stationed here.

Under Jehu's reform, King Ahaziah was slain in Megiddo. In 610 BC, Pharaoh Necho killed Josiah at Megiddo (I Kings 23). From atop Megiddo there is a marvelous view of the Valley of Armageddon to the east and south. From here the three mountains of the Jezreel Valley can be clearly seen. Right to left the mountains are Tabor, Moreh and Gerazim.

Aerial view of Tel Megiddo

Mount Tabor lies to the southwest of Nazareth. From a distance, the mountain looks like the top half of a circle. It rises 1843 feet above sea level. Tabor was the boundary between Issachar and Zebulun (Josh. 19:22-23). Deborah and Barak gathered forces here to defeat Sisera in the valley below (Judg. 4:6-17). The brothers of Gideon were slain here (Judg. 8:18-21). Catholic tradition teaches that Jesus was transfigured on Mt. Tabor, and a beautiful transfiguration church adorns the peak. However, Mt. Hermon in the Golan Heights seems the more likely place. Josephus, in the Jewish Revolt of 66 AD, held the top of the mount as a stronghold before he defected to the Romans.

En Dor (fountain of Dor) is located on the western base of Mt. Tabor. Here Saul visited the witch on the eve of his battle with the Philistines (I Sam. 28:7-25). Returning across the Valley Jezreel, he died in battle the next day. Earlier, many fugitives of Sisera's army perished in this valley (Psa. 83:9-10).

Modern En Dor is located on the slope of Mt. Tabor. Ancient En Dor is where Saul went for advice from the witch about his battle with the Philistines.

Mount Moreh (Hill of the Teacher) rises in the center of the Valley of Jezreel. From her slopes Gideon attacked the Midianites with pitchers and lamps, routing their entire army (Judg. 6-8; Psa. 83:10-11). The Mount has seen two young men raised to life from death – one in Shunem by Elisha, and the other in Nain by Jesus.

Nain (pleasant) is where Jesus raised the widow's son to life after stopping the funeral procession (Lk. 7:11-15). The city is built of basalt stone, and it can only be entered by a narrow road winding through grain fields. The town was in Issachar's tribal area.

Photograph shows Shunem's open air village ovens for the baking of bread.

Shunem (uneven) sits on the west side of Mt. Moreh and belonged to the tribe of Issachar. Here Elisha raised the widow's son to life (II Kings 4:8-37). Shunem is located about two miles over Mt. Moreh from Nain. Abishag, David's wife of his old age, was born here. The Philistines gathered their forces at Shunem to fight against Saul and Jonathan.

Jezreel (God sows) is the city where King Ahab and Jezebel had their summer palace. Influenced by her Gentile background, she promoted Baal worship in Israel. After Ahab took Naboth's vineyard, Elijah warned Ahab of the drought to come. After Elijah killed the Baal prophets at Mt. Carmel, he ran ahead of Ahab's chariot to the gate of Jezreel (I Kings 18:42, 46). After Ahab's death and under Jehu's reform, Jezebel was thrown from the palace and her body was eaten by dogs in the street (I Kings 21:17-25, 22:37-38). Ahab was wounded in battle, and later died in Samaria, where dogs lapped his blood from the chariot, as prophesied.

Mt. Moreh lies across the Valley of Jezreel, and ruins of Ahab's palace in Jezreel, in the foreground.

Mount Gilboa is 10 miles long and rises 1,696 feet above sea level. Saul and his sons were killed by the Philistines here (I Sam. 28:4, 31:1-6; II Sam. 1:5-10, I Chron. 10:1-6). David lamented the death of Saul and Jonathan, and he prayed that no dew would fall on Gilboa (II Sam. 1:19-27). Until today, sparse plant life grows on her slopes.

Pools at Beit Alpha National Park are formed from the water flowing from Gideon' Spring to Ein Harod. It was here that Gideon brought his troops. God selected 300 qualified men for this battle (Judges 7). Mt. Gilboa rises in the background.

Gideon's Springs/Ein Harod (fountain of terror or trembling) flows from the base of Mt. Gilboa. Gideon gathered his troops here prior to the battle with the Midianites. God told him to reduce his forces, and he sent home all who *"laps the water with his tongue as a dog laps"* (Judg. 7). Gideon entered the battle with only 300 men, but God gave him the assurance of victory (Judg. 7). Saul and his men encamped at this spring the night before his death, in the battle against the Philistines on Mt. Gilboa.

Beit Alpha has a 6th century synagogue with an incredible mosaic floor. Nearby is a national park with warm springs, pools and great swimming. These pools are rated among the top ten of the world.

Tel Beth Shean's excavations began in the 1920's. A stella to the goddess Ashtoreth has been found there, and relates to Saul's death (1 Sam. 31:10). Photographed by author in 1959.

Beth Shean's city gate - Mt. Gilboa in background, 1959

Roman Amphitheater seated 5000 people in 200 AD

Beth Shean's Roman main street

Beth Shean (house of quiet security) was the city that protected the entrance to the Valley of Jezreel from the Jordan Valley. It rose above the Jordan Valley, and was inhabited as early as 3000 BC. The tel reveals eighteen occupation levels with six pagan temples. According to Joshua 17:11, the tribe of Manessah inherited the city, but they could not subdue the Canaanites at Beth-Shean (Judg. 1:27).

The bodies of Saul and Jonathan were hung on the city gate facing Mt. Gilboa, where they died. Saul's head was placed in the Temple of Dagon, but the brave men of Jabesh Giliead crossed the Jordan by night and removed Saul and Jonathan's bodies. They took their bodies to the east side of the Jordan for burial (I Sam. 31:8-13; II Sam. 21:12-14).

Beth Shean was one of the ten Greek cities of the Decapolis, and the only one west of the Jordan. During the time of Christ, the city was named Scythopolis. To our knowledge, Jesus never entered the city, but He often passed Beth Shean on the "pilgrims route" through the Jordan Valley. Excavations of the Roman ruins have revealed an enormous city with magnificent temples, streets, a theater and a large amphitheater for games.

Today tourists can visit the Roman baths, walk the main east-west street (the cardo), view the great pillars of the temples and stroll through the market and public buildings. The extensive Roman city was destroyed by an earthquake. Sitting in the basalt stone theater, one can visualize the life-style of the people who lived, worked and played here.

Beth Shean is one of the largest Roman excavations in the Middle East. The Old Testament tel rises above the Roman ruins to the east.

Ancient Beth Shean - The Jordan River lies beyond, with the Mountains of Gilead in the background.

Mediterranean Coast

PHOENICIAN COASTAL CITIES

Phoenicia of the Hebrew Scriptures (Old Testament) was located on the Mediterranean Sea coast in what is now present day Lebanon and northern Israel. This narrow strip of land included the cities of Tyre, Sidon, Acco and Achzib. The inhabitants were Semitic maritime traffickers who were instrumental in colonizing many islands of the Mediterranean Sea. Their Greek name comes from the word "Phoenix", meaning "the People of the Purple Dye".

King David developed alliances with King Hiram I of Phoenicia, who supplied him with materials and craftsmen for the Temple in Jerusalem (II Sam. 5:11; I Kings 5:1-18). The Old Testament often makes reference to Phoenicia, Israel's neighbors to the north.

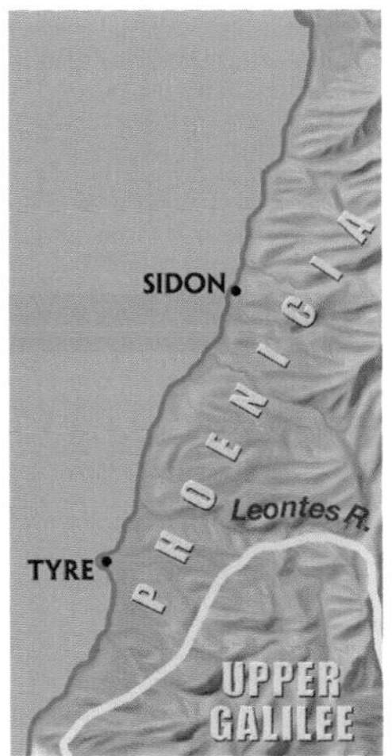

Sidon was located in the territory of the Canaanites (Gen. 10:19). Today, Sidon, along with her twin city of Tyre, is part of Lebanon. Scripture records Jesus leaving Israel only once as an adult, and on that occasion He visited Phoenicia and ministered to the Syro-Phoenician woman (Matt. 15:21). Paul stopped in this port city en route to Rome (Acts 27:3).

Tyre was the home of King Hiram, who was a friend to both King David and King Solomon (II Sam. 5:11). Hiram furnished timbers, "*the Cedars of Lebanon*", for the construction of the Temple. Tyre lies just south of Sidon, and is 25 miles closer to Israel.

The white-chalk rocks of Rosh ha Niqua are honey-combed with beautiful caves. This rock forms the present day border of Israel and Lebanon.

Acco/Acre is located in the northern coastal plain of Israel, at the northern extremity of Haifa Bay on the Mediterranean Sea.

Looking south along the Mediterranean coast, the Plain of Asher spreads before us.

Israel's Northern Coast

***"Listen to Me in silence, O coast lands; let the people renew their strength; let them come forward and speak."* (Isaiah 41:1)**

Rosh ha Niqua / Ladders of Tyre is located on the Israeli-Lebanon border at the southernmost point of the Lebanese Mountains. Legend has it that Abraham was led here by God, and he proclaimed, "*This is the place*", meaning the *Land of Promise.* This narrow passage was the entrance into Israel used by Alexander the Great, the Crusaders and the Allied Forces in 1914 and 1941.

The waves of the Mediterranean Sea have carved out beautiful grottos from the white chalk rock cliffs. These can be visited by cable car as time permits. This area is seldom included in tours due to its distance from other important sites.

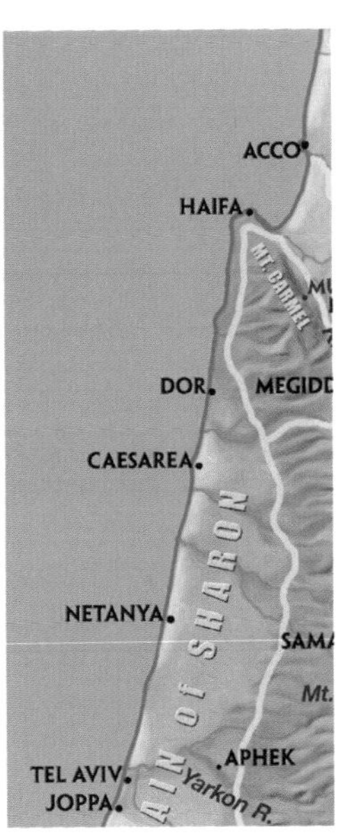

The Plain of Asher stretches south from Lebanon along the sea coast. The Plain is 25 miles long and about 8 miles wide. Most coastal towns were either seaports or fortresses. (Inland fortresses helped guard the interior). In Bible times, this plain was of little importance, since Israel was not a seagoing people. God instructed Israel through Joshua, "*...You have the Great Sea and its coastline; this shall be your west border*" (Num. 34:6). Unfortunately, this area was never really secured by Israel due to the powerful Phoenicians. Israel held territorial control from Mt. Carmel south, including Athlit and Dor to Philistia.

Achzib (lying) is a northern coastal city which continued to be occupied by the Canaanites for years after Israel invaded the land (Judg. 1:31).

Acco was the Crusader's headquarters on the Mediterranean Sea.

Acco/Acre (hot sand) existed for nearly 4000 years as a major seaport. It was first a Canaanite and later a Phoenician port which guarded the pass into the Valley of Jezreel. Acco was targeted for acquisition by the Pharaohs of Egypt. In the Old Testament period, the city was assigned to the tribe of Asher, but it was never conquered by them. At that time it was called Acco (Judg. 1:31).

In 261 BC Ptolemy II fortified the city and renamed it Ptolemais. It later became the main port of Israel until Herod the Great built Caesarea, Acco/Ptolemais came under Roman rule in 65 BC.

Acco was the Crusader port in the Holy Land and their capital for over 100 years. The city has experienced 17 sieges. Napoleon was unable to take the city from the Turks.

One can visit the underground Crusader city, the walls, buttresses and ramparts, the Citadel and the Mosque. Acco is not included in most tour itineraries for Israel since there are so many more important Biblical sites.

Acco was in Asher's territory but seldom was it under Israel's control. Paul stopped here in Acts 21:7 and "*visited the brethren*", which indicates that a community of believers/followers of the Messiah was here in the New Testament period.

Haifa is one of the most beautiful cities in the world. Some say that it was founded by Caiaphas, the High Priest of Jesus' trials. The city was destroyed by the Muslims, and then later by the Crusaders. The British built a modern harbor here, and today Haifa is Israel's main port and home of the Israel's Navy.

Haifa is located where Mt. Carmel dips into the Mediterranean Sea. The bay is the home of the Israeli Navy. The entrance to the Valley of Jezreel is to the right.
Photo 1960

Millions have returned to their "Home" Land through the Port of Haifa. She has been the *"first sight of Heaven"* for many homeless Jewish refugees. Today, the city's population is nearly half a million. The city sits on the northern slope where Mount Carmel dips into the Mediterranean Sea, and overlooks the beautiful entrance to the Valley of Jezreel. Acco lies across the bay to the north.

Caesarea's coastline with the theater, aqueduct, Roman port and hippodrome

Dor (habitation) was for many centuries the most important coastal town, with a strong tower fortress guarding the bay in Canaanite and Israelite times. Her king fought against Israel and was conquered by Joshua (Josh. 11:2). The victory did not last because the tribe of Manasseh was unable to hold the port city. Actually, Dor was on the dividing line between the tribes of Asher and Manasseh. King David captured the city from the Philistines, but Dor remained a Phoenician/Gentile city well into the Roman period. Pompey granted autonomy to the city in 64 BC.

In ancient days, Dor was a center for the production of a dye called *Tyrian/Royal purple.* It was the color of royalty and was used by emperors, kings and nobles. The color was a purplish blue, and was extracted from a tiny gland in the mollusk/murex snail. They abound along the coast toward Athlit. Not until the 19th century was this royal color matched by other sources. In Roman times the Jews were famous for dyeing cloth. *(See detailed notes at the end of this section.)*

Caesarea was Rome's headquarters in Israel for 500 years. Rome's port and enormous breakwater stones have sunken into the sand of the Mediterranean. Photo taken in 1959

In the 1950's the Roman theater at Caesarea was discovered beneath the sand. The beginning of the excavations are seen below, 1959.

Caesarea (pertaining to Caesar) is located 30 miles north of Joppa and 70 miles from Jerusalem. It was built by Herod the Great in 25 BC as his summer palace, on the site of Old Testament Strato's Tower. Caesarea was the capital for the Roman government in Israel for nearly 500 years. It was named after Caesar Augustus (Lk. 2:1). Caesarea was truly the "Rome of the Middle East". It was the home of Pontius Pilate. Herod Agrippa died here, and *"an angel of the Lord struck him... he was eaten by worms and died"* (Acts 12:19-23).

Vespasian was crowned Emperor of the Roman Empire in

Caesarea's theater is were Paul was tried, and King Agrippa died.

Caesarea, after leaving his son Titus in charge of the Jerusalem siege. Later, Titus celebrated his father's birthday by forcing 2500 Jews to fight wild animals to their death in the amphitheater. Terrible cruelties were inflicted upon the Jews under Felix and Festus. While in prison at Caesarea, Paul witnessed to Felix, Festus and Agrippa (Acts 26).

At Caesarea, Peter preached to Cornelius and the "Gentile Pentecost" followed (Acts 10). Philip lived and preached here (Acts 8:40, 21:8-9). Paul visited here three times, and here Agabus warned him not to go to Jerusalem (Acts 9:30, 18:22, 21:8-16, 25:3-6). Later, riots between Gentiles and Jews led to the final Jewish War in 135 AD.

Rabbi Akiva was martyred here by the Romans after the Bar Kokhba rebellion. Many Jews and Christians were thrown to the lions at that time. In the third century, the Christian scholar Origen directed a school at Caesarea. Eusebius was the Bishop of Caesarea from 313 to 340 AD.

The city was conquered first by the Muslims in 638 AD. Then, the Crusaders controlled the city for a brief time. But, it fell back into Muslim hands. It was the scene of a Muslim massacre of Christians in 1101. In 1265 it was conquered by the Turks. Today, there are many Roman ruins, Crusader fortifications and Muslim buildings on the site.

Caesarea's Roman aqueduct, before and after excavation

Incredible excavations have uncovered a 2nd century Roman aqueduct, built by the Roman Fifth Legion. It brought water twelve miles from Mt. Carmel to the city. Here the first archaeological evidence of Pontius Pilate has been unearthed. An inscription confirms his rule from 26 AD. Some believe the "Holy Grail" was found here when the Crusaders conquered Caesarea.

Important excavations include the Crusader fortress, the Roman palaces, hot and cold baths, ornate columns, beautiful statues and sea walls of the ancient port city. Herod the Great built a temple to honor Caesar Augustus. The recently excavated Roman Hippodrome is over 1000 feet long and could seat 20,000 people. But the most beautiful building of all is the Roman Theater, which is located near the seashore. It is used today for Israeli concerts and performances. As late as 1960 it was completely covered with sand. Only the upper rim was then visible. It is said to have been discovered by a pilot in Israel's air force flying a coastal patrol.

The aqueduct was built by the Roman 5th legion.

At Caesarea a dry moat protected the Crusader city.

Tzitzit Blue was a royal blue. God commanded that a *"blue cord"* be woven into the tallit (prayer shawl) (Numb. 15:37-41). The blue thread was woven into the tzitzit/tassel/fringes located at the four corners, and tied in five knots to remind every Jew of the five books of Torah/Law. The four spaces between remind one of ***Y H W H***, God's unpronounceable name.

In our day synthetic blue is prevalent. In Biblical days blue dye was very expensive and reserved for royalty and the wealthy. The only source was the snail/mollusk. It took 12,000 snails to fill just one thimble with blue dye. In 200 BC one pound of blue cloth cost the equivalent of $36,000. By 300 AD it cost $96,000.*

Lydia, the *"seller of purple"* and an early follower of the Messiah, was one of the wealthiest women in the Empire (Acts 16:14). Blue represented the divine, and it set people apart in the Roman world. To own a blue thread was a special honor.

On the tallit, it reminds the wearer that he is significant in God's eyes. This is fitting, as God calls his children a *"Royal Priesthood"*. Blue threads were passed from father to son.

The first Israeli flag was a white and blue tallit. Today, the blue stripes in the flag symbolize that Israel is a chosen and a special nation in God's eyes. The Israeli flag represents God and his relationship with his people, who are to be a testimony to Him.

*Tzitzit information is from Clarence Wagner's book, ***Lessons from the Land of the Bible***. His book - ***365 Fascinating Facts About the Holy Land***, is also recommended. Both books can be ordered from bridgesforpeace.com

Jewish tallit/prayer shawl is shown with tzitzit/ "wings of the garment", tied on all four corners. Author explains the tzitzit at Capernaum.

A MEMORABLE MORNING at PORT DOR
With Dr. Kurt Raven, Archaeologist

Notes from the October 8, 2004 visit with Abe Azoulay, Bob and Barbara Ross

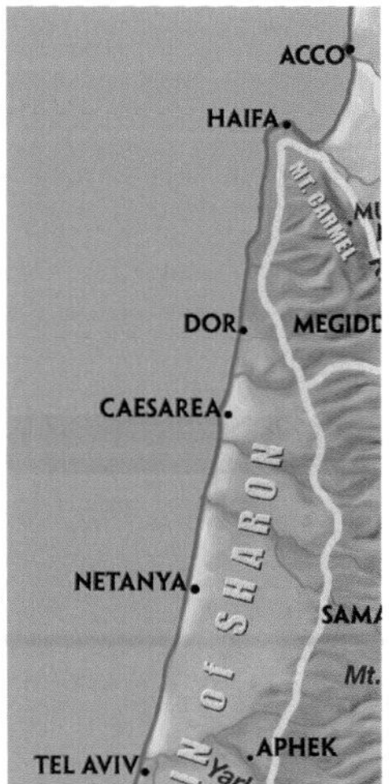

We arrived in Dor and met with Dr. Kurt Raven and Frans Yout. Frans, a naval officer with NATO, was the technician for the underwater archaeological excavations. He insured that the sand was properly removed, videos were taken of all artifacts that were found, and that proper sketches were made of these artifacts in their location. Then, he removed the objects to be studied by on-site archaeologists.

Kurt and Frans lived on the beach in the nearby moshav. Kurt was a professor at Haifa University's Department of Archaeology and Underwater Excavations. Kurt came to Dor in 1973 for a 3-week stint and stayed for 30 years. He now has spent 22 years excavating the Dor port. Kurt was in charge of the underwater excavations of this ancient port, and he led the excavation of the **"Jesus Boat"** at **Nof Ginnosar** on the Sea of Galilee.

When we visited Dor, Dr. Kurt Raven was waiting for their next excavation team (60-70 volunteers) from around the world. The following day, National Geographic was scheduled to photograph the excavation site for their next issue.

Dor has seen 5,000 years of shipping on the coastal trade route. It was the only natural harbor between Alexandria, Egypt and Phoenicia. Prevailing winds and strong currents led captains to seek this natural harbor. Kurt estimates that one ship per year was lost, resulting in thousands of ship wrecks.

The natural breakwater extends about one kilometer in length, but the entrance is no longer than a football field. Twenty two wrecks have been discovered at the port entrance. The ships ran into sandbars and broke apart. There is no coral in the Mediterranean Sea, only sand, shells and rock. Storms in the winter months often produce waves up to 24 feet, and this could spell tragedy for small boats of that day, which were all sailing vessels. For many years there was no safe shelter along this coast. The wrecked ships and cargo have been preserved beneath layers of sand.

One underwater excavation revealed provisions from one of Napoleon's campaigns. In two days, Napoleon jettisoned the arms for a 12,000 man army – to lighten the load. The sandy bay has kept these treasures for over 200 years. After Napoleon's failure to capture Acco, he sailed for Europe, trying to beat the fierce winter storms.

Author's wife, Barbara enjoys the warm sun, the beautiful harbor and the beach at Dor.

Today, underwater teams work from small boats in 6-15 feet of water. This shallow depth is marvelous considering the comparative costs of deeper excavations. Therefore, Dor is an ideal haven for underwater archaeology. Six people are assigned to each excavation boat, and there are approximately 18 people working in the water at any one time. The scuba tanks can last a full hour at this shallow depth. No decompression is ever necessary. One could sit on the bottom all day and simply observe the sea life and sunken treasures. Barb and I were greatly attracted to this dive site since diving has been a hobby for us for about 30 years.

All wrecks are buried under the sand, and it takes much energy to remove the silt and sand before being able to concentrate on the archaeological finds. By comparison, Caesarea to the south is 24 feet deep. At Athlit, to the north, they have found an underwater village 15 meters beneath the surface, with 65 full skeletons of the "Carmel Valley people". Public buildings and homes have also been excavated at Athlit.

Red Tulips on the coast of Tel Dor

Incredible treasures have been found at Dor: 1500 kilos of coins, 800 kilos of jewelry, 3800 candlesticks, plates, silver trays, bowls, images and vases. Canons, rifles, pistols and many swords have been excavated from the Napoleonic wrecks found scattered on the sandy bottom.

What about Biblical finds? Though Kurt has found many Roman and Byzantine wrecks, they have little relationship with Biblical history. Nor has any 13th century BC Phoenician ship been found, which carried the cedars for the construction of the Temple. Evidently the Phoenicians were a knowledgeable seagoing people. At one time, Kurt thought they had found a Phoenician ship, but it turned out to be an ancient Russian ship from the Black Sea. One wrecked ship, however, did carry Byzantine building stones.

On our visit we were invited to the moshav where Kurt and his wife had a beach home. He brought items to a beach-side picnic table for viewing. The artifacts were from the Greek, Roman, Crusader and Napoleonic periods. His finds included swords, canons, wine bottles, vases, rope, and a 1936 anchor. Sea shells and sand encrusted all the excavated items. The prior day he found seven swords, a cannon and pistols from Napoleon's time. Anything less than 300 years old may be kept by the excavator. Older artifacts belong to the Israeli Department of Antiquities. We held a skull from the Athlit excavation of the Carmel people. Strangely, the skull had no sockets for teeth. Kurt showed us a large Roman jar from the 2nd century. We recorded on video his site map of shipwrecks in the bay. The map showed all previous excavations and plans for future dives. Some wrecks have been discovered in water only nine feet deep, including one ship carrying bottles of perfume. Thirty types of wood from the shipwrecks have been identified.

Below - Ancient ruins of Tel Dor

One of Kurt's most important accomplishments thus far, was directing the excavation of the "Jesus Boat" at the Sea of Galilee.

Tel Dor (dwelling) is located north of today's port and is the second largest tel in the Land - only Hazor is larger. Tel Dor consists of 17 cities, or levels of habitation, built one upon another over 5,000 years. Richard the Lionhearted spent much time in this city. To the east toward Mt. Carmel there are many vineyards and a local winery.

The visit was a real *serendipity* for us since we had desired to visit underwater archaeology sites along Israel's Sea Coast for years. The next day Dr. Kurt Raven was to direct a National Geographic camera crew as they filmed the underwater site and discoveries.

Tel Dor across the bay

Plain of Sharon

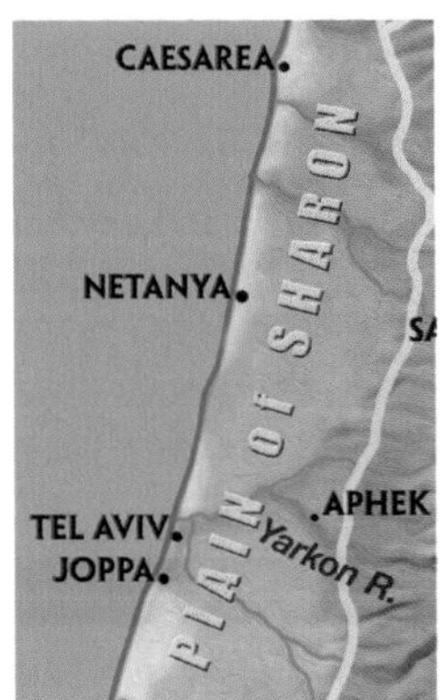

The Plain of Sharon is 8-12 miles wide and about 30 miles long, running from Mt. Carmel in the North to Joppa in the South. Here King David's shepherds cared for his herds (1 Chron. 27:25, 29). Isaiah spoke of *"the beauty of Sharon"* (Isa. 35:2, 65:10).

Natayna, in the northern part of Sharon, is called the "Pearl of Sharon". Her main industry is diamond cutting, started by Belgian refugees during WWII. Located on the Mediterranean Sea coast, she was founded in 1929 as a resort city. Natayna quickly became a recreation center for war weary soldiers of the U.S. and Allied Forces in the Middle East. Citrus groves and tourists provide livelihood for her 100,000 residents.

Tel Aviv (hill of the spring) was the first city built by the returning Jews in the 20th century. This was prophesied in Jer. 31:8. Today, Tel Aviv is the second largest city in Israel after Jerusalem. She is the center of Israel's business, commerce and industry, as well as the center of Israel's culture. Her name means "the Hill of the Spring".

Tel Aviv on the Mediterranean - Photo from Jaffa

Joppa/Jaffa/Yafo (beautiful) is the oldest seaport in the world, and is more than 3500 years old. Under Solomon, it served as Jerusalem's port of entry for cedar and other materials from Lebanon used for the building of the Temple. The city was located on the Via Maris, which connected Egypt to Mesopotamia; strategic for any foreign invader. The port city has undergone numerous attacks and sieges. It was a city allotted to the tribe of Dan, but the Philistines prevented Israel from possessing the territory. Thus, the Tribe of Dan moved to the North Country and conquered Laish, and renamed that city Dan.

Jonah set sail from Joppa, trying to escape God's call. He boarded a ship headed for Tarshish, with a one-way ticket (Jonah 1). His return trip was a "whale of a journey".

Conquerors like Alexander the Great, Ptolemy I, Antiochus III and Antiochus Epiphanes all marched against Joppa. Antiochus Epiphanes used Joppa as his port when he attacked Jerusalem. He coaxed 200 Jews onto ships in the harbor, and then killed them. In retaliation, Judas Maccabee burned the harbor. Under Pompey's reign, the city was under Roman rule, but it was later returned to the Jews by Julius Caesar.

In the days of the early church, a community of disciples lived here. In Joppa, Peter had his rooftop vision at Simon the Tanner's home. The messengers from Cornelius came seeking Peter (Acts 9–10). This is where Dorcus died and was raised to life by Simon Peter (Acts 9: 36-42).

Vespasian destroyed Joppa during the Jewish Revolt. The seaport was rebuilt. Her winding streets are refreshing and memorable. Today, Joppa is an artist colony with unique homes and quaint streets which rise above the ancient Mediterranean port. Joppa sunsets and the views across the bay towards Tel Aviv are beautiful. "Yoffe"!

Narow street in Jaffa's artist colony

Sunset over ancient Joppa, the world's oldest sea port

Aphek (strength or fortress) was also located on the ancient Via Maris. Joshua killed Aphek's king here (Josh. 2:18). The plain was a natural muster point for the Philistines. Here they fought with Israel and captured the Ark of the Covenant (I Sam. 4). On another occasion, the Philistines gathered their forces to attack Saul in the Valley of Jezreel at Mt. Gilboa. Saul and Jonathan were both killed in that battle (I Sam. 29:31).

Aphek was changed to **Antipatris** (belonging to Antipater) after it was rebuilt in 9 BC by Herod the Great, to honor his father. Paul was brought here by night under the protection of 270 soldiers (Acts 23:31). The city marked the border between Judaea and Samaria.

The springs of **Rosh ha'Ayin** are located below the fortress, and form the head waters of the **Yarkon River**, which flows into the Mediterranean and empties near Tel Aviv.

Lydda/Lod was a fortified city in the time of Joshua. It was rebuilt by the Benjamites when they returned from the Babylonian exile (Ezra 2:33; Neh. 7:37, 11:35). There was an early Christian community here, and Aenaeas (the paralytic) was healed by Peter in Lydda (Acts 9:32-35). Word of this miracle spread quickly throughout the entire Plain of Sharon.

Kefar Ha Baptistim - Village of the Baptists near Petach Tikvah... The orphanage was relocated here from Nazareth. The author and his wife lived and taught here in 1959-60.

Kefar Ha Baptistim (village of the Baptists) is located to the east of Petach Tikvah. In 1955-56 the Nazareth Baptist orphanage was moved to this location. By 1960, Kefar Ha Baptistim had become the conference center for Israel's evangelicals.

The author and his wife lived and served at this village as Southern Baptist "pre-journeymen" in 1959 and 1960, with their new son Randy. Randy, being a native born Israeli, is called a *sabra*, fruit of the prickly pear cactus, which is "sweet on the inside and prickly on the outside".

Modin is located near Aphek (six miles east of Lod/Lydda). It was the home of Judas Maccabaeus and his family. "Modi'in" was the home of the high priest Mattathias and his five sons. It was located in the same area as the modern city. The Jewish Maccabees won their freedom from the Greeks in 167 BC. This century old freedom was lost to the Romans in 63 BC. The name "Maccabim" is Hebrew for the Maccabees and is a common nickname given to Mattathias and his five sons. You may read about this Hasmonean dynasty in *I Maccabees.*

The Mountains of Samaria are the Biblical *"**Mountains of Israel**"* in the Hebrew Scriptures (Shomron). God promised to return His People Israel to this area in the *"latter days"*. God is presently keeping that promise.

Today's Palestinians claim this area is their territory, naming it the "West Bank" of Jordan. This area belonged to Israel for 1380 years. The Jordanians were there from 1948-1967, a mere 19 years.

Samaria

God's Word calls this area *"The Mountains of Israel"*. The "Palestinians" call it "The West Bank" of the Jordan River.

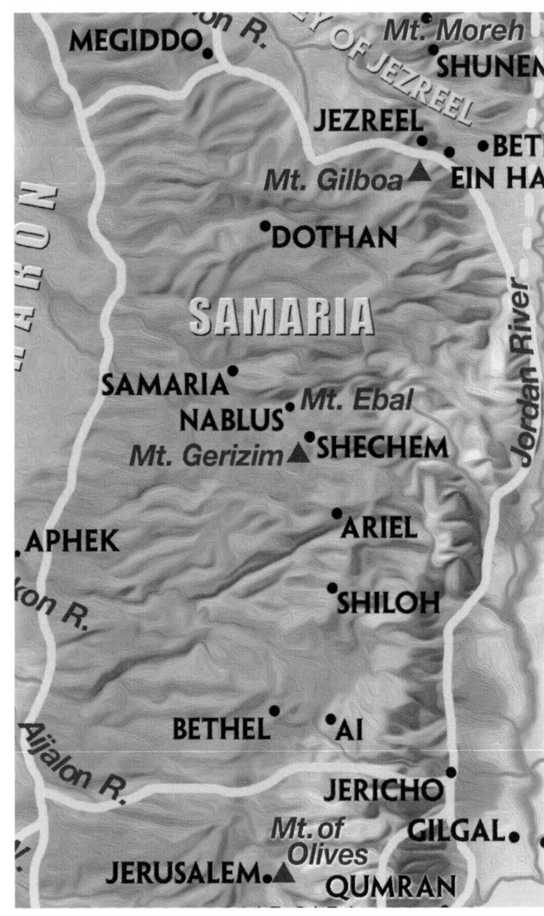

Jenin En-Gammin (Fount of Gardens) is located on the southern edge of the Valley of Jezreel on the highway leading from Galilee to Jerusalem. It was mentioned in *Joshua,* and according to tradition was the location where Jesus healed the 10 lepers (Lk. 17:11-19).

Dothan (double feasts) was a military post guarding an entrance into the Valley of Jezreel, and is 13 miles south of Jenin. This is the area where Joseph's brothers, while tending their father's flocks, sold Joseph to the Ishmaelites and into slavery, which took him to Egypt (Gen. 37:13-32). Elisha was from Dothan, where the Syrian invaders surrounded him and his servant (II Kings 6:13-23).

King Omri selected this incredible location for the capital of his Northern Kingdom. This mountain could easily be defended on all sides. He named the city Samaria, after the entire territory. Photo 1950 by Dr. George Redding, head of the Bible Department of Georgetown College, KY. His life and teachings deeply influenced our author.

Samaria/Sebaste/Shomrom (city of the watcher of the mountains) sits atop a 300-foot hill, dominating the countryside. King Omri (876-869 BC) wisely chose this incredible site as the capital of the Northern Kingdom (the 10 tribes of Israel). The whole country took its name from the city. It was located in the tribal area of Ephraim and Manasseh.

After a six year reign, Omri's son, Ahab, built a palace of ivory, which was strongly condemned by the prophet Amos (I Kings 22:39; Amos 6:1,4). Ahab's wicked wife Jezebel convinced him to build a temple to Baal in the Israelite capital (I Kings 16:29-33). After God killed Ahab, Jehu slaughtered his 70 sons and destroyed all idols in the city (II Kings 10). Still, the following four wicked kings – Jehu, Jehoahaz, Joash and Jehoash – were all condemned for their continued idolatry by God's prophets Isaiah, Jeremiah, Ezekiel, Hosea, Amos and Micah.

Naaman, the Syrian military captain, went to Samaria to be healed of his leprosy by Elijah (II Kings 5). Elisha sent him to wash in the Jordan River to be healed.

Omri's son Ahab built an incredible ivory palace at Samaria. The Prophets of Israel were critical of his evil rule, his wife, Jezebel, their worship of Baal and their opulent lifestyle.

Samaria was besieged by Benhadad of Syria twice, but he could not take the city. God's prophet Elisha smote his entire army with blindness (II Kings 6-7).

As had been prophesied, Samaria was finally conquered by Sargon of Assyria in 722-721 BC. The northern *"ten tribes"* were taken captive and became "lost" (until recent discoveries). The *Royal Annals* of Nineveh record that 27,290 Israelites were taken into exile. Those who were left in Israel intermarried with the repopulated Gentiles imported by Assyria from Babylon, Cuthah and Hamah. Descendants of these mixed marriages were called *"Samaritans"*, whose influence continued to affect God's people into the New Testament period.

Herod the Great rebuilt Samaria, making it one of his key cities in Israel. Note the avenue of the pillars from Herod's time.

Alexander the Great besieged Samaria in 331 BC. Later, it was destroyed by John Hyrcanus in 120 BC. Pompey, of Rome, rebuilt the city, and Herod the Great embellished it with a promenade of large granite columns. He changed her name to Sebaste, in honor of Caesar Augustus. It was here that Herod had one of his sons, and his beloved wife Mariamne, killed.

The palaces of Omri and Ahab have been excavated, as has the Temple of Augustus, the Roman Forum, the theater and the street of the columns. The Church of St. John the Baptist dates from the Crusader period.

Tradition holds that here Salome presented the head of John the Baptist to her mother. However, the author believes that Tiberias is where John was beheaded. Samaria is quite a distance for the elders of Galilee to have traveled to attend Herod Antipas' banquet (Matt. 14:11-12). Tradition also asserts that Elisha and Obadiah were buried in Samaria. According to Acts 8:5-25, the Samaritan Pentecost took place here.

Nablus seceded from ancient Shechem, which was destroyed by the Romans in 70 AD. Two years later it was replaced with **Neapolis** (new city). After the Arab conquest that name was corrupted to Nablus. Ancient Shechem lies about one mile to the east.

Nablus is the largest commercial and industrial city in the "West Bank". It is a center of passionate Palestinian nationalism, with a history of unrest, violence and political killing. (See Fodor's *Exploring Israel,* 1996, page 220). Few tourists feel comfortable here, and Arab guides and drivers are required. Hotels, mosques and Islamic sites are closed to non-Muslims.

Shechem (shoulder) lies in the valley between Mt. Ebal to the north and Mt. Gerazim to the south. This was the first city where Abraham settled, and where God told him *"Unto you and your seed, I will give this Land"* (Gen. 12:1-7). After returning from Mesopotamia, Jacob made Shechem his home. He dug a well which still carries his name today. Here, his daughter was defiled (Gen. 34), and his wife worshipped *"strange gods"* (Gen. 35).

Joseph sought his brothers at Shechem, and years later his bones were brought from Egypt and buried here. Abimelech, son of Gideon, set himself up as head over all Israel and reigned 3 years (Judg. 9). Later, when Rehoboam was rejected, the kingdom was divided (I Kings 12). Jeroboam was chosen as king and made Shechem his capital. When Samaria fell to Assyria, the king repopulated the exiled land with people from Babylon, and placed them in the central cities. The Jews that were left in the Land intermarried with the imported Gentiles and became the Samaritans of the New Testament. Their descendants are the Samaritans of today.

Nablus/Shechem 1960 photo, as seen from Mt. Gerazim

Mt. Ebal (barren or Mount of Cursings) rises 3077 feet above sea level, and was the mount where the *"curses"* were recited by Israel when they entered the Land of Israel and renewed their vows to God (Deut. 11:29-30, 27:11-26; Josh. 8:30-34). Joshua erected a monument honoring the Law of Moses on Mt. Ebal (Josh. 8:30).

Woman drawing fresh water from Jacob's well

Mt. Gerazim (waste places or Mount of Blessings) rises 2848 feet above sea level (Deut. 11:29-30, 27:11-26; Josh. 8:30-34). Today this mountain is the main home of the Samaritans.

Samaritans consider Mt. Gezarim to be a sacred mountain (Jn. 4:20). Recall the beautiful event in the Lord's life when He encountered the Samaritan Woman in Sychar at **Jacob's Well** (Jn. 4:4-42). The well was dug by Jacob when he pitched his tent outside Shechem (Gen. 33:19).

After this **Sychar** woman came to experience Jesus Christ as her Messiah, she shared her personal discovery with her village. The Samaritans graciously received Jesus, and He remained there several days teaching and ministering with his disciples.

Today a beautiful Greek Orthodox Church has been constructed on a Crusader foundation over that well. The priest, Father Justinian, who has done most of the construction, is usually found working around the church until today. The construction, the mosaics and most paintings are his handiwork. The church is absolutely amazing!

Remains of the ancient Samaritan Temple on Mt. Gerazim

The ruins of **The Samaritan Community** and museum atop Mt. Gerazim are well worth visiting. The community is very safe and they love to have visitors.

Though they are not considered Jews, they have a special relationship with Israel and are closely connected religiously to Judaism. The Israeli high court ruled that Samaritans may have full Israeli citizenship. The Samaritans had petitioned for some to leave Mt. Gerazim and the "West Bank" city of Nablus to live in Holon near Tel Aviv. Today the Samaritans, from five main family groups, are split about fifty-fifty.

The Samaritans Believe :

- There is one God.
- Moses is the only prophet and the intercessor for man in the final judgment.
- The Law given through Moses is the only divine revelation.
- Mt. Gerazim was the place chosen by God and is the center of their worship. They believe it is where Adam offered sacrifices – "the navel of the earth".
- On Judgment Day the righteous will be resurrected into paradise, and the wicked will descend into eternal fire.
- Six thousand years after creation, a "Restorer" will arise and restore their fortunes. He will live for 110 years.

Samaritan High Priest 1960

In the Samaritan synagogue and museum one can view the Samaritan Pentateuch Parchment. It is believed by the community to be 3650 years old, the oldest copy of Moses' writings. However, many scholars date the copy from 1100 AD. The fact is, it is very old! The Samaritains are a remnant of the ten northern tribes of Israel. They are the people who remained in Samaria during the Assyrian exile. Because they intermarried with the repopulated Gentiles, the Samaritans have historically been shunned by the Jews, just as they were in Jesus' day. Yet, they claim a pure bloodline, tracing their lineage back to Aaron, Moses' brother and Israel's first high priest.

In New Testament times there were over 2 million Samaritans, but today only about 500 remain. Nearly half live on Mt. Gerazim with the remainder in Holon, south of Tel Aviv near Joppa.

Ariel, the modern capital of Samaria, is located less than two miles south of Shechem. The new community has been raised up by Jewish settlers since 1979. It is the Jewish corridor that joins Samaria to Israel. This "finger corridor" extends east from Tel Aviv/ Petach Tikvah through the Aphek pass. The bustling new city is proud of its frontier nature. It hosts Ariel's extension of Hebrew University, a shopping area, and a unique hotel, Eshel ha Shomron.

Looking toward the extension of Hebrew University in Ariel.

For seven years a dear friend, Homer Owen, operated a miniature golf course in Ariel – serving Texas hamburgers and homemade ice cream. That place was extremely popular, but Homer has since returned to Texas. Sorry, famished pilgrims!

The Valley of Lebonah lies just to the south of Ariel. In Jesus' day the grapes for the temple wine were raised in this fertile valley. In Judges 21:16-25, the wifeless tribe of Benjamin *"captured"* the maidens of Shiloh as they danced at a festival in the valley.

A dry summer field in Lebonah

Shiloh (peaceful or place of rest) was Israel's first capital for 300 years before it was moved to Jerusalem. Here Joshua allotted the Land of Israel to the tribes after the conquest (Josh.18). Shiloh became the home of the Ark of the Tabernacle during the time of the Judges. Eli was the judge when Hannah prayed for a son, Samuel, who later grew up under Eli's tutelage. Samuel was called by God as a child and served the Lord in Shiloh (I Sam. 3).

Eli's two sons, Hophni and Phinehas, committed evil before the Lord at Shiloh. From there the Ark was taken to Aphek in the battle against the Philistines. Though captured, the Ark was later returned to Israel. To the southwest is the Valley of Dancing Maidens/Valley of the Thieves.

Ancient Shiloh was located in the very heart of Samaria. The **Ark of the Covenant** was moved from its first home in ancient Gilgal to Shiloh.

Bethel (House of God) lies 11 miles north of Jerusalem. Originally it was known as Luz. Here Abraham built an altar to God (Gen. 12) and first worshiped ***YHVH*** by His holy name.

Based on satellite photography, many believe that God "branded the Land" with His name, the Hebrew letters ***Yod, Heh, Vav, Heh = YHVH.*** This possible "branding" of the landscape is about one-half kilometer high and one kilometer long and reads in Hebrew by facing east. Strangely, the inscription doesn't follow the erosion patterns of the rest of the area. Only after satellite photography revealed this strange pattern did the possibility come to light. If this is what God intended, it was discovered 3500 years after God placed His Holy Name in the landscape at Bethel. After all, God said, *"the Land is Mine..."* (Lev. 25:23).

At Bethel Abraham built an altar. After his sojourn to Egypt, he prayed to God, and called Him YHWH (God's unpronounceable name). Some believe that God inscribed His sacred name in the landscape. This area is *"the Mountains of Israel"* (the heart of ancient Samaria), which God promised to Israel.

Map above - courtesy of Moshe Atiya of Atiya Productions at **HolylandChristian Maps.com**

From Bethel Lot departed from Abraham and moved to Sodom and Gomorrah (Gen. 13). Here Jacob dreamed of a ladder with angels ascending and descending from Heaven, and God promised him and his descendants the Land. Jacob built an altar to God (Gen. 28:10-22). Deborah lived nearby, and the Ark of the Covenant was here briefly. Jeroboam sought to make Bethel the religious center of the Northern Kingdom by setting up the golden calf.

Both Elijah and Elisha ministered at Bethel. Here, King Josiah destroyed Jeroboam's altar.

Ai (ruined mound) dates back to 3000 BC. It was the second city attacked by the Israelites under Joshua. Israel took the city in their second attack (Josh. 8:1-29), after dealing with Achan's sin in the camp (Josh. 7:2-5).

Ramah in the Heights of Samaria

Ramah (height/loftiness) has ancient *"graves of the children of Israel"*. Deborah judged from beneath a palm tree between here and Bethel. Samuel was born here, lived and judged Israel (I Sam. 1:18-20, 2:11, 8:4). Here Samuel anointed Saul as the first king of Israel (I Sam. 10:1). David fled from Saul's anger and sought safety with the prophet Samuel in Ramah. Samuel was buried here. Ramah was built up by Baasha, King of Israel. Jeremiah was released from chains here (Jer. 40:1-4). Joseph of Arimathea, in whose tomb Jesus was buried, was born in this city (Matt. 27:57-60; Mk. 15:42-45; Lk. 23:50-51; Jn.19:38-42).

"Samuel died and all Israel gathered and lamented him and buried him in his hometown of Ramah" (I Samuel 25:1).

Gibeon (hill) boasts a rock-cut water system and pool (82 feet deep x 37 feet in diameter). A water channel was cut to bring the water beneath the city. David defeated the Philistines at Gibeon. Twelve of Ishbosheth's fighters under Abner and twelve of David's best fighters under Joab fought to their death at this pool (II Sam. 2:12-1-9). When five kings of the Amorites fought against Gibeon, Joshua came to their rescue. Near here God sent hailstones from Heaven, and the Valley of Aijalon is where the son and the moon stood still until Joshua could complete the battle (Josh. 10:1-27).

Mizpah (watch tower) / **Nebi Samwil** (Prophet Samuel) is located four miles northwest of Jerusalem in Benjamin's territory. It was a prominent religious center during Samuel's time as a prophet. A tall minaret marks the site from a distance.

Israel gathered and conferred here about the outrage of the Levite concubine (Judg. 20:1-3). Here Samuel rededicated Israel and attacked the Philistines (I Sam. 7:3-14). Saul was proclaimed Israel's first king here (I Sam.10:17-25). King Asa fortified the city, and Gedeliah reigned over the remnant left by Nebuchadnezzar (II Kings 25:22-26; Jer. 40:5-16).

Ancient Gibeah of Benjamin

Gibeah (hill of Gabaah) was Saul's capital over Israel. King Hussein of Jordan started to build a palace for himself over the ruins of Saul's fortress, but the construction was interrupted by the Six Day War of 1967.

Gibeah was in Benjamin's territory, and was the place where most of the tribe was destroyed (Judges 20:12-48). It was also Saul's hometown. Here he held court (I Sam. 14:2-3) and summoned Israel to war (I Sam. 11:1-13). When he was overthrown, the bodies of his seven sons were hung on the city wall (II Sam. 21).

The Jordan Valley intersecting the Valley of Jezreel – Gilead and Jordan in the background

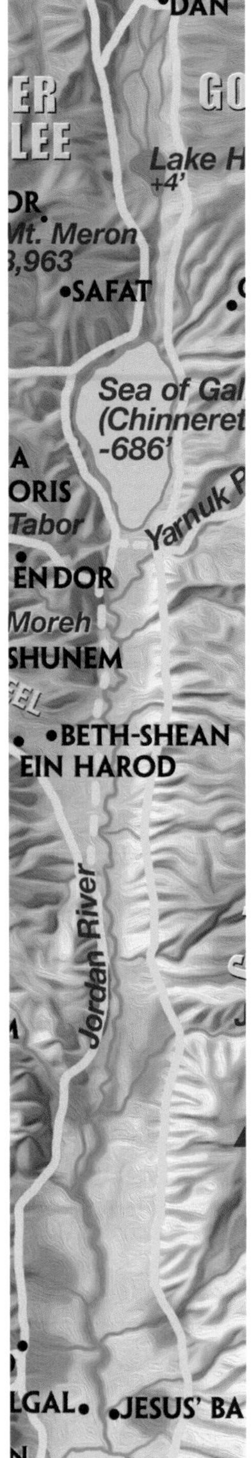

Jordan Valley

From the SEA OF GALILEE to the DEAD SEA

The Jordan River begins its flow in northern Galilee and the Golan, with three tributaries (Iyon, Dan and Banias Springs) which join together in the Huleh Basin, 4' above sea level. From there the Jordan (meaning "flowing down" or the "descender")drops through rocky gorges and winds its way to the beautiful Sea of Galilee, 686' below sea level. From its exit at the southern end of the Sea, the Jordan snakes through the Ghor, where the Jordan overflows during the spring flood season. On either side of the valley, mountains rise up as high as 1500' above the river. As the Jordan flows south, the country of Jordan lies to the east, with Israel to the west. North of the Dead Sea, Lot chose the Plain of the Jordan (Gen. 13:10-11), and later settled in Sodom. Ancient Israel entered the Land by crossing the Jordan at flood stage near the city of Adam (Josh. 3:13-17, 4:1-9, 4:20-21; Ps. 114:3). There God blocked the flow of the Jordan for His people to cross. In the Old Testament period, lions and other tropical animals lurked in this valley (Jer. 49:1; Zech. 11:3).

Striking the water with his mantle, Elijah and his disciple, Elisha, crossed the Jordan on dry ground (II Kings 2:7-8). Later, God caused an iron axe head to float to the surface for

Elisha (II Kings 6:1-7). The Syrian General Naaman, at Elisha's instruction, dipped seven times in the Jordan to cure his leprosy (II Kings 5). King David crossed the Jordan to escape his son Absalom's conspiracy (II Sam. 17:22). Absalom pursued his father David, but it was a one way trip when he was hung by his hair in the oaks of Gilead (II Sam. 17:22).

The **"Pilgrim's Road"** of Jesus' day, followed the Jordan from Galilee, and intersected the Jericho Road, which led to Jerusalem. Pilgrims traveling to the Holy City would usually take this route instead of traveling through Samaria. However, I suggest that Joseph and Mary took the shorter Samaritan route to Bethlehem, prior to the birth of Christ (Lk. 2:4). They probably took the "Pilgrim's Road" when Jesus accompanied them to Jerusalem prior to the Passover (Matt. 2:19-23; Lk. 2:41-52).

John the Baptist was baptizing in the Jordan (Matt. 3:6) when Jesus came to him to be baptized (Matt. 3; Mk. 1:4-11). After His baptism, Jesus spent the evening with His first disciples somewhere in this area (Jn. 1:25-51).

Near where the Jordan River leaves the Sea of Galilee, is the beautiful baptismal site of **Yardenit**. This modern, convenient baptismal site was developed by Calvary Chapel Churches of America. Though the popular site is located some 70 miles north of where Jesus was baptized, most Christians simply want "to be baptized in the Jordan", to identify with their Lord.

The average width of the Jordan is less than 100 feet. By canoe one must travel 210 miles from Galilee to arrive at the Dead Sea, yet the actual distance is only 70 miles in a straight line. The Jordan is the only river in the world whose course flows below sea level.

The Jordan River is a 156 miles long river flowing to the Dead Sea. Israel borders the river to the West, while Jordan lies to its East. The Hashemite Kingdom of Jordan takes its name from this river. The river has significance in both Judaism and Christianity. The Israelites crossed the River to enter the Promised Land. It was in this area, Jesus of Nazareth was baptized by John the Baptist.

Belvoir, a 12th century French Crusader fortress, is located about 10 miles south of the Sea of Galilee. The mountain peak where the fortress stands affords an incredible sweeping view of the entire northern end of the Jordan Valley and the Mountains of Gilead, east of the Jordan Valley. Five miles further south, the Valley of Jezreel drops 300 feet to join the Jordan Valley. At this intersection, the city of Beth Shean proudly protected the pass into the Valley of Jezreel.

The **Alexandrium** was built by Alexander Jannaeus (103-76 BC) as a fortress overlooking the Jordan River. It stands 800 feet above the river. Herod the Great rebuilt it, but Vespasian of Rome destroyed it in 70 AD. Because of his fears and suspicions, Herod had two of his own sons drowned in Jericho, and buried them at the Alexandrium. (Herod tried to destroy anyone who threatened his throne, whether it was his wife, his children, or a new-born baby in Bethlehem. Caesar said of Herod, "It is safer to be a pig in his household than to be his son").

Gilgal (stone circle). The Department of Tourism has marked the location of Gilgal several miles north of the Dead Sea. There Israel has built a beautiful memorial. However, there is strong evidence to suggest that Gilgal was located immediately north of the Dead Sea, with the Jordan River flowing through the camp of Israel.

A team led by Vendyl Jones of the Institute of Judaic-Christian Research, made a discovery in February 1994 that seems to support the above claim. The ancient camp of Israel was discovered by Remote Satellite Imaging. The exact location of the Tabernacle, a raised area in the center of the camp, was identified. Infrared signatures indicate where Israel camped for 14 years. The location of the tribes within the tent city of Gilgal can be identified by this satellite imaging.

At Gilgal Joshua set up 12 memorial stones to remind Israel of their crossing at the Jordan (Josh. 4:1-13, 20-24). At Gilgal the men of Israel were circumcised (Josh. 4:19-24, 5:2-10, 9:6, 10:7, 14:6, 15:7; Deut. 11:30). Here Israel ate the Passover, and the manna ceased. Outside the camp, God sent *"the Angel of the Lord"* to Joshua (Josh. 5:10-15). Israel encamped here while conquering Jericho (Josh. 6).

Later, Saul was crowned as king at Gilgal (I Sam. 11:14-15). Here Samuel preached (I Sam. 12) and Agag was slain (I Sam. 15). Elisha and Elijah both lived at Gilgal for a period of time (II Kings 2:1). Elisha purified the pottage at Gilgal (II Kings 4:38-41). Nearby God caused the axehead to float in the Jordan (II Kings 6). Unfortunately, Gilgal was later referred to by the prophets as a place of idolatry (Hosea 4:15; Micah 6:56).

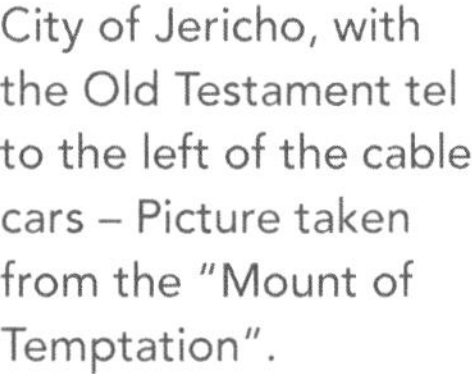

City of Jericho, with the Old Testament tel to the left of the cable cars – Picture taken from the "Mount of Temptation".

Jericho (City of Palms) is the world's oldest city. Some think it was built as early as 8000 BC. It is a virtual oasis in the barren Judean wilderness between Judaea and the Jordan. Joshua sent spies here, and Rahab sheltered them (Josh. 2). Jericho became the first city conquered by Israel in the Land (Joshua 6:1-21). Here Achan broke God's commands and was stoned (Josh. 7). With salt Elisha healed the *"bitter water"* (II Kings 2:19-22).

The Old Testament city of Jericho was located near **Elisha's Spring**. Excavations here have revealed the oldest structures on earth. A tower of stone and mud was constructed around 8000 BC – 4000 years older than the pyramids of Egypt. The tower is the oldest building on earth.

In Johsua's time, the walls of Jericho fell outward, pointing to the supernatural destruction of the city by God (Josh. 6:13-17). The city was given to the tribe of Benjamin, and was still called the "City of Palms" during the time of Judges.

After fleeing through underground cave passages from Solomon's Jerusalem quarries to the Jericho Plain, Zedekiah was captured and blinded near Jericho (II Kings 25:5-7; Jer.39:5-7, 52:8-11).

Zacchaeus climbed a sycamore tree to see Jesus passing by. Jesus ate at his home that day, and was criticized for eating with tax collectors (Lk. 19:1-27). Multitudes from Jericho followed Jesus (Matt.20:29), and here Jesus healed blind Bartimaeus (Matt.20:29-34; Lk. 18:35-43).

St. George's Monastery rises above Wadi Kelt

The traditional Mount of Temptation rises to the north of Jericho. Today a cable car can take a person to the Greek Orthodox Monastery halfway up the mountain.

Mount of Temptation rises to the north of the Jericho Plain. This is the traditional site of Jesus' 40 days and nights of fasting. After that period, Satan came to tempt Jesus (Matt. 4:1-11; Mk. 1:12-13; Lk. 4:1-13). The mount is honeycombed with caves. An 1895 Greek Orthodox monastery is perched halfway up the trail, that leads to a distinctively Maccabean fortress on top.

The Jericho Road is the seventeen mile road connecting Jerusalem to Jericho. That road drops 3600 feet in those seventeen miles. It is a steep, winding, descending and remote road that for centuries has been a place of robbers.

The Jericho Road climbs from the Jericho Plain into the wilderness of Judea. It follows the **Brook Cherith** to the place where God's ravens fed Elijah while he was hiding from Queen Jezebel (I Kings 17:1-7). This traditional Cherith Brook flows into and through **Wadi Kelt**. The beautiful gorge houses a Greek Monastery which clings like a swallow's nest to the sheer cliffs. There is a problem with this traditional location of the Brook Cherith. The Scripture says, it was *"east of the Jordan"* (I Kings 17:3,5). This does not take away from the breathtaking beauty of this location.

The road leads through **Maale Adummin** (ascent of blood), where we are reminded of the parable Jesus told of the Good Samaritan (Lk. 10: 34-35). Passing through the ***"valley of the shadow of death"*** (Psa. 23), we climb to the plateau of the Wilderness of Judea.

Jericho Road ran beside Brook Cherith in Wadi Kelt. This was likely the "Jericho Road" of the New Testament.

The impressive Greek Monastery of St. George rises above Wadi Kelt, or Brook Cherith. The Monastery clings to the Judean mountain like a swallow's nest.

Dead Sea at sunset, with the Mountains of Edom (meaning *"Red"*) in the background

Dead Sea

The Dead Sea receives the fresh water flow of the Jordan River just south of ancient Jericho and Gilgal. The rugged country bordering the sea on the west is the Wilderness of Judea. To the east are the ever-changing colors of the high mountains of Moab, and to the southeast are the red mountains of Edom.

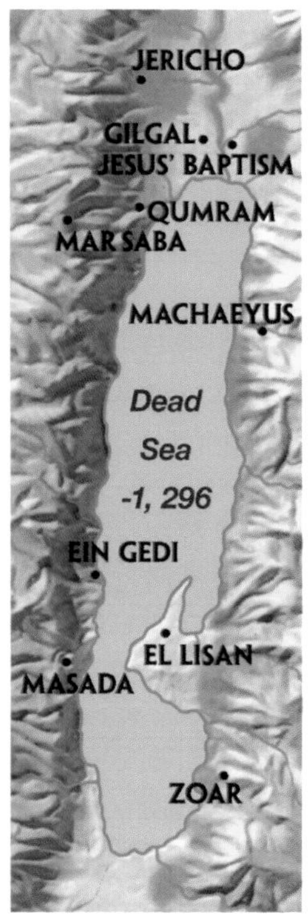

The Dead Sea is approximately 47 miles long and 10 miles wide. It is nearly 1300 feet deep, and the surface lies 1292 feet below sea level – the lowest point on the surface of planet Earth.

The water is 27% mineral (containing potash, salts, bromine, gypsum, calcium chloride, and magnesium). Tons of water evaporate from the sea daily. The Dead Sea contains more economic value than all the Arab oil in the Middle East. Processing plants are located near the southern end. The receding waters have affected the entire area.

The Dead Sea is "dying", and several plans have been proposed to give stability to the Sea. One such plan is to cut a canal for water from the Mediterranean Sea and control its downward flow, which would generate enough power for the entire Middle East. The drop would be five times greater than that of Niagara Falls, and controlled lakes could be strategically placed in the northern Negev. Another suggested plan would bring water through the **Arabah Valley** from the **Gulf of Eilat**. Scientific studies indicate that mixing ocean water with the unique chemical qualities of the Dead Sea, would destroy her integrity and usefulness.

Traveling south from the Dead Sea (1,300′ below sea level), the road "snakes" through the Arabah Valley of the Great Syrian/African Rift. The valley floor rises and prevents the present Dead Sea from connecting with the Red Sea, located 105 miles south at the Gulf of Eilat or **Aquaba**.

Today, the Dead Sea cannot sustain any plant or animal life, but prophecy says that there will come a day when fishermen will spread their nets *"from Ein Gedi to En Eglaim…their fish will be according to their kinds, like the fish of the Great Sea* (Mediterranean Sea)*… and very many"* (Ezek. 47:10). In light of this passage, the author believes that the replenished water will be ocean water.

Wadi ha Kippah was identified by Vendyl Jones in the 1970's. He has conducted excavations at the Cave of the Column over a period of 25 years, as he and his teams have searched for the "Kalil" containing "the ashes of the red heifer"/ashes of cleansing.

Qumran (two moons) was a monastery on a hill overlooking the ***"City of Salt"*** (Josh. 16:52). Qumran was built in the 1st century BC by a religious sect that left Jerusalem because of religious corruption. For many years this group was incorrectly referred to as Essenes. Today they are called **"The Sect of the Wilderness of Judea"**. They were an ascetic group which copied the Hebrew scrolls of the entire Old Testament, known today as the **Dead Sea Scrolls**. Later they hid these scrolls in isolated caves near the Dead Sea. Many believe that John the Baptist lived here, practiced many of their customs, and studied at the yeshiva/seminary in Qumran.

Qumran community

In March of 1947, a 35-year-old shepherd discovered some leather parchments in **"Cave # 4"** when he tried to scare his goat from the cave. He sold the scrolls to a merchant in Bethlehem. Dr. Sukenik of Hebrew University purchased three of the scrolls on November 29, 1947. On that very day the United Nations voted to re-create the Jewish nation of Israel after 2,000 years. What a coincidence! Right? Many other scrolls have been discovered since, dating from 300 BC to 70 AD, and all were written in Hebrew, save one.

Qumran Cave #4

Recent studies of the Dead Sea Scrolls have revealed some amazing discoveries. This Sect of the Wilderness of Judea believed in two Messiahs, one returning to deliver Israel from Gentile rule and to reign over Israel from David's throne, and the other a "pierced Messiah" who would rise from the dead. Did Jesus fulfill the latter expectations through His death and resurrection? In light of these discoveries, many today (even among Jewish scholars) refer to Qumran as being a pre-Christian community.

Fresh waterfalls and pool at Ein Gedi

Ein Gedi (fountain of the kid/goat). The goat's rocks are part of the awesome and rugged Wilderness of Judea. Boxed in between the mountains and the Dead Sea is a beautiful Israeli kibbutz, which farms the fertile soil with the help of fresh water from the Fountain. Here the desert "blooms" and produces fruits and vegetables in abundance (Isa. 35:1).

David hid at Ein Gedi, in a cave near the waterfalls, from King Saul who was pursuing him (I Sam. 23:29-24:22). Ein Gedi's wonder and beauty is mentioned in Song of Solomon 1:14 and in Ezek. 47:10.

The acacia tree, from which the Ark of the Tabernacle was built, grows abundantly in this area (Ex. 25:5, 10, 13, 23, 28). Nearby

Author's son, Randy Ross reads the Jerusalem Post while floating in the Dead Sea.

is a marvelous place to swim in the Dead Sea and to enjoy refreshments while relaxing in the desert.

The Dead Sea is so buoyant that one can read a book or newspaper while floating on the surface. The buoyancy of the water amazes most visitors.

After an all-night spring rain in Jerusalem in 1993, the water rushed down the wadis of the Wilderness of Judea, cascading toward the Dead Sea. The next morning we traveled to Masada. As we passed the rugged cliffs in the wilderness of Judea, the indentations in the cliffs turned into gushing waterfalls.

Returning from Masada, near Ein Gedi, traffic was forced to stop for over three hours until the water subsided. The road had to be cleared of rocks and boulders from the Wilderness of Judea. The water had risen to 4-6 feet over the roadway. Front-end loaders moved boulders weighing between two and three tons from the highway before traffic could pass.

Masada (fortress) is one of the most important mountains in world history. It is a rock fortress one half mile long and 220 yards wide, which rises 2000 feet above the surface of the Dead Sea. It is located opposite the large Dead Sea peninsula called **El Lisan** (tongue) in Hebrew.

Masada is the Hebrew word for "Stronghold/fortress" (female gender in Hebrew). David may have used this stronghold, but the Hebrew gender for the "Masada strongholds" that he used is in the male gender. As author of the praise-book of our Bible, David often spoke of *"the Stronghold* or *Rock"* in *Psalms.*

On Masada, Herod the Great (37 BC–4 BC) built an incredible winter palace and isolated retreat for security. Herod's fortress walls were 18 feet thick, with 38 towers that were 75 feet tall encircling the mount. He feared for his life and throne because of Mark Anthony, Cleopatra of Egypt and the Jewish subjects he ruled. All of hated him. Herod the Great is the Herod who tried to have the *"newborn King of the Jews"* killed in Bethlehem.

Masada is the world's most famous mountain. Her history is unparalleled. The awesome mountain, pictured from the bank path, rises majestically above the Dead Sea and Moab in the background.

After Herod's death, Jewish Zealots took Masada and held it from 66–73 AD. After Jerusalem fell, the Romans laid siege to this fortress for three years. Jewish slaves from Jerusalem were forced to construct a siege ramp to the top of the wall on the west side. An enormous battering ram broke through the wall. When the end seemed inevitable, 960 Jewish defenders on top determined to put themselves to death, rather than fall into the abusive hands of the Romans. The fall of Masada in 73 AD marked the end of Jewish Independence in the Land of Israel, until May 1948.

We suggest you watch the classic movie *Masada.*

Wadi ha Kippah, cave and visiting tour group, above. Below, Rabbi Goren was very interested in finding the "Kalil" and the "ashes of cleansing". He believed that was necessory prior to the Third Temple, the ordination of the Sanhedrin and the renewal of the Temple sacrifices. Both men died without the items being found.

Archaeologist Vendly Jones discusses the ashes of the Red Heifer with Chief Rav Shlomo Goren at Wadi ha Kippah.

The awesome mountains of the Judean Desert tower above En Gedi

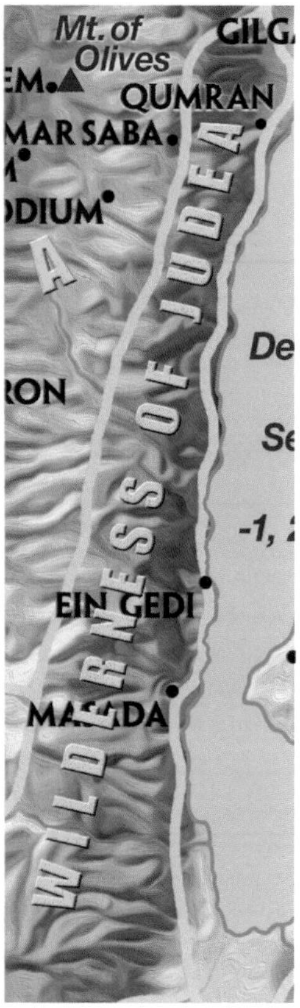

Wilderness of Judea

"The scepter shall not depart from Judah, nor the ruler's staff from between his feet,
Until Shiloh comes to whom it belongs,
To whom the peoples shall render obedience." **Gen. 49:10**

Judea is very small (1350 square miles), and one half of it is desert or wilderness. Yet, it served as the stronghold and sanctuary of The Land. Judea was physically barren and unattractive, yet it became the seat of Israel's most enduring dynasty. Judea was the site of the Temple, and the pulpit for Israel's greatest prophets. In the "*fullness of time*" (Gal. 4:4). Judea was chosen as the birthplace of our Lord. Judea was the scene of Jesus' temptations, His ministry, His agony, and the place of His death. He was buried in a Judean sepulcher.

It was in Judea where that first startling announcement was made: *"He is not here, HE IS RISEN!"* (Matthew 28:6). In Judea, our Risen Lord first appeared to His disciples. At Pentecost He returned in the power of His Holy Spirit.

In Judea, Jerusalem was destroyed by Titus, the Roman general, in 70 AD. Three years later the remnant Jewish garrison of Masada fell on April 15, 73 AD. The Jewish freedom fighters failed to gain freedom, but they chose death over Roman slavery – 960 gave (or took) their own lives. In 135 AD, under Emperor Hadrian, 2,000 towns and villages were destroyed by the Romans. Judea became the sepulcher of God's people.

The colorful Wilderness of Judea stretches eastward toward the Dead Sea.

See ***The Jewishness of Jesus***, Book 1, Section 2, Chapter 1, for details concerning the route that Joseph chose between Nazareth and Bethlehem.

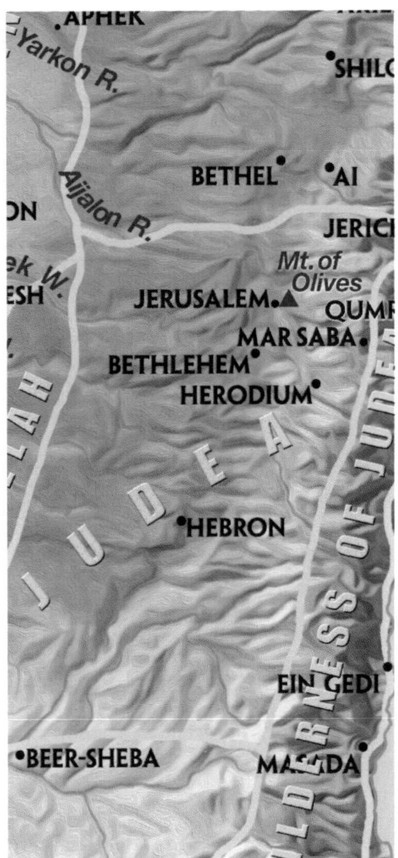

Judea

GOD CHOSE JUDEA AS THE STAGE FOR THE MOST IMPORTANT EVENTS IN BIBLICAL HISTORY

Jacob and his family traveled to Bethlehem from Bethel. While some distance from *Bethlehem Ephrath*, Jacob's wife, Rachel, died giving birth to Benjamin. She was buried by the highway (Gen. 35:16-20). Rachel's tomb has traditionally been shown on the road between Jerusalem and Bethlehem. However, recently archaeologists have identified her tomb in Ephraim. Since the Scripture simply implies that she was buried "*in route to Bethlehem...some distance from Ephrath*" (Genesis 35:16), the location in Ephraim seems more likely. Jews always bury the dead on the same day of their death.

We believe Joseph and Mary traveled the Samaritan route from Nazareth to Jerusalem, then made their way to Bethlehem. They arrived and immediately sought lodging as the birth of our Lord drew near (Lk. 2:1-7).

Wheat field in Israel

Bethlehem (House of Bread) is located five miles south of Jerusalem, and is 2350 feet above sea level. Returning from a sojourn in Moab, the widowed Naomi and her Moabite daughter-in-law, Ruth, came to Bethlehem. They arrived at the beginning of the barley harvest. While Ruth was following the barley gleaners, she met Boaz, and later married him (Ruth 1-4). This Moabite *Gentile* became the grandmother of King David (I Sam. 17:12).

Bethlehem was David's home, and God directed Samuel to anoint him to succeed Saul (I Sam. 16:1-17). Later, when Bethlehem was controlled by a garrison of Philistines, one of David's mighty men came from the Cave of Adullam, or Masada, to offer David a drink of water from his father's well (II Sam. 23:14-17). The prophet Micah prophesied that the Messiah would be born in Bethlehem (Micah 5:2).

Bethlehem courtyard

Joseph and Mary came here to register for taxes since they were of David's lineage. Luke 2:7 tells us that *"there was no room in the kataluma"* (Jewish guest room), for Joseph and Mary. They were not turned away by an "inn keeper" – as most have been taught. Actually, Bethlehem had no inn. The town was too close to Jerusalem (4 miles) to have an inn in the New Testament period. Why were Joseph and Mary turned away from using a "kataluma" by Joseph's own family? Could it have been that the families in Bethlehem had not been invited to their wedding? To those families in Bethlehem, there was much doubt about Jesus' questionable birth, a stigma Jesus had to carry throughout His life.

(Extensive details will be discussed in the author's coming book, ***The Jewishness of Jesus***. Please visit **www.jewishnessofjesus.com** for updated information on the publication date and availability).

We assume that a member of the family had mercy on the desperate couple and provided a cave or succa/succot. ***The Jewishness of Jesus*** discusses in great detail the timing and events surrounding Jesus' birth. Consider the possibility that Jesus was born during the Feast of Tabernacles/Succoth, mid to late September, in 4 BC (around the 20th). Jesus was born in David's city of Bethlehem, as God promised (Matt. 2:1-6; Lk. 2:4-7).

This Judean cave, served as a kataluma for a village home.

Jesus was born in Bethlehem (Micah 5:2; Matt. 2:1-6; Lk. 2:4-7). Shepherds in the field at **Migdal Eder** (Watchtower of the Sheep–Micah 4:8) were the keepers of the Temple flock of sacrificial lambs. The good news of the birth of Jesus was first proclaimed to these shepherds (Lk. 2:8-20).

Some believe that the "birthing tower of the sheep" at Migdal Eder was the specific location of Jesus' birth in Bethlehem. References to a manger and Jesus being wrapped in swaddling clothes add support to this view.

Scripture tells us that wise men came from the *east* to Bethlehem. They had followed the *star* to see the *"new born king."* It is believed the *"star"* was the *"Shekinah" (Glory of God)* which led them to the place. When they left Herod's palace in Jerusalem (4-5 miles away), *"they rejoiced to see the star"* (Matthew 2:10) and were led to the child. No normal star anywhere in God's universe could have done this without God's supernatural action. The *"Shekinah" (Glory of God)* that guided the Children of Israel in the wilderness guided the *wise men* to Bethlehem (Matt. 2:8-12).

The "Shekinah" Star guided the *wise men.*

In 4 BC, by the order of Herod the Great, and just before his death, all male children in Bethlehem under the age of two were killed (Matt. 2:16). From here Joseph and Mary fled to Egypt to protect Jesus (Matt. 2:13-23; Jer. 31:15).

In 325 AD, Queen Helena, the mother of Constantine, had the **Church of Nativity** built over the *traditional cave where Jesus was born* in Bethlehem. This is the oldest church building in the world. Sections of the church have been destroyed and rebuilt many times.

The Interior of the Church of Nativity

In 1998, Bethlehem was about 90% Christian. Since the PLO and Hamas have taken over this area many Christians have fled due to persecution. Today, fewer than 15% of Bethlehem is "Christian". Even though the city is under Muslim control, many tours visit the area. Highlights of this area include the Church of Nativity, shepherd's fields, olive wood factories and marvelous stores. The Arab food in Bethlehem is wonderful, and brave visitors who come are greatly appreciated.

The Herodium, the cone-shaped mountain on the edge of the Judean Wilderness, was built by Herod the Great. He moved one mountaintop (with slave labor) to form the top half of the present Herodium. Then he fortified the fortress and built his beautiful palace in the top of the cone. The extraordinary mountain palaces were built in 24 BC to honor Herod's victory over the Parthians in the plain below. That victory was perhaps his fondest memory. Here Herod was "secretly" buried in 4 BC. The excavations of 1962-64 revealed a palace of luxury.

Herod's Herodium

Jesus obviously referred to Herod the Great when He mentioned the *"kings in their palaces"* (Matt. 11:8). In the spring of 2007, Herod's Tomb was finally discovered deep within the heart of the Herodium directly beneath

Herod's great palace. Herod so carefully arranged for his tomb to be hidden that it has taken over 2,000 years to find it. Obviously, many took their memory of Herod's burial to their own premature graves. How did Herod arrange it all? Thousands viewed his burial procession. Herod had a special theater built near the base of the north eastern edge of the Herodium, which was used for Herod's burial ceremony (Josephus, Jewish Wars I, 33, 9). Amazingly, that theater has been discovered and excavated. A special section of the Israeli Museum in Jerusalem is now dedicated to the discoveries from Herod's tomb. This is a "must see". (After the discovery of Herod's burial site, the archaeologist in charge, fell to his death into the theater below).

Solomon's Pools were a source for Jerusalem's ancient water system and were credited to him (Eccl. 2:6). When Pontius Pilate installed a water system for Jerusalem, he repaired the pools. A "sealed fountain" was discovered here, and aqueducts supplied water from several springs in the area. Rainwater was also channeled into the system (Psa. 65:9-10).

Olive Wood **Carving of Spies** carrying a cluster of grapes from Eschtol

Valley of Eschol is where the 12 spies cut down the branches of grapes to demonstrate to the congregation of Israel the fertility of the Land (Num. 13:23-24). Today, the largest grapes in Israel are still raised in this valley.

The "Oak of Mamre" is actually a grove of ancient oaks, and was Abraham's dwelling place (Gen. 23:19, 35:27). Here God made His covenant with Abraham (Gen. 15 and 17:9-14), and here Ishmael was born (Gen. 16). At Mamre the three angels visited Abraham, announcing the birth of Isaac (Gen. 18: 9-15). In this place Abraham was told of the eventual destruction of Sodom and Gomorrah (Gen. 18:22-23). Isaac died here shortly after Jacob returned with his family (Gen. 35: 27-29). From here, Joseph went to seek his brothers, who responded by selling him into slavery. God's destination for him was Egypt (Gen. 37:14).

Hebron (company) was founded before Zoan in Egypt, and it is one of the oldest cities in the world. Built in 2000 BC, Hebron was first called Kirjatharba (Gen. 23:2). Here the Anakim giants of the Canaanites dwelt (Josh. 14:15).

In Hebron Abraham built an altar to God (Gen. 13:18). Sarah died near Hebron, and was buried in the **Cave of Machpelah** (Gen. 23). Later Abraham, Isaac, Ishmael, Jacob, Esau and Leah were all buried here.

Joshua conquered Hebron (Josh. 10:36), and it became part of Judah's inheritance. Here Caleb claimed victory over the Anakim giants as he took the city. After Saul died, David made Hebron his capital before relocating to Jerusalem.

Abraham was buried in the Cave of Machpelah in Hebron, beneath the mosque.

Both Jews and Arabs of Hebron claim ownership of and worship at the Cave of Machpelah. Arguments over rights of possession have resulted in armed conflicts. Few tourists visit Hebron due to the tensions and spasmodic outbreaks. Unfortunately, Hebron gets a lot of bad press when the "news makers" create their own news stories by stirring up conflict. In most years quiet prevails.

The Great Lavra of St. Sabbas the Sanctified, known in Arabic as Mar Saba, is a Greek Orthodox monastery overlooking the Kidron Valley in Israel. The traditional date for the founding of the monastery by Saint Sabas of Mutalaska, Cappadocia is the year 483. Today it houses around 20 monks. It is considered to be one of the oldest inhabited monasteries in the world, and still maintains many of its ancient traditions.

Jerusalem is considered the world's holiest city by both Jews and Christians. Many claim that Jerusalem belongs to three faiths. However, though Muslims claim spiritual links to the city, Jerusalem is never mentioned in the Qur'an.

Jerusalem

"Great is the Lord, and greatly to be praised.
In the city of our God, His holy Mountain.
Beautiful in elevation, the joy of the whole earth,
Is Mount Zion in the far north, the city of the great King.
Walk about Zion, and go around her;
Count her towers; Consider her ramparts; Go through her palaces;
That you may tell it to the next generation.
For such is God. Our God forever and ever..."
Psalm 48: 1-2, 12-13

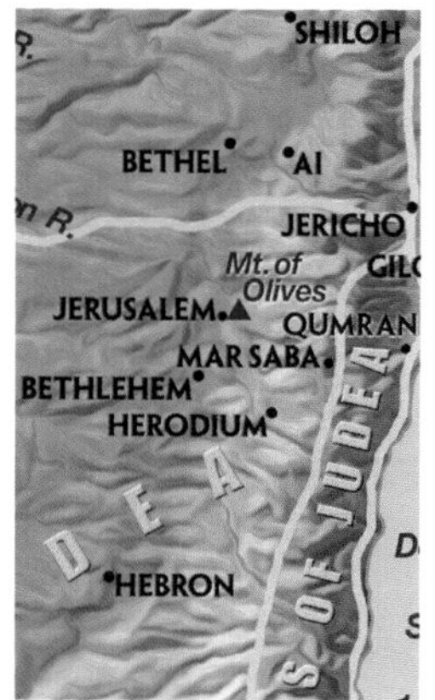

Jerusalem had been known as **Jebus** and **Salem.** Today it is called **The City of Peace, Zion, City of David** and **The Holy City.** Muslims call it **Noble Sanctuary.** The first mention of Jerusalem in the Scriptures is related to Melchizedek, *"Priest of the Most High God"* (Gen. 14:18). Today, Jerusalem is considered to be the most sacred city in the world, and was the most important in Biblical history.

Ironically, this **"City of Peace"** is the most fought over city in world history. She is located in the heights of the mountains of Judea, 2740 feet above sea level, and her natural water supply has always been very poor. The city is 38 miles from the Mediterranean Sea and 14 miles from the Dead Sea.

In 996 BC, David took the city and made Jerusalem his capital. He brought the Ark of the Tabernacle to the city (II Sam. 5:6-16, 6:1-2; I Chron. 11:4-7, 13-16; Psa. 24). When the city was preserved from pestilence, the site of the future Temple was purchased by King David (II Sam. 24). Solomon, who ruled from 965-922 BC, remodeled Jerusalem, making it one of the most beautiful cities on earth. He built the temple to God, built palaces for himself, strengthened her walls and filled the city with treasures (I Kings 6-9).

King David with harp

After Solomon's death, his kingdom was divided. In the following turbulent history of Judea and Samaria, many kings ruled. A few were good, but most were evil in God's eyes. In 609 BC the Egyptian Pharaoh Necho captured the city. Then, in 598 BC, Nebuchadnezzar of Babylon captured Jerusalem, and in 586 BC destroyed the city (II Kings 24-25; II Chron. 36:15-21; Jer. 39:9-14). In exile, the Jews lamented over Jerusalem (Lam. 1-2; Psa. 130, 137). Isaiah and Micah prophesied the restoration under Cyrus (Isa. 44:24-28, 45:12-13; Micah 5). These prophesies were fulfilled under Zerubbabel (Ezra 1:1-11). In 538 BC, after 70 years of captivity, Cyrus of Persia restored the Jews to their homeland (Isa. 45:1). Only a remnant of Jews returned to restore the walls and build the Second Temple.

Mosaic of Alexander the Great, Sepphoris

In 332 BC the Greeks, under Alexander the Great, captured Jerusalem. In 170 BC her walls were razed by the Selucid ruler Antiochus Epiphanes. In response, the Maccabees led a revolt, overthrowing the invading Greeks. The Jews gained independence in The Land, and welcomed self-rule from 167 to 63 BC, under the Hasmonean kings.

Then came Rome! In 63 BC the city was conquered. In 37 BC Herod, half Jew (spiritually) and half Arab/Idumaean (ethnically), was appointed king over the Jews by Rome. He rebuilt Jerusalem, and built a magnificent temple over the smaller temple built by Ezra. This was still considered the "Second Temple Period". Herod died in 4 BC, but the city in Jesus' day was the city that Herod and his descendants built. The temple complex was under construction throughout Jesus' entire ministry, and was finally completed in 64 AD.

Jerusalem of Solomon's Day – Temple upper right

Jesus was dedicated in the Temple (Lk. 2:22), and was later brought there to be examined for His bar-mitzvah (Lk. 2:41-52). Jesus often ministered in Jerusalem and attended many feasts. Near the close of His ministry, He entered the city "triumphantly" at the beginning of His Passion Week (Matt. 21:1-11). Jesus wept over the coming destruction of Jerusalem and foretold her doom but did nothing to prevent it (Matt. 23:37-24:51; Mk. 13).

Roman coin "Judea Captiva" depicts the destruction of Jerusalem in 70 AD.

In Jerusalem, He was tried and crucified (Matt. 27; Mk. 15; Lk. 23, Jn. 19), arose from the dead, and at Pentecost, His Spirit descended to *"fill"* the disciples and lead the early Believers/Messiakim (Acts 2).

In 68 AD the Jews again revolted against Rome, and Titus destroyed the city in 70 AD, These events fulfilled Jesus' prophecy of Luke 19:41-44 and 21:20-24.

In 135 AD, the Bar Kokhba revolt brought an end to the rebellion and the final destruction of Jerusalem and Judea. Hadrian built pagan temples over the sacred sites in 138 AD. Jews were forbidden to enter the city on penalty of death.

Constantine tried unsuccessfully to convert the city to Christianity. Jerusalem was conquered by the Persians in 614 AD, and again by the Muslim Arabs/Saracens in 639 AD. The Temple Mount eventually became a Muslim shrine. A mosque was built there in 690 AD. It remained under Muslim control for 500 years, until the time of the Crusaders. The Crusader victories were short lived, and the city came under Turkish control for nearly 400 years. In 1917 General Edmund Allenby brought the city under the British Mandate. In May, 1948, the new city of Jerusalem became the capitol of the new nation of Israel.

"No Man's Land" and Mandelbaum Gate was the only passage between Israel and Jordan from 1948 to June 1967.

From 1948 to 1967 the city was divided between the Arabs and the Jews – the Old City to the Arabs and the New City to the Jews. Mandelbaum Gate was the only passage between the two sections. During the Six Day War of June, 1967, the Israelis captured the Old City. Jerusalem was united for the first time in 19 centuries. Jerusalem had come under Jewish control as God promised (Lk. 21:24).

ISRAEL'S PROPHETS AND ISRAEL'S RETURN

1400 BC	**Moses**	(Lev. 26:44-45; Deut. 30:1-5)
800 BC	**Amos and Micah**	(Amos 9:14-15; Micah 4:1-2)
740-701	**Isaiah & Nehemiah**	(Neh. 1:8-9; Isa. 5:25-30, 11:11-12, 14:1, 35:4, 43:4-6, 54:7-8, 61:4)
600 BC	**Jeremiah**	(Jer. 3:12-18, 12:14-15, 16:14-16, 23:2-8, 30:3, 31:7-12, 32:37, 33:7-11, 50:4-5)
575 BC	**Ezekiel**	(Ezek. 11:16-18, 20:34-42, 28:25-26, 34:11-16, 37:21-27)
34 AD	**Jesus**	(Matt. 24:31, Jn. 10:16)

IMPORTANT NOTE:

This manual's explanations for Jerusalem's sites are slightly more abbreviated than for other parts of Israel. To provide the history of Jerusalem in detail would fill many books and be impractical for this study. While in Jerusalem we intend to provide basic facts and Scripture references for each site. Your guide will fill in the details at his/her discretion.

**This manual is meant to be your "on tour" study guide,
not a detailed research publication.**

Jerusalem from Mount Scopus - Colorized Photo 1896

East Jerusalem

Mount Scopus/Nob (to abandon) forms the northern end of the Mount of Olives and is home to the beautiful Hebrew University. Looking toward Jerusalem from the mountain, we overlook the deep Kidron Valley. When Jerusalem was under seige in 68-70 AD, the Roman Legion camped between Mt. Scopus and the city.

The **Mount of Olives** is located between Bethany and Jerusalem. The limestone ridge rises 240 feet above the Temple Mount, and 2450 feet above sea level. Jesus often rested here while

Aerial photograph of the Mount of Olives, with Jerusalem to the left and Bethany to the right

Church of All Nations and the Garden of Gethsemane are located on the western edge of the Mount of Olives.

visiting Jerusalem. The Garden of Gethsemane is located on its western slope. The tombs of the Prophets Haggai, Zechariah and Malachi are near the summit, just to our left as you descend the Mt. of Olives. The traditional place of Jesus' ascension is marked by a small Dome of the Ascension, with his "footprint" preserved in the limestone rock.

Present day road down the Mount of Olives

During His **"Triumphant Entry"**, Jesus descended the Mount of Olives, crossed the Kidron Valley, and entered the Temple Mount (Matt. 21:1-11; Mk. 11:1-10; Lk. 19:41-44). Later, Jesus withdrew from Jerusalem to the Mount of Olives to teach his disciples about Jerusalem's pending doom, and "End Times". This teaching is called "The Olivet Discourse" (Matt. 24; Mk. 13). Forty days after his resurrection, Jesus ascended into heaven from this mountain (Mk. 16:19; Lk. 24:50-51; Acts 1:9-11).

Zechariah prophesied that when Jesus returns to the Mount of Olives it will be split in two, and be divided by a wide valley. Water will flow from the Temple Mount through this new valley toward the Dead Sea (Zech. 14:4-8).

Mosaic of Mary and Martha with Jesus in Bethany

Bethany (house of dates or figs) is located 1.7 miles East of Jerusalem. Lazarus, Mary and Martha lived here. They often extended hospitality to Jesus and His disciples when they visited Jerusalem (Jn.11:1; Matt. 21:17; Mk.11:11). Here Jesus taught Mary as Martha complained (Lk.10:38-42). In Bethany Jesus raised Lazarus from the dead (Jn. 11:1-44). Jesus attended a feast in His honor given by Simon the Leper, and Mary anointed his feet (Matt. 26:1-13; Mk. 14:3-9; Lk. 7:36-50; Jn.12:1-8). For political reasons, Bethany has been given to the PLO, and tours seldom go there. Visiting there recently has been a hassle and disappointment.

The Garden of Gethsemane is located on the western edge of the Mount of Olives.

GARDEN OF GETHSEMANE

Gethsemane (garden of the olive press) is maintained by Franciscan monks. It has eight olive trees, which many botanists claim are 2000 years old. However, Josephus records that all trees in this area were cut for campfires during the Roman siege in 70 AD. According to the Mishna, olive oil pressed in the Garden of Gethsemane was sold to the Temple. Those records indicate that the Garden belonged to Mary Magdalene's family.

The Garden lies just across the Brook Kidron from the Golden Gate and Temple Area (Jn. 18:1; Lk. 22:39). Here Jesus prayed *"Father not my will, but Thine be done"* (Matt. 26:36-56; Mk. 14:32-49; Lk. 22:30-53). The Garden is the scene of Jesus' betrayal by Judas, and the place of His arrest (Matt. 26:47-56; Jn.18:1-13).

From the Garden of Gethsemane one can view Jerusalem's walls and the Golden Gate rising above the Kidron Valley. Our devotional thoughts will focus on Matthew 24 and Jesus' trials. **The Garden is a wonderful place for prayer.**

KIDRON VALLEY

The Kidron Wadi (dark, turbid, gloomy) is only 3 miles long, yet it flows through the entire Valley of Jehoshaphat and into the Wilderness of Judea, or Wilderness of the Scapegoat. (During the rainy season the turbid Kidron flows 400′ below the temple platform). David crossed the Kidron as he fled the anger of his son, Absalom (II Sam. 15:23). Asa destroyed and burned his mother's idols here (I Kings 11:16). When Asa cleansed the Temple, he threw the idols into the Kidron. (II Kings 23:4-12; II Chron. 29:16, 30:14).

By Josiah's time, the area had become a cemetery for Jerusalem (II Kings 23:6; Jer. 26:23, 31:40). The Muslims believe it will be their place of judgment, and Joel mentions God's judgments in the valley (Joel 3:2, 12).

Kidron Valley with the "Tombs of the Kings" - photographed from the Temple Wall

The **Valley of the Kings** is located across from the eastern corner of the Temple. Four ancient tombs are found here. The first is called Absalom's Tomb, although the structure was probably built some 700 years after Absalom's death.

Jewish Law required that all tombs be whitewashed at Passover so pilgrims would not touch a tomb and become unclean for the Feast. Jesus may have referred to tombs in the Kidron Valley, or on the Mount of Olives, when he accused the Pharisees of being like *"white washed sepulchers"* (Matt. 23:27).

When Jesus died on the cross, there were many who got up from their graves and appeared in the city of Jerusalem. There was quite a stir in this cemetery (Matt. 27:52-53).

GOLDEN GATE

The Golden Gate, as it is called in Christian literature, is the oldest of the current gates in Jerusalem's Old City Walls.

The present **Sealed Gate** is Turkish. An older 7th century Byzantine structure, nearly buried, lies to the south of the present gate. This gate was sealed by the Muslims to prevent and postpone *"the day of judgment"* (Matt. 12:36). In 1530 the Turkish governor of Jerusalem ordered the gate sealed, to prevent the Messiah from returning through it. The Golden Gate is the only gate that led directly into the Temple area. Prophecy indicates that the Messiah will *"again"* enter this gate (Ezekiel 44:1-3). It was the route that Jesus and his disciples took from Gethsemane. The Golden Gate was not used by Jesus' when He entered Jerusalem during His triumphant entry, as donkeys were unclean and not allowed in the Temple area (Matt. 21:8-11; Lk. 19:35-38; Mk. 14:26). The Sheep Gate/Lion's Gate to the north was probably the gate of his triumphant entry.

There is much scholarly discussion about the location of the Golden Gate/The Gate Called Beautiful in the New Testament period. The placement of this Golden Gate helps determine the location of Herod's Temple.

Dr. James Fleming, then professor at Hebrew University, was photographing the Golden Gate when an earthquake hit Jerusalem. The ground opened in front of the gate, and he fell and slid several feet into a dusty cavern. When the dust cleared, in front of him was another gate forming the foundation on which the present gate had been built. A hurried examination led Dr. Fleming to date the lower gate to the Byzantine period. Question; was the New Testament Gate remodeled by the Byzantines, and is the Gate of Jesus' time still deeper?

With the sun setting he departed, returning early the next day, to research what the earthquake had uncovered. By then, the Muslim authorities had completely filled the cavern with new concrete. Had they done this for safety reasons, or to prevent investigation?

Donkey tied at Bethphage

Bethphage (place of young figs) is located on the eastern slope of the Mount of Olives, toward Bethany. This was the starting point for Jesus' triumphal entry. Here the disciples found the colt tied and ready for his ride into Jerusalem (Matt. 21:1-11; Mk. 11:1-11; Lk. 19:29-40; Zech. 9:9).

JERUSALEM'S WALLS

The present wall is a patchwork of many periods, but most of the visible structure was built under the Turkish reign of Suleiman the Magnificent in 1542. There are now 8 gates and 34 towers along its two and a half mile length. The wall averages a height of 40 feet. Near the Kidron Valley, below the southeastern peak of the wall, one can easily contrast the wall of Nehemiah's day with the stones of Herod's Temple. Most of the stones used in building the temple and temple wall were carved from Solomon's Quarries, the ancient quarry area just south of Golgotha. Here quarry operations were suspended when the rock became too porous for construction. Thus Golgotha was left looking like a skull with two eyes, a nose and a mouth.

Jerusalem Wall – The southeastern corner of the Temple Mount is a stone patchwork from the ages of Jerusalem's history.

South Jerusalem

Mount Ophel (high place) extends from Mount Moriah to the Pool of Siloam. The early City of David was situated on this slanted plateau which descends toward the south. Mt. Ophel separated the Valley of Kidron on the west from the **Valley of the Tyropoeon (Cheesemaker)** on the east. In the Old Testament period, Mount Ophel's sheer cliffs and plateau were easily defended. The cliffs of that time could be compared with Masada's cliffs of today. The Jebusite city seemed impregnable. The only way David was able take the city from the Jebusites was through the water shaft (II Sam. 5:8). Most tours to Mt. Ophel visit Joab and Hezekiah's Tunnels. Joab dug a separate tunnel to drain away the water so that his men could enter the shaft that led to the city above. Visitors view the exact passages from 3,000 years ago. Mount Ophel continues north and connects with Mt. Moriah, where David built his palace. The city wall was extended in Solomon's day to include the entire Temple area. There Solomon built the magnificent temple for God. (Note: New evidence has identified David's Tomb near the Pool of Siloam, but tradition will be difficult to overcome.)

The southwestern corner of the Temple Mount was the "place of horn-blowing" (blowing of Shofar).

One of the exciting adventures of visiting Jerusalem's Mount Ophel is a wet trek through Hezekiah's ancient tunnel.

GIHON SPRING / HEZEKIAH'S TUNNEL and POOL OF SILOAM

Exit from Hezekiah's ancient tunnel to the Pool of Siloam

Gihon Spring was the Jebusite source of water when David conquered the city. He combined the twin cities of Jebus (caravan city) and Salem (walled fortress), gave it the name Jerusalem, and made it his capital. Water shafts from the plateau led to the spring below.

In the 8th century BC, Hezekiah, in anticipation of the siege by Sennacherib of Assyria (701 BC), built a tunnel beneath Mt. Ophel and brought the water completely within the city walls to the Pool of Siloam. The tunnel is 1777′ in length, but only 1090′ if it had been possible to dig it in a straight line. It cut through solid rock approximately 651′ beneath Mt. Ophel. It was completed just before the Northern Kingdom fell to Sennacherib in 721 BC.

This was a remarkable feat of engineering. Workmen started digging from each end and met in the middle, within 3′ of each other. The Siloam Inscription, memorializing that meeting, was found in the tunnel near the Pool of Siloam. In 1880 the Turks took the Siloam Inscription to the Istanbul Museum. The Israeli government has requested the return of the inscription, but the Turks have refused. To this day, the Inscription is located in the Istanbul Museum.

Hezekiah's Tunnel is mentioned in the Old Testament in Neh.3:15; Isa. 8:6, 36-37, 22:11, as well as II Kings 20:20 and II Chron. 32:2-4, 30. Isaiah had prophesied that the King of Assyria would not come against Jerusalem (II Kings 19:32-33) and an angel of the Lord smote the Assyrian army (II Kings 19:35).

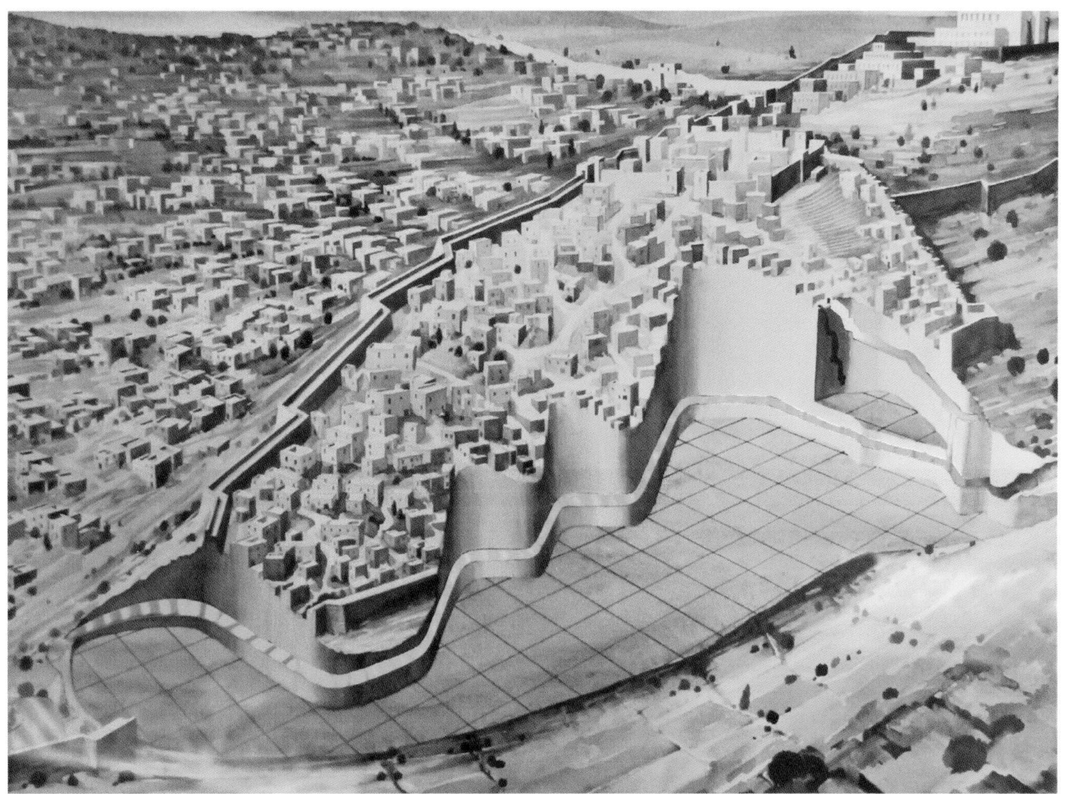

This crosscut of Mt. Ophel illustrates the route of Hezekiah's Tunnel, from Gihon Spring to the Pool of Siloam. (Courtesy of King David's City Displays)

Pool of Siloam – This part of the old city of Jerusalem is very complicated. Most homes above ground are Arab with the ruins beneath being Canaanite and Israelite.

Option: Depending on the weather and the season, many tours schedule a walk through Hezekiah's Tunnel. The water is ankle to knee deep, so visitors need to be in good health, wearing old jeans, cut-offs and tennis shoes. A flashlight or head-light is essential. This walk is usually scheduled near the end of the touring day, so those who do not want to hike the tunnel can return to the hotel by taxi. What an experience to stroll through the wet tunnel!

In the New Testament the Tower of Siloam fell, killing 18 people (Lk. 13:4). Jesus sent a blind man from the Temple to wash in this pool, and he was healed (Jn. 9: 7-11). In 2007 excavations of the Pool of Siloam revealed both the size and beauty of the first century pool. Every tour visits this location.

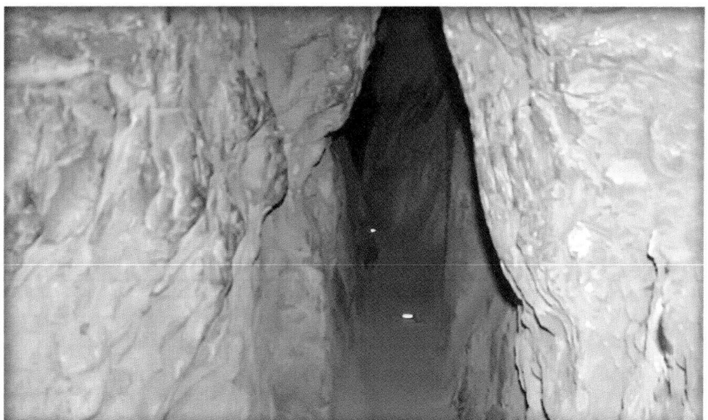

Today one can walk through **Joab's "dry tunnel"**. Joab used it to divert the water from the Gihon Spring so he could enter and conquer the Canaanite city of Jebus (one early name for Jerusalem).

Model of David's City

King David's City has proven to be a monumental excavation. The discoveries are too numerous to mention in this study. Tour groups walk down Mt. Ophel of David's city and consider how Joab conquered the city for David in 1000 BC. The ruins are enormous and cover several Biblical periods. Joab's entry into the Jebusite city was an incredible act of bravery.

The Royal Stairs, from the Pool of Siloam, lead up Mt. Ophel to the Temple. A visiting tour group can arrange to climb the stairs all the way to the Davidson Center, at the Temple area. The stairs were opened in the fall of 2010.

Confluence of the Kidron, Hinnon and Cheesemaker Valleys, where they join the Valley of Gehennah

The Valley of Hinnon/Valley of the Slaughter runs from the foot of Mt. Zion and joins the Kidron Valley at **Gehenna** (Place of Burning). Here perpetual fires burned the refuse of Jerusalem. It was a place of defilement, and the New Testament likens it to "*eternal punishment*" (Matt. 5:22, 29-30, 10:28, 18:9, 23:15, 33; Mk. 9:43, 45, 47; Lk. 12:5; James 3:6).

This was the place of Molech worship (II Kings 23:10; II Chron. 28:3, 33:6; Jer. 7:20-34) where King Ahaz and Manasseh offered their sons to Molech (II Chron. 28:3, 33:6; II Kings 23:10; Jer. 32:35).

Field of Blood where Judas hung himself

Potter's Field/Field of Blood/Aceldama is the place where Judas hanged himself, just as Zechariah had prophesied (Zech. 11:12-13). The field was bought as a burial place for strangers in Jerusalem with the "blood money" of "*thirty pieces of silver*" given to Judas for the betrayal of Jesus (Matt. 27:3-10; Acts 1:18-19). A Greek monastery marks the traditional site. There is an incredible view of the whole area from a platform above this Valley of Gehenna.

A mile to the south is the **Mount of Evil Counsel**, where Solomon kept his harem of nearly 1,000 wives. Ironically, today the United Nations headquarters is located on this mount in the old government buildings of the British Mandate command. Fittingly, it is still called "The Mount of Evil Counsel".

The Western Wall, Wailing Wall or Kotel is located in the Old City of Jerusalem at the foot of the western side of the Temple Mount. Parts of the wall are remnants of the ancient wall that surrounded the Jewish Temple's courtyard, and is arguably the most sacred site recognized by the Jewish faith outside of the Temple Mount itself. It has been a site for Jewish prayer and pilgrimage for centuries.

Church of the Domitian Abby on "Mount Zion", viewed from the Jerusalem city wall

West Jerusalem

MOUNT ZION

The literal translation of **"Mount Zion"** is "Fortress". Zion was the name David gave to the citadel of the Jebusite area of Jerusalem (the lower eastern mount of the city). Today tradition has applied the name wrongly to this mountain. Mt. Zion in the Old Testament was the Temple Mount (Psa. 137:1-3; Isa. 8:18; Jer. 31:6; Mic. 4:7). In Psalm 102:21 and Micah 3:10-12, Zion was the name given to the whole city of Jerusalem. In 340 AD, the Basilica Hagia Zion / **Dormition Abbey** was built near Zion Gate. Subsequently, the hill received its name from the church. The church was destroyed by the Persians in 614 AD, but the mount kept its name. The area is sacred to the Jews because most believe King David was buried here. Recent archaeological discoveries have revealed that David's Tomb is located on Mt. Ophel, below David's City.

Traditional "Upper Room" at "Mount Zion"

The **"Upper Room"** is the traditional site of the Lord's Supper (Matt. 26:17-30; Mk. 14:12-25; Lk. 22:7-30; Jn. 13:1-30). Tradition indicates that the Lord led his final Passover in the Upper Room. Here Jesus appeared to the disciples, and later to Thomas (Jn. 20:19-29). After Jesus' ascension, 120 disciples gathered to pray in the "upper room" (Acts 1:13-14). Here they prayed until the Holy Spirit came upon them at Pentecost (Acts 2:1-42). The problem with this traditional site is that the room is rendered in Crusader design and construction. However, it is accurate to say that this was the general area of the occurrence of these important New Testament events. It is located in the same area as the traditional David's tomb.

The Traditional Tomb of King David is on Mt Zion. A more likely location of David's Tomb is near the Pool of Siloam.

Shown here are the dungeon pillars where Jesus was beaten (caned) prior to his scourging by the Romans. It seems that this beating in Caiaphas' house was prior to the Sanhedrin interrogation or Jewish trials.

House of Caiaphas/St. Peters in Gallicantu is the traditional site of the House of Caiaphas, the high priest in Jesus' day. Jesus was brought here after his arrest in the Garden of Gethsemane. He was imprisoned here overnight, and it is believed He was likely beaten with canes by His Jewish captors. A visit to the cell and dungeon is most enlightening. This same prison may have been the place of the later imprisonment of the apostles (Acts 4:3, 5:17-23).

In Caiaphas' courtyard Peter denied the Lord three times (Matt. 26:34, 69-75; Mk. 14:66-72; Lk. 22:54-62; Jn. 18:15-18, 25-27). After His trial by the Jewish Sanhedrin, Jesus was condemned, and sent to Pilate (Matt. 26:57-63; Mk. 14:53-65; Lk. 22:54; 63-71; Jn. 18:12-14, 19-24).

Temple Area
AND THE WAILING WALL

Wailing Wall/Western Wall/Kotel is the remaining portion of the outer courtyard wall Herod built on the west side of the Temple. It is the holiest site in the Jewish world. The section open to the public is 60 yards long and 60 feet high. Some of Herod's stones in the wall are 30'x3'x5' in size.

The wall is called "the Wailing Wall" based on three traditions: (1) Jews come here to weep over the loss of the Temple. Today, their tears are tears of joy because the Jews have returned to their land. (2) In the late evening the wall is covered with dew, which legend holds, are the tears the wall sheds for Jews in exile. (3) Legend indicates that in the dead of the night, a white dove comes to the Wall and coos sadly with the Jewish mourners. Coincidentally, today a family of white doves dwell in the niches of the wall.

The Western Wall/ Wailing Wall / Kotel at sunset

Jews were not allowed to worship at, or even come to, the Wailing Wall prior to the Six Day War, in June of 1967. At that time, Israel took over the entire city of Jerusalem for the first time since 70 AD. Today, Jews can be found wor-

Artist concept of the Wailing Wall prior to 1967

shiping here any time of the day or night. Before the sun begins to set on Friday evenings, crowds of orthodox Jews gather for regular Shabbat services. They often place written prayers in the cracks of the wall. Cameras are not allowed on the Sabbath. Monday is usually the day for bar-mitzvahs.

Before the Six Day War, the present worship area was hemmed in by Arab buildings, and few worshipers could be accommodated. This part of Jerusalem was under Jordanian control from 1948 to June 1967. Today, the entire area has been cleared, and thousands can worship at the wall. New recruits in the Israeli military take their oath of commitment at the Wailing Wall.

To the southeast, the excavation of the First and Second Temple complex has been going on since 1968. Items have been found that date from Solomon's time to the days of Jesus. On the north end of the Western Wall, beneath Wilson's Arch, Jews gather for prayer before going to their synagogues. In the Second Temple period this arch bridge connected the Temple area to the upper city.

Rabbi's / Western Wall Tunnel – With Israeli clearance and permission, groups are allowed to examine the underground excavations along the Temple Wall. Here one can view the foundation stones of Herod's Temple complex.

At right angles from the Tunnel, sealed passages lead beneath the Temple Mount where the Temple once stood. (Information gleaned from any of the investigations beneath the Temple has been kept secret, to prevent conflict between Arabs and Jews).

Muslims were given control of the Temple Mount by secularist General Moshe Dyan just two days after Israel won it in the Six Day War of June 1967. Whenever Jewish archaeologists propose research or dig near the Temple complex, Muslim outcries of protest are heard in Jerusalem. Even necessary repairs can create problems. Muslims have built one of the world's largest mosques beneath the Temple Mount. In doing so, they hauled out tons of dirt and ancient artifacts to trash dumps. They claim that Israel never had a Temple on the mount, and it all belongs to them. It seems it is no problem for the Muslim community to rewrite history in their favor.

The largest foundation stone of Herod's Temple complex is 50′ long, 6′ tall and 5′ wide

The **Dung Gate** leads out of the city of Jerusalem to the refuse dump in Gehenna. Today this gate has become the main entrance for worshipers, leading to the Wailing Wall.

TEMPLE MOUNT

The Temple complex was located on Mt. Moriah. Many believe that the cupola to the left, the "Dome of the Spirits", covers an outcropping of Mt. Moriah which was the location of the ***"Holy of Holies"***.

The wall enclosing **Mount Moriah/Mt. Zion/Mountain of Sacrifice** encompasses 35 acres. Abraham brought his son Isaac here to offer him as a sacrifice. God stopped him, and provided a ram caught in the thicket as a substitute (Gen. 22:1-2).

Eight hundred years later David purchased the threshing floor of Araunah to build an altar to God (II Sam. 24:18-25).

This Temple hill was then known as Zion (the dwelling place of God). The position of the Temple was determined by God (I Chron. 21:15, 18; 22:1; II Chron. 3:1), and Solomon built it here in 950 BC (I Chron. 22:14-15, 28:11-20).

After the **Ark of the Covenant** was placed in the Temple, Solomon dedicated the Temple and God filled it with His Glory. This First Temple was destroyed by Nebuchadnezzar in 586 BC.

When the Jews returned to Jerusalem from captivity, they built the Second Temple under Zerubbabel's leadership (Ezra 3:8-13, 4:23-24, 5:15, 6:15-18). Herod built a larger Temple over Zerubbabel's temple (still called the Second Temple), and built the entire complex around it. To support this elaborate Temple Complex, Herod built arches supporting the south end of the Temple platform (where Mount Moriah slopes to meet Mt. Opel, of David's City). Later, the Crusaders wrongly named the area beneath the platform **"Solomon's Stables"**.

After Herod's Temple was completed, Zerubbabel's Temple was dismantled by the Jewish priests. Herod's Temple was started in 20 BC and completed it in 64 AD, 6 years before it was destroyed by the Roman armies, under Titus in 70 AD. The Temple area was under construction during the entire ministry of Jesus.

Today, the Muslim's have taken over the "stables" beneath the Temple Mount, to construct one of the world's largest mosques. The construction process has destroyed historical artifacts related to Israel's Temple Periods. They have endangered the support structure of their Dome of the Rock. An earthquake could destroy the Mosque above, (which of course would be "Israel's fault").

Gabriel announced the coming birth of John the Baptist to Zacharias as he ministered in the Temple (Lk. 1:1-25). Jesus was dedicated at His Pid Yom ha Ben (redemption of the first born) by the priest Simeon. Jesus came here in preparation for his Bar Mitzvah (Lk. 2:41-47). He cleansed the Temple on two occasions (Jn. 2:12-25; Lk. 19:45-48) and healed many here (Jn. 8:20; Mk. 12, Lk; 19:47; Jn. 8). He ministered to the woman who was caught in adultery (Jn. 8:7). He called attention to the widow who cast her two mites into the treasury (Mk. 12:41-44). Jesus taught many religious leaders in the Temple area (Matt. 21:23-23:29).

At Jesus' death, the veil of the Temple was torn from top to bottom. (Matt. 27:51) Here Judas cast his "blood money" back at the priests. (Matt. 27:5) Peter healed the lame man at the Gate Called Beautiful/ Golden Gate of the Temple (Acts 3). Paul was captured by an angry crowd in the Temple area, and eventually sent to Rome for trial (Acts 21:11-15).

Left – "Solomon's Stables" were built by Herod the Great to support the Temple platform

Right – Muslims renovated the "Stables" as seen below.

The Roman army, led by general Titus, destroyed Herod's temple complex in 70 AD.

The Temple and the complex were destroyed in 70 AD by the Romans, but Zechariah prophesied that it would be rebuilt (Zech. 8:7-9; Ezek. 40-48). Ezekiel's Temple, in the end days, will have water flowing from the Temple Mount (Ezek. *47:1-2*), and Malachi indicated that *"the Lord whom you seek will suddenly come to His Temple"* (Mal. 3:1).

In the center of the present Temple complex is the Muslim mosque, the Dome of the Rock. It is a gold domed, octagonal mosque decorated with brilliant Persian tiles. The Dome is 180′ in diameter, and is 108′ tall.

Some believe that the Dome stands over the site of Solomon's Temple. However, there is much controversy as to where the Temple actually stood. Many believe it was to the north, with the Holy of Holies located where the **"Dome of the Spirits"** now stands. From there, one has a direct view across the Eastern Gate to the Mount of Olives, where the *"Red Heifer"* (Num. 19:2) was sacrificed to provide the *"ashes of the heifer"* (Num. 19:19; Heb. 9:13), thus the *"ashes for purification of sin"* (Num. 19:2, 9, 17).

The Muslim Dome of the Rock stands over the traditional location of the *"Holy of Holies"*.

Muslims consider the **Dome of the Rock** to be their third most sacred site, after Mecca and Medina in Saudi Arabia. They believe Mohammed went up into Heaven, on his white winged steed, from the rock which is beneath the Dome. His horse was named El Baruck, meaning "Lightning". Muslims claim that the Wailing Wall was just a hitching post for Mohammed's horse. The **Waqf** are the Muslim custodians of the Temple Mount today.

The Jews consider the Temple Mount so holy that the previous Chief Rabbi, Shlomo Goren, did not allow Jews to walk on the Mount for fear that they might tread on the site of The Holy of Holies. Jewish guides, however, are allowed to lead tours to the Temple Mount.

The **Mosque of El Aksa** is located at the southeast corner of the Mount, where Solomon's palace once stood. It was built as a church to the Virgin Mary by Justinian in 536 AD. It was reconstructed into a Muslim mosque in the years 709-715 by the son of the builder of the **Dome of the Rock**. The present structure was built on the foundations of the older Byzantine Church, and can hold 5000 Muslims at prayer. In 1187, Saladin captured it for the Muslim hordes. Just to the left of the door Abdullah, king of Jordan, was shot and killed in 1951. His grandson King Hussein was saved when a bullet struck a medal he was wearing.

הודעה ואזהרה
אסור לפי דין תורה לכל
אדם להכנס לשטח הר-הבית
מפני קדושתו.
הרבנות הראשית לישראל

NOTICE AND WARNING
ENTRANCE TO THE AREA OF THE TEMPLE MOUNT IS FORBIDDEN TO EVERYONE BY JEWISH LAW OWING TO THE SACREDNESS OF THE PLACE.
THE CHIEF RABBINATE OF ISRAEL

Muslims are monotheistic and observe Friday as their Sabbath. They eat no pork, drink no alcohol, and do not gamble. They practice polygamy, and can have up to four wives if they are wealthy. Therefore, most produce more children than other ethnic groups in the world. They pray five times a day while facing Mecca and Medina (backs to Jerusalem). However, they claim that Jerusalem is their third most holy site. Arafat and PLO propaganda sought to convince the world that Jerusalem, containing the Dome of the Rock, was the most important piece of Muslim property in the entire Islamic world.

The PLO has used this political banner to raise military funds, and gain Arab support. Their goal is to return to the borders prior to the Six Day War (June 1967). Their real goal is to eventually drive the Jews from Israel, and into the Mediterranean Sea. Today, Muslims are rewriting history to convince the world that the Jews never possessed Jerusalem or the Temple Mount. To that end, they have destroyed archaeological artifacts which would provide hard evidence that the Temple Mount belonged to Israel. With lack of concern, front end loaders and enormous dump trucks have removed centuries of historical layers. Israeli archaeologists have had to sift through the dump. Meanwhile, Muslims have built one of the largest mosques in the world beneath the Temple platform.

1) Moon crescent... Allah was the name of the moon god of Mecca, adopted by Muslims.
2) Interior of the Dome of the Rock. This is the traditional sacred rock where Abraham prepared to sacrifice Isaac, according to the Bible. Contrary to the Scriptures, in the Qur'an Abraham prepared to sacrifice Ishmael.
3) Muslim man washes his hands, feet and face in preparation for his daily prayers (5 times per day).
4) Muslim faces Mecca for one of his daily prayers. The Dome of the Rock is to his back, stating emphatically that Jerusalem is of less importance to the Muslims than is Mecca.

Old City of Jerusalem

ST. STEPHEN'S GATE TO THE JAFFA GATE

St. Stephen's Gate, or Lion's Gate, is located on the eastern side of the city, with reliefs of lions on the façade. Through this gate the Israeli Defense Force's paratroopers/stormtroopers penetrated the Old City on June 6, 1967. One battalion secured the Temple Mount and the Wailing Wall where Rabbi Sholomo Goron led the first Jewish worship service at the Wall in 1897 years. A second battalion, led by Yehudah Hecht, secured the area from Via Dolorosa to the Damascus Gate, as well as the Arab Quarter. Every step was met with heavy resistance from the Jordanian military.

Stephen was taken through this gate to the place of stoning, located in the quarry area in front of Golgotha (Acts 7:54-60). Before Stephens' death the gate was called the **Sheep Gate**.

The **"Via Dolorosa"**, the Catholic **"Way of the Cross"**, winds through the narrow streets of the Old City to the Church of the Holy Sepulcher. This "Crusader route", with its thirteen stations of the cross, memorializes traditional events (not Biblical) en route to Calvary. The accuracy of this traditional route, and the location of Calvary, is questioned by many. Few of the Via Dolorosa events are based on the events in the Gospels. There is also a question as to the location of Golgotha and the Garden Tomb. If Jesus was crucified at the northern site of Calvary, then Jesus would have been taken from the Pratorium, through the Sheep Gate, along the eastern wall to the place of crucification.

The **Pool of Bethesda** (house of mercy or grace) is an ancient pool about 60′ below the present ground level. The pool in Jesus' day had porches on each side. Here Jesus healed the lame man at the *"troubled waters"* (Jn. 5:1-16). The **Church of St. Anne**, built near the pool, is one of the finest examples of Crusader construction in the land. The acoustics in particular are incredible.

The Crusader Church is built over a 5th century Byzantine Church, which supposedly was built over the cave where Joachim and Anna, the Virgin Mary's parents, lived. This is the traditional Catholic site of the "immaculate conception". (Roman Catholics believe that Mary never had a sexual relationship from her birth to her death).

In June of 1967, an elite unit of the Israeli paratroopers entered the courtyard to take a break from the intense fighting, as they secured the Arab Quarter of Jerusalem. Here a miracle from God saved them from certain death.

Tower of Antonia was named after Mark Antony, and was the site of Herod's Fortress. The Antonia overlooked the Temple Area, and Rome stationed troops here to quell any Jewish uprising.

The Praetorium/Pilate's Judgment Hall is where Jesus was robed, mocked, beaten, given a crown of thorns and sentenced to death (Jn. 19:13; Matt. 27:2-31). Here Pilate "washed his hands" of Jesus' blood. The first Catholic "Station of the Cross" begins the traditional Via Dolorosa at this point.

Others, with strong support, place the Praetorium near the Jaffa Gate, at the location of Herod's Palace. The argument continues. Your author may even be leaning in this direction, but the subject is still being researched with his friend Dr. Gary Crossland, author of *The Merged Gospels.*

The Roman fortress, the Praetorium, overlooked the Temple complex. From here Rome controlled the activities of the Jews on the Temple Mount.

The **Pavement** is located on the Roman courtyard level and reveals **"the King's Game"** or ***Basileus***. This game determined who would be next to die, and the Romans used it to mock Jesus (Matt. 27:27-30). The guide will discuss the details as the group visits the site.

Ecce Homo is the traditional site where Pilate said to the Jews, *"Ecce homo"*, meaning *"behold the man"*. According to the Scriptures, Pilate had Jesus severely beaten by the Roman guards; so severely was his body ravaged that the Jews requesting his death did not even recognize Jesus when He was brought back to them (Jn. 19:5).

Catholic pilgrims on the Via Dolorosa come to the final three stations of the cross at the Church of the Holy Sepulcher.

The "Via Dolorosa" is the traditional Catholic "Way of the Cross" from the **Praetorium** to the **Church of the Holy Sepulcher**. The Catholics have memorialized 14 **"Stations of the Cross"** en route to the Holy Sepulcher. Catholics walk this route, as a pilgrimage, praying at each station, hoping to attain special blessings from God. The Via Dolorosa leads to the Church of the Holy Sepulcher in the Christian Quarter of Jerusalem.

(*Biblical references related to the Crucification* are as follows; Simon of Cyrene was ordered to carry the cross for Jesus (Matt. 27:32). Jesus spoke to the women along the way (Lk. 23:27-32). At Calvary, He was stripped of his garments, given gall to drink (Jn. 19:23) and nailed to the cross (Lk. 23:33). At Calvary He was crucified and died (Matt. 27:50; Mk. 15:25, 37; Lk. 23:46; Jn. 19:30). His body was then taken down from the cross, and He was laid in a garden tomb (Matt. 27:57-61, 28:1-10; Mk. 15:42-16:8; Lk. 23:50-24:8; Jn. 19:38-20:31).

Constantine became the first "Christian" Emperor of the Roman Empire.

Church of the Holy Sepulcher (traditional site), is the most sacred place on earth to millions of Christians. According to Byzantine, Catholic and Greek traditions, the church was built over Mt. Calvary and Jesus' Tomb.

Emperor Hadrian first built his pagan temple to Jupiter and Venus on this site in 135AD, supposedly to discourage early Christians from venerating the site. That temple remained until 335 AD, when Emperor Constantine built the first church on the site. His church was destroyed in 614 by the Persians, but many other churches followed, with the Crusader church of the 12th century being the basic outline of the present church.

When Saladin defeated the Crusaders in 1187, he allowed Christians to continue to worship in the church if the key remained in Muslim hands. In 1330 he placed the church's key in the hands of the Nuseibeh family, and its care remains in their hands until today. This was done to keep peace and prevent conflict between the Roman Catholic, Greek and Russian Orthodox sects.

Many earthquakes have greatly changed the ancient church. It has continued to stand as a testimony to the death and resurrection of The Lord Jesus. The 1927 earthquake nearly destroyed the church, but the British, in 1936 and 1944, shored up the building with ugly steel girders. In 1958 a total renovation was finally decided on by the controlling six communities who use the facility (Roman Catholic, Greek Orthodox, Armenian Orthodox, Jacobite-Syrians, Coptic and Abyssinian Catholics).

Station 10 is the Crucifixion of Jesus inside the Church of the Holy Sepulcher

After entering the Church, steps on the right ascend to the Latin and Greek chapels, where the Crusader Via Dolorosa leads up to "Calvary", and concludes with "Stations of the Cross" 10–13. Tradition says that Adam's skull was buried at Calvary; thus the name *"hill of the skull"*.

The Franciscan chapel has Station 10, where Jesus was stripped for crucifixion, and Station 11 is where He was nailed to the cross. The Greek altar is Station 12, where Jesus died. Between the supports for the altar one can touch the rock of *"Calvary"*. Above is the Greek treasury with relics and "two pieces of wood from the cross".

Scene from the Dome of the Holy Sepulcher, looking down upon the Easter morning mass, 1960.

Back at the entrance of the Church is the "Stone of Anointing/Unction", where Jesus' body was prepared for burial. To the left is Station 14, where according to tradition, Jesus was buried. Entering, one passes through the Chapel of the Angel, where the angel spoke to the women on Easter morning. Beneath the present renovated dome is the traditional slab where Jesus was laid in death. Behind this burial area is the Jacobite chapel with several rock-hewn tomb shafts. It is said that these were part of the "Tomb of Joseph of Arimathea".

Dome of the Church of the Holy Sepulcher

In the Greek Cathedral is a large chalice marking the Crusader's "center of the earth". From here a flight of stairs leads down to the Chapel of Queen Helena. In 327, according to tradition, she found 3 crosses in the cave beneath Hadrian's Temple. She decided that the center cross was Jesus' cross, and that the hill above was "Calvary". Thus, she had her son, Emperor Constantine, build the first church on the site.

Without a guide, visits to the church are very confusing. Incense, candles, and dark passages are everywhere. It is difficult to know which church is in control of which chapel, and perhaps not necessary. Many who visit the Church of the Holy Sepulcher are spiritually disappointed. However, committed Catholics and Orthodox are usually blessed.

The long standing tradition, that Calvary and the Garden Tomb were located here at the Church of the Holy Sepulcher, will be discussed in detail as we visit **North Jerusalem.** The other possible site of Jesus' death and resurrection is Gordon's Calvary and the Garden Tomb. (As a reader, you will be encouraged to draw your own conclusions). Departing from the Church of the Holy Sepulcher, one passes through the narrow streets of the of the Old Jerusalem market/shook.

Herod's Palace/Citadel, built by Herod the Great, is located near Jaffa Gate. The exterior wall of this fortress was not destroyed during the Roman attack by Titus.

Herod's Palace, at the Citadel and the Museum

"David's Tower" is actually a Muslim minaret, and has nothing to do with King David. It was built centuries later during the Muslim conquest. The *"Wise Men"* came from the East to Jerusalem seeking the *"new born King of the Jews"*. They were directed to King Herod at this palace (Matt. 2:1-2).

Pilate stayed here when he was in Jerusalem. Pilate interrogated Jesus at daybreak, and then sent Him to Herod Antipas, who was staying in the same complex. Jesus refused to speak to Herod, *"the old fox/dog"*, after which Herod returned Him to Pilate. This was the site of Jesus' second trial. By this time Pilate had gone to work at the **Praetorium.** There, at the **Tower of Antonia,** Jesus' final trial took place. Catholic tradition places the timing for this event on "Good Friday" morning (Matt. 27:11-26; Lk. 23:1-25).

The present citadel stands on Crusader foundations. The present wall was built by Suleiman the Magnificent in 1540 and was for 500 years the Turkish Citadel in Jerusalem.

The **Citadel/Tower of David Museum**, in unique ways, presents an incredible 3000 year history of Jerusalem. The Museum and the Sound of Light concerts (held most of the year) are well worth viewing.

British Gen. Allenby entered Jerusalem for a bloodless surrender.

The **Jaffa Gate** led out of the Old City toward the port of Jaffa/Joppa on the Mediterranean Sea. General Edmund Allenby of the British Command entered this gate on Christmas Day of 1917, to accept Jerusalem in a bloodless surrender from the Turks.

Jewish Quarter

The Jewish Quarter was systematically destroyed by the Jordanian army between 1948 & 1967.

The **Lion's Gate** is bullet-riddled due to the heavy fighting in this area in 1948. Entering the gate, one proceeds to the south central portion of the Old City, the Jewish Quarter.

The **Jewish Quarter of Jerusalem** was the center of Jewish life in the city for 800 years, until 1948. In 1948, during the War of Liberation, the Jewish community in the quarter was cut off from the rest of the world. In the Jewish Quarter, God performed many miracles to protect His people from starvation.

A Jewish convoy tried to get food and supplies into the Jewish Quarter to sustain the Jews there. Many lives were lost in heavy fighting to keep the community supplied. The memorial vehicles along the "Jerusalem Corridor" leading up to Jerusalem help tell the tragic story. You are encouraged to view the video *Cast a Giant Shadow* with Kirk Douglas. The movie accurately portrays those events.

A Jewish convoy transports supplies to the besieged and starving Jewish Quarter - 1947.

Between 1948 and 1967 this quarter was bombed the Jordanians, and almost totally destroyed. The Jews struggled to remain and rebuild meager homes. Life was hard for them. When the Jordanians were asked why they did not destroy all of the Jewish Quarter, they responded, "We knew that the Jews would someday return."

In June of 1967 Israel took control of the Old City of Jerusalem. Nearly 100 synagogues had been destroyed by the Jordanians, under the so-called "moderate" King Hussein. Israel has never attacked or destroyed any church or mosque. (The only time any places of worship have come under attack by Israel has been when terrorists used mosques for their protection or ammunition storage).

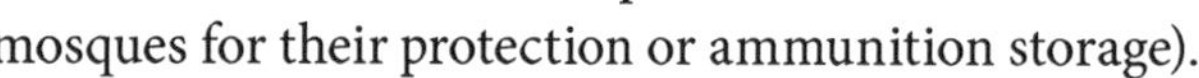

Due to the terrible destruction of the Jewish quarter, Israeli leaders made the wise decision to do archaeological excavations of the quarter prior to rebuilding. Today, the Jewish Quarter has been beautifully rebuilt, while protecting archaeological discoveries of First Century Jerusalem beneath the new buildings.

Model from Nehemiah's time – construction of the city wall, Citadel Museum, Jerusalem.

Nehemiah's Wall of today is a visible portion of the wall which was constructed when the Jews returned from Babylon/Persian exile. Your guide will discuss the interesting details of the wall.

Cardo Maxima, a street in the Jewish Quarter, is located above the First Century Roman pavement of Jerusalem's main street. Today in the Cardo you will want to visit the Jewish art and tallit shops.

First century eating utensils – Burn House

The "Burn House", in the **Herodian Museum,** is an incredible display of a wealthy First Century home. This area was first excavated in 1967, when the Jews returned to the Jewish Quarter. The "Burn House" was destroyed in 70 AD by Rome. Artifacts, discovered from Jesus' day, indicate how the wealthy residents in the Herodian Quarter lived. Here are many stone jars, glass items, pottery and furniture from that period. It seems likely that Jesus and his disciples observed the Passover in such a home, and in this area of the city, rather than at the traditional *"Upper Room"* site. After the meal, the Lord gave the ordinance of the Lord's Supper, using items from the Passover table (unleavened bread and wine).

Golden Jewish menorah, Jerusalem

The Temple Institute, located in the Jewish Quarter, is a group of scholars and artisans who are making items, in accordance with the Biblical instructions, to be placed in the Third Temple. These items include the vessels, menorah, priestly garments, and even the 24-carat gold crown for the High Priest. The Institute is well worth one's visit, especially if you are interested in prophecy and the "end days".

North Jerusalem

Damascus Gate

Damascus Gate is pictured on the Madeba Map as the "Gate of the Pillar". Today it is the most beautiful gate of the city. For centuries it has been the main entrance to Jerusalem. Today's gate was built in 1537 by Suleiman the Magnificent.

To the left of the present gate, and several feet lower, the remains of a first century wall and gate can be seen. Many believe this was the gate through which Saul departed as he made his way towards Damascus. Beneath the Gate is a small museum, and the entrance to the Wall Ramparts. Steps lead to the top of Jerusalem's Wall where one can stroll and view the city.

Solomon's Quarry cave passage was the Jerusalem escape route for King Zedekiah. Cave passages from the quarry led 17 miles to the Jericho Plain (II Kings 25:4-5). There he was captured by the Babylonians. (Many believe that the Temple treasures were transported secretly through this passage to the Dead Sea area, or to the mountains of Moab).

From the northern wall one can clearly discern the nose, eyes and mouth of the "Hill of the Skull"/Golgotha. The strata at Golgotha matches the limestone strata beneath the narrow path on the Jerusalem Wall.

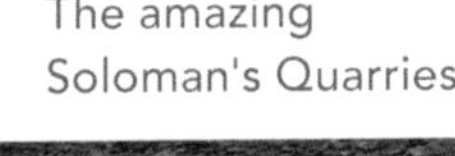
The amazing Soloman's Quarries

South is the Muslim Quarter of Jerusalem. In 1960 the view was very different. At that time one could look down a grassy slope which angled toward the Temple Mount. The 1960 view made it crystal clear that we were standing on *"Mt. Zion in the North"* (Psalm 48:2). The strata beneath, and the area between the wall and Golgotha, were part of Solomon's Quarries in the Old Testament period. The huge cavern below reaches 214 yards beneath the city and into the heart of Mt. Zion. Limestone from this quarry was carefully cut for the construction of Herod's Temple (I Kings 5:15, 6:7; II Chron. 3).

Hill of the Skull today

GOLGOTHA AND GARDEN TOMB

Mount Zion ***"In the North"*** - Golgotha was a part of the Temple Mount/Moriah/Zion. According to recent bedrock studies, it extended from the Temple to the north. Some suggest that the Temple Mountain is the same mount on which Jesus, the Perfect Lamb of God, became a sacrifice for the sins of the world.

Jesus was crucified at **Golgotha/Hill of the Skull**. Here He *"laid down His life"* (Matt. 27:32-56; Mk. 15:21-41; Lk. 23:26-46; Jn. 19:16-37). Just south of Golgotha/Calvary was the Jewish "place of stoning". Stephen was stoned here by the "Bloody Sanhedrin" (Talmud). This was the only Jewish High Court to take a man's life. They demanded the death of both Jesus and Stephen.

Pictured above is Jeremiah's Grotto, where he was imprisoned.

Jeremiah's Grotto, according to Jewish tradition, is the cave pit to the eastern side of Skull Hill where Jeremiah was imprisoned (Jer. 38:6). Here he wrote, *"Is it nothing to all you, who pass by this way? "Is it nothing to all you who pass this way? Look and see if there is any pain like my pain, which was severely dealt out to me, which the Lord inflicted on the day of His fierce anger.* (Lam. 1:12). Amazingly, Jeremiah describes Jesus' coming crucifixion 600 years before it took place. He gave that prophecy a few yards from where Jesus died. **God's finger of prophecy is both incredible and accurate!**

The Garden Tomb lies just west of Skull Hill. General Gordon of Khartoum, in 1885, proposed that this rock-hewn limestone tomb was the biblical Garden Tomb. The tomb was that of a *"rich man"* and had two chambers; one where the family could gather and mourn, and a second where the body was laid on a burial slab. The entrance was closed with a *"rolling stone"*, which was rolled like a giant millstone. A sealing/locking stone was set above the rolling stone in its groove, thereby *"sealing"* the doorway in the face of the tomb.

This tomb has niches above the entrance, and there are indications that a pagan temple had been built over the tomb to prevent early Christians from worshiping there. In Jesus' day there was a large garden outside the tomb, with an enormous water storage cistern, the second largest in Jerusalem. A large wine press has been excavated in this First Century garden. The Scripture says that Jesus was buried in a *"garden"* near the place where He died on Calvary (Matt. 27:57-66; Mk. 15:42-47; Lk. 23:50-56; Jn. 19:41-42). His tomb was guarded (Matt. 27:62-66) and secured by a large rolling stone (Mk. 16:3-4). The garden is located about 500 yards from the Damascus Gate.

Entrance to the Garden Tomb

After His resurrection, Jesus appeared to Mary Magdalene in the garden (Mk. 16:9; Jn. 20:11-18). Peter and John raced to the garden tomb, and looked in to find the *"...linen wrappings lying"* (in their place, implying undisturbed), and they knew immediately that Jesus had risen (Matt. 28:1-15; Mk. 16:1-11; Lk. 24:1-12; Jn. 20:1-18).

Jesus is alive forever!

WHERE WAS CALVARY AND THE GARDEN TOMB?

This question is difficult to answer. It has been argued in theological circles for centuries. Here we will share thoughts from both sides of the argument. Two key sites are offered as possibilities. The first is Gordon's Calvary/Hill of the Skull and the Garden Tomb (located outside the Jerusalem Wall near the Damascus Gate). The second is the traditional Catholic site of the Church of the Holy Sepulcher (which is today inside the Old City of Jerusalem near the Christian Quarter).

Hill of the Skull, "Gordon's Calvary", 1859 photograph restored – note the absence of any Muslim cemetery on top of the hill.

Recently, when the **Church of the Holy Sepulcher** was renovated, the only new find was a Jewish cemetery.

Queen Helena, a noted "Christian pilgrim" and mother of Constantine, came to the Holy Land to locate the holy sites. When she located "Biblical sites", she had her son construct churches over these locations. These were the first churches in Christendom. Sometimes her "research" was based upon "word of mouth" and local traditions. It seems she chose sites according to her "spiritual leading", personal intuition and convenience of travel. (The latter was true in the Crusader's choice of Cana in Galilee). Little evidence supports her chosen sites.

Helena's choice of the Holy Sepulcher is accepted today by many church traditions to be the site of Jesus' death and resurrection. The Eastern Orthodox, Armenian, Coptic, Syrian, Abyssinian, Latin and Roman Catholic Churches all accept the church as the holy site. The ownership of the church is split among them, and has been disputed since Saladin broke up the Christian Crusader Kingdom in 1187. The Crusaders ruled over Jerusalem and controlled the church for only 88 years. Since their defeat, the "Church" pays the Muslims "tax" for the use of the Holy Sepulcher, even to this day.

The Romans destroyed Jerusalem in 70 AD, and many Christians fled to Pella. A few returned forty years later, around 110 AD. Because of the Roman-Jewish conflict in Jerusalem early in the second century, Christians were simply struggling to stay alive. It seems logical that those who returned from Pella (110 AD) would not have given time or energy to locate the sites of Jesus' death and burial. To the contrary, they worshiped in secret and hid their identity. There were no Christian tourists to identify holy sites in the second century.

Emperor Hadrian conquered Jerusalem in 135 AD and sought to revise Jerusalem's Jewish history while paganizing the city.

The second Jewish Revolt was brewing, and Hadrian would soon destroy Jerusalem (135 AD). His goal was to annihilate Judaism and Christianity. He built pagan temples everywhere, and mocked any religion that worshiped the God of Abraham. As a result of Hadrian's hatred and edicts against Judaism and Christianity, no churches would be built until 325 AD.

When Hadrian rebuilt Jerusalem in 136 AD, he dedicated the city to the Roman god Jupiter and renamed Jerusalem **Aelia Capitolina**. Many assume he built a pagan temple to Venus over what he believed was the site of Jesus' crucifixion. I doubt that he had many Jewish or Christian confidants to assist him in identifying the correct location, since he was persecuting them with fervor. Some believe he was trying to destroy Christianity by desecrating their holy places. The real question is, did Christians seek to worship at, or venerate such sites,

Roman Temple of Jupiter at Baalbeck is the best preserved Roman temple.

under Hadrian's reign? Who knows? Hadrian built pagan temples all over Jerusalem, as he had in Rome. So, was the Venus Temple actually built over the location of Calvary and the Garden Tomb?

If Hadrian did that in Jerusalem, he may have done exactly what he did *not* want to do; namely, preserve the holy places for future Christian worship. During the days of Constantine, Eusibus tells us that Helena ordered Hadrian's temple to Venus be torn down, and the mount cleared. She then arranged for her son to build the first Christian church on the site.

Helena believed the site was the location of Calvary. According to tradition, she brought a woman with an issue of blood to a cave beneath the place where the pagan temple had stood. There were three crosses in that cave. The ill woman touched the crosses on either side and nothing happened. But when she touched the cross in the middle she was healed. Helena proclaimed that cross was the very cross on which Jesus died, and proclaimed the place to be the mountain where He was crucified. Helena then had the Church of the Holy Sepulcher constructed over that "sacred cave".

The remains of the Venus Temple in Rome. It is likely that the Temple of Venus, in Jerusalem, was similar to Jupiter's Temple at Baalbeck.

Did Queen Helena always find the holy sites she was looking for? Her approach might well be illustrated by Jewish scholars in centuries past, who were discussing a passage in Genesis. The Jewish rabbis were asking why travelers *"discovered a plain in Sinar"*. Their answer was, "because they were looking for a plain in Sinar". It is human nature to find what we are looking for.

Why did Hadrian and his pagan construction crews leave three crosses undisturbed in the cave beneath their temple. Were these crosses not discovered when the foundation was laid for that pagan temple?

By the fourth century nearly all pilgrims accepted the Holy Sepulcher to be the place of Calvary, *without questioning* the location. No one dared question the king's mother, or Constantine, concerning the location choice of the holy site.

In a topographical study of Jerusalem Dr. Vendyl Jones, director of the Institute of Judaic-Christian Research, used a computer-generated map of Jerusalem to overlay the bedrock of the city. He believed the study showed that Queen Helena's site of Calvary was within the city walls of Jesus' day. Yet, crucifixions were required to take place outside the city walls.

Exterior - Church of the Holy Sepulcher

Across the years, Catholic and Greek churches have built and rebuilt over the remains of Helena's church. Earthquakes and fires have destroyed sections of the early and subsequent constructions. Today the Holy Sepulcher is a virtual hodge-podge of altars, domes, pillars, tombs and worship chapels for the various Christian sects, who claim ownership of "Calvary" and "Jesus' Tomb". For the first time visitor, it is difficult to get a mental picture of what the area would have been like in Jesus' day. The *faithful* cling to the historical traditions. Approximately one million pilgrims worship there annually.

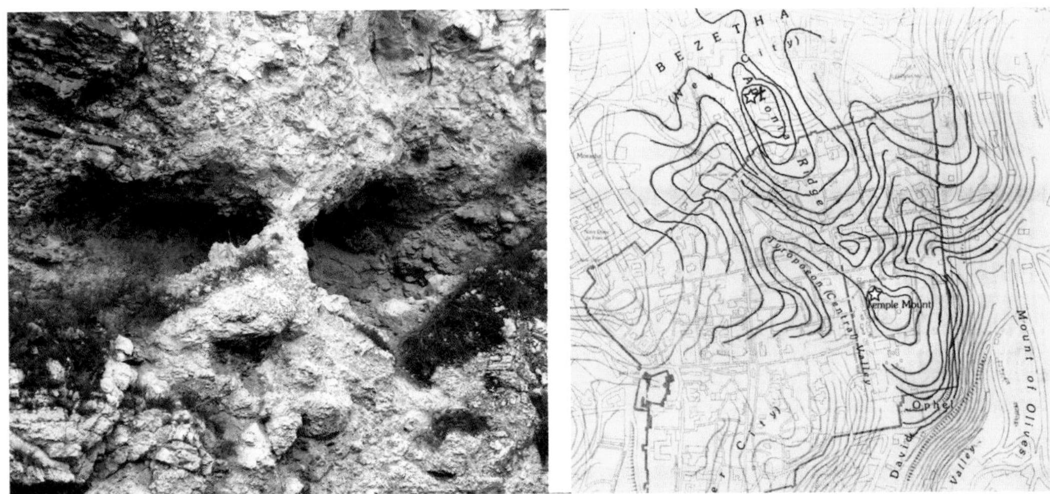

Left – Close-up of the Hill of the Skull

Topographical map of Jerusalem showing the bedrock strata from the Temple Mount northward to the *Hill of the Skull.* (Psalm 48:2)

GORDON'S CALVARY AND THE GARDEN TOMB THE SECOND POSSIBILITY – WITH ADDITIONAL CONSIDERATIONS

Many people today believe that the Hill of the Skull was the extreme northern end of Mt. Moriah/Mount Zion/Temple Mount/the Mount of Sacrifices. The bedrock of Moriah extends, in a gentile rise, from the Temple Mount to the north wall of modern Jerusalem. Solomon's Quarries lie beneath the present city wall, just east of the Damascus Gate. A modern street, which was the First Century road to Damascus, runs parallel to the wall and then turns north. The ancient Quarries of King Solomon were in the area between the wall and a hill that rises about 300 yards to the north. Solomon and other kings used the quarry to cut limestone for the construction of Jerusalem. When they quarried to the north the rock became too porous to be usable. They abandoned the quarry operation, leaving a portion of the hillside resembling two eyes, a nose and a mouth - hence the name, Hill of the Skull/ Goul' Gohlt (Heb). From the study of the bedrock of Jerusalem it is known that the limestone inclined to the north, and was simply the extension of the northern end of Mt. Moriah/Zion. In light of this information, we believe that Calvary was located on the northern extension of the Mountain of Sacrifice. The Psalmist may have prophesied concerning this site...

> *"Great is the Lord, and greatly to be praised, in the city of our God, His Holy Mountain. Beautiful in elevation, the joy of the whole earth, is* ***Mt. Zion in the far North,*** *The city of the Great King."* (Psalm 48:2)

Several Bible scholars from the mid-1800's have judged this to be the site of Calvary. The quarry area between Jerusalem and Calvary has been known since Roman times as the Jewish *"place of stoning"*, and is where Stephen died. The Roman highway passed where the modern street is today. It is possible that Jesus was crucified near the roadside rather than on the hill itself, since the Romans were trying to deter rebellion and insurrection. This made the crucifixion *up close and personal.* Only in our Christian hymns is it inferred that Jesus died on a

Hill of the Skull with Arab bus station below and new Muslim minaret to the east

hill. It is never mentioned in the Gospels.

In 1883 General Charles George Gordon, a British officer and Bible teacher, concluded that The Hill of the Skull was indeed Calvary. Because of this many call it "Gordon's Calvary". Locked gates of the Muslim cemetery on top of the hill prevent Christians from going there. Muslims do not allow "infidels" in their holy cemetery. The Arab bus station below Calvary was built in 1953, and is the loudest in the Middle East. A Muslim mosque and minaret have been built to the east of Skull Hill. The minaret loud speakers blast the call for Muslim prayer 5 times a day. The combination of sounds often disrupts the quiet mood of the garden for Christian worshipers.

Skull Hill fits the New Testament descriptions in John 19. Jesus carried his cross to *"the place of the Skull"* (v.17) *"near by the city"* (v.20). In Hebrews 13:12 we are told that Jesus suffered and died *"outside the city gates"* and likely near the highway, since *"those passing were hurling abuse at Him, wagging their heads...'save yourself if you are the Son of God, come down from the cross'"* (Matt. 27:39, 40). Others watched Him from *"far off"* (Lk. 23:49).

The garden fits several New Testament descriptions. The tomb was in a garden. *"Now in the place where He was crucified there was a garden..."* (Jn. 19:41). The Garden Tomb area hosts one of the largest cisterns in Jerusalem, with a capacity of some 200,000 gallons. The Garden held a vineyard, as indicated by the excavation of a beautiful wine press from the first century. Crosses carved in the cistern may indicate its use by early believers.

This First Century Wine Press is located in the Garden. Some reconstruction has been done to preserve it.

The Garden Tomb is located about 100 yards west of Calvary, and is a part of the same limestone structure as Skull Hill. The first century tomb seems to fit the account from the Gospels. (The entrance of the tomb was enlarged in Crusader times). Early Christian symbols have been discovered on the vaulted limestone ceiling. An "anchor cross", an early Christian symbol, is found on the rock face of the tomb, to the left of the door. Inside the family vault, drawings of two Byzantine crosses have been discovered.

The Garden Tomb (though it does not have the historical claims as does the Holy Sepulcher) seems to best fit the accounts in the Gospels. The tomb was definitely owned by a wealthy Jew of the Roman/Herodian period (Matt. 27:57-60). It was *"hewn out of rock"*, and was not a cave adapted for burial (Matt. 27:60); *"a new tomb in which no one had yet been laid"* (Jn. 19:41). It was a tomb where the body could be viewed from the entrance of the tomb (Jn. 20:5). Most First Century tombs were only a slit in the rock to receive the body horizontally. In comparison, this Garden Tomb has room inside for a number of people to stand near the body (Lk. 24:1-4). In this tomb there was room for the angel, who sat to the right of the women who came to anoint Jesus' body (Mk. 16:5). The tomb could be closed with *"a great stone"* (Lk. 24:2; Mk. 16:3-4; Matt. 27:60, 28:2) and it had a "weeping chamber". It was a spacious sepulcher. The tomb could have been "sealed" with a sealing stone like those used at the Tombs of the Kings in Jerusalem.

Was this the Garden Tomb from which our Lord Jesus arose? It seems to best fit the criteria mentioned in the Gospels, but I choose not to be dogmatic.

When at the Garden Tomb, I suggest that you obtain a copy of Peter Walker's book, *The Weekend That Changed the World* by Zondervan. It is a most interesting book on this subject.

The natural beauty of the Garden Tomb draws one's heart to the site. Here one can experience Calvary and the Garden Tomb as it most likely appeared in Jesus' day.

This Jewish tomb on Mount Carmel gives a perfect concept of a First Century tomb with an authentic rolling stone.

Most tours worship at the Garden and observe the Lord's Supper.

A visit to the Garden Tomb is an unforgettable experience.

The entrance to the Garden Tomb

New City of Jerusalem

Yad Vashem Memorial/Holocaust Museum is an unforgettable experience. There one can walk through the portals of WWII Jewish history and grieve at the inhumanity of the Nazi Holocaust. It is heartbreaking to realize that other European nations participated while the world looked on in silence. You will brush shoulders with Jewish survivors of the Holocaust and their relatives. Therefore, a somber and respectful demeanor is appropriate. One can't visit the museum and come out the same person.

Scene from Nazi death camp in Europe at the close of WWII

MODEL OF FIRST CENTURY JERUSALEM

This model of First Century Jerusalem is on a 1 to 50 scale (1/4 inch per foot) and is housed at a choice location in the Israel Museum. This model took 7 years to complete. It was originally constructed by the owner of the Holy Land Hotel in memory of his son, who was killed in the 1967 war. It greatly helps the visitor to "put together" the locations of the ancient city and its many Biblical sites.

The incredible Model of First Century Jerusalem is housed at the Israeli Museum.

Israel's Knesset/ Parliament is composed of 120 members, democratically elected from Jews, Arabs, Secularists and other Israeli citizens.

The **Knesset** is the **Israeli Parliament**. The building sits atop Jerusalem's "Acropolis". Nearby stands a beautiful 16-foot-tall bronze menorah, which was a gift from Great Britain.

The **Shrine of the Book Museum** is a beautiful rounded dome structure that was built to resemble the top of the clay jars in which the **Dead Sea Scrolls** were found. It is located on the campus of the **Israel Museum**, and houses the incredible collection of the Dead Sea Scrolls, plus artifacts from the Qumran community. The Hebrew of the Isaiah scroll can be read by any Israeli lad from beit safer, since Hebrew is the language of Israel today. A special section of the Israel Museum is dedicated to the presentation of Herod's tomb, recently discovered in the Herodium, near Bethlehem.

Home of the Dead Sea Scrolls

The **New City of Jerusalem** is a thrilling and amazing sight. Most visitors are shocked to see such beautiful architecture, shopping malls, soccer fields, synagogues, a zoo and marvelous housing projects; all a part of the New City. The layout of the new city complements the beauty of the mountains of Judea.

Hadasseh Hospital is home for the beautiful Chagall Windows, which depict the 12 Tribes of Israel, and are located in the hospital chapel. These windows are considered to be one of the finest art presentations in the world.

An extensive new addition to Hadasseh Hospital was designed by the author's friend, Ron Skaggs, a world renowned architect from HKS Inc. of Dallas, TX. He first visited Israel on a study tour over a decade ago. Ron's visit caused him to fall in love with God's Land.

Hadasseh Hospital showing addition of the new wing

Ein Karem (Spring of the Vineyard – Gen. 49:11) was one of the villages assigned for the priests that served in the Temple. This village was the home of Zacharias and Elizabeth. Here John the Baptist was born and Mary praised God (the Magnificat–Lk. 1:39).

View over the Shephelah showing the Valley of Elah, where David killed Goliath.

Shephelah

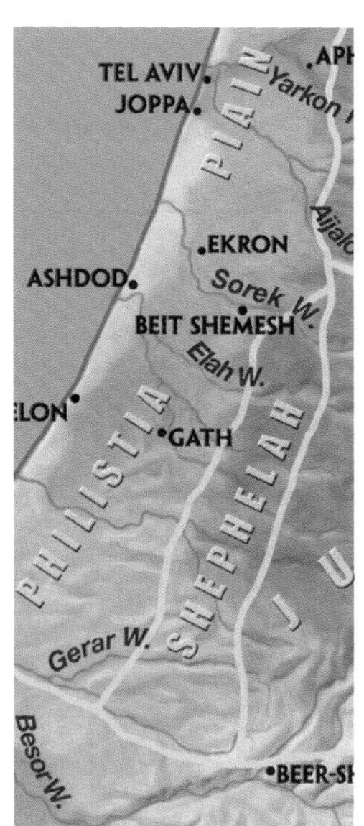

Kirjath-Jearim is an Arab village 9 miles west of Jerusalem. A Crusader church dates to 1142 AD, and was built over a Roman fortress. Interestingly, the Ark of the Covenant was located here in the House of Abinadab for 20 years (I Sam. 7:1-2; II Sam. 6:1-16; I Chron. 15:25-29). Strangely, the location of Abinadab's house is marked by a huge statue of Mary and Jesus. We need to ask how the church Christianized David bringing the Ark from Abinadab's house to Jerusalem (II Sam. 6).

The **Valley of Aijalon** (deer place) lies 14 miles northeast of Jerusalem. In this valley the Israelites, Philistines, Maccabees, Romans, Arabs, Crusaders, British and modern Israel have all fought. Aijalon is the battlefield where Joshua fought the Amorites. Hailstones killed many, and the *"sun and the moon stood still"* (Josh. 10:6-27). And here Saul defeated the Philistines (I Sam. 14:31).

The city was conquered by the tribes of Joseph, and it later became a *"city of refuge"*. Rehoboam fortified the city, but it was captured by the Philistines in the days of Ahaz.

Emmaus (the traditional site) is located about 11 miles west of Jerusalem. This location presents a problem, since the Scripture speaks of the distance being only *"about 7 miles"* (Lk. 24:13). The problem is that a village fitting that description has not been found. The exact location will be found in God's timing.

The **Emmaus Road** was the route taken by Cleopas and his wife as they walked with the risen Lord on His Resurrection Day (Lk. 24:13-35). Cleopas told Jesus, speaking about the

Messiah, "*...we were hoping that it was He who was going to redeem Israel...*" (Lk. 24:19-21). The people of Israel loved Jesus and believed He would "*redeem*" them from the Gentiles who ruled over them - the Romans and Herodians. The people wanted to enthrone Jesus, but the threatened rulers wanted Him dead.

As they broke bread together in their home, Cleopas and his wife recognized Jesus. Perhaps they saw the nail scars in his wrist when He spoke the Jewish blessing over the bread.

Forested area outside Jerusalem toward the Shephelah

Latrun is located about one mile from Emmaus. This strategic fortress was captured by the Israelis in the 1948 War of Independence. The fortress guarded the entrance to the Jerusalem Corridor. While traveling the corridor to Jerusalem it is possible to see the overturned trucks and vehicles left as a war memorial to those who lost their lives trying to get food and supplies to the Jewish Quarter in Jerusalem. The movie *Cast a Giant Shadow* portrays the events of 1948.

The forest contains approximately 90 million trees (pine, carob and locust). Reforestation was prophesied by (Ezek. 36:8). Turkish law taxed landowners by the number of trees on their property, thus, these citizens destroyed all the trees to escape taxation. This "scorched earth policy" of the Turks, during their 500 year control of God's Land, resulted in a "barren desert". And thus, the Turks raped the land as had the Romans before them. Israel has planted over six million new trees since 1970. The Tabor Oaks in this area are some of the oldest trees in Israel. They were left by the Turks for the mosque nearby.

The Latrun Monastery was made famous by the War of Independence, 1948.

Eshtaol (Hollow Way) is located 13 miles west of Jerusalem. The village was within the inheritance of Judah (Josh. 15:33). Samson was buried here (Judg. 16:20-31).

Zorah comes from "Zor," meaning (Prominent or Wasp). Zorah sits atop a hill overlooking the Valley of Sorek. The village was allotted to Judah (Josh. 15:21,33), and was the birthplace of Samson (Judg. 13:2,25). The city was fortified by Rehoboam (II Chron. 11:5,10), and was repopulated by Jews after the exile (Neh. 11:19).

The wall of Beth Shemesh shows burn indications from the attack by Nebuchadnezzar en route to Jerusalem in 586 BC.

Beth Shemesh (house of the sun) was a Canaanite town where they worshiped their sun god. It is located on a hill on the eastern edge of the Valley of Sorek. The Ark was returned from Philistia, through this Valley, and was first spotted by the Israelites of Beth-Shemish (I Sam. 6:7-21). The city was destroyed by Nebuchadnezzar on his march toward Jerusalem. The burned strata from that period can be seen at the excavation. The walls of David's day reveal fortifications built to protect Israel against the Philistines.

Timnath was located on a small hill between the Valleys of Sorek and Elah. In this area Samson celebrated his marriage to the Philistine, Delilah (Judges 14:1-15:6).

Sampson courted Delilah in the Valley of Sorek.

Valley of Sorek (Valley of the Vineyard) lies near **Zorah /Eshtaol**. This was the home of Delilah, where Samson spent his time with her during their relationship (Judges 16:4-21). Through this valley, the *"Ark of the Tabernacle"* was returned to Israel (I Sam 6).

Valley of Elah was named for the special elah/tabernith tree, which only grows in this valley. This was the place of the battle between David and Goliath (I Sam. 17: and 21:9). The Valley's wadi extends eastward toward Bethlehem, where David pastured his father's sheep. He was sent to check on his brothers, who were serving in Israel's military under King Saul. When he arrived he found the Philistine's taunting the Israelites and God.

David picked up *"five smooth stones"* from the stream bed, and one found its way into Goliath's forehead. The warrior Goliath stood nine and a half feet tall. When David killed Goliath, the Philistines fled to their cities, Gath and Ekron. The Wadi is a perennial stream, and was named after the Elah trees in the area.

The Israeli/Philistine battle site is just below ancient **Effes Dammin** (zero bloodshed). The ancient tradition of zero bloodshed at the location was respected by all. The location may well explain the strange battle agreement between Israel and the Philistines; that is, both armies sending out one representative to fight for their entire army.

Valley of Elah where David picked up five smooth stones and killed Goliath.

Azekah overlooks the Valley of Elah. Joshua defeated the Canaanite kings here (Josh 10:5.10), and later Rehoboam fortified the city (II Chron. 11: 5, 9). This was the last city in Judah to fall to Nebuchadnezzar before he took Jerusalem in 586 BC (Josh. 15;21, 35; I Sam. 17:1-3).

The Cave of Adullam is where David hid from King Saul, and trained his *"mighty men of valor"*. It lay a few miles from the Valley of Elah. From here, three of David's *"mighty men"*, slipped through the Philistine position to Bethlehem, where they drew water for David from his father's well at the city gate. When they returned to Adullam, David would not drink it, instead pouring it out as a *"sacrifice to God"* (II Sam. 23:13-17). Many *belie*ve that David's men made the journey across the Wilderness of Judea from Masada to Bethlehem. In either case, the commitment to their commander-in-chief was extraordinary.

Bell Caves of Beit Govrin, perhaps carved out, to supply building materials for the Romans in the First Century. Later these caves became hiding places for Christians under persecution.

Beit Guvrin (House of Bell Caves). In Roman times the name was changed to City of Liberty. Here are found dozens of breathtaking caves, dating back to the Roman and/or Byzantine periods. Most believe the caves were formed when the Romans used the raw materials for cement. Others believe they were burial caves. They are shaped like bells or beehives, with round holes in the top. Under persecution, Christians hid here, and left chiseled marks of Christian crosses. Recently the caves have been off limits to tourists due to minor cave-ins. (No pun intended).

Lachish (Height) was an ancient Hyksos city. Joshua conquered Lachish, and it was allotted to Judah (Josh. 10:31-33, 15:21, 39). The city guarded the approach to the Judean hills and Jerusalem. Rehoboam strengthened its defenses, and Amaziah was murdered here. Sennacherib of Assyria, attacked the city and sent emissaries to parley with Hezekiah in 701 BC (II Kings 18:13-17). In 586 BC, the city was one of the last to hold out against Nebuchadnezzar's attacks (Jeremiah 34:7). After the Babylonian captivity, the city was resettled by returning Jews. Micah denounced Lachish for encouraging Jerusalem to sin against God (Micah 1:13). Nearby, **Moreshet-Gath** is where Micah was born and lived (Micah 1:1).

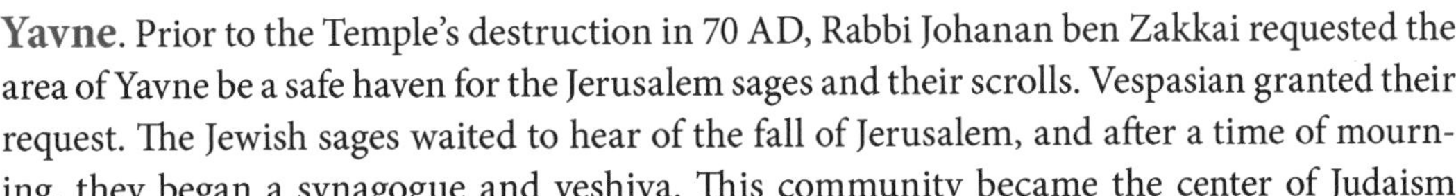

Yavne. Prior to the Temple's destruction in 70 AD, Rabbi Johanan ben Zakkai requested the area of Yavne be a safe haven for the Jerusalem sages and their scrolls. Vespasian granted their request. The Jewish sages waited to hear of the fall of Jerusalem, and after a time of mourning, they began a synagogue and yeshiva. This community became the center of Judaism and Jewish learning for all Israel. The canon of the Hebrew Scriptures, the Old Testament, was established here. The recording of the Oral Law/Mishna was begun here, but completed in Galilee. The tel has not been excavated.

Saul, later the Apostle Paul, attended yeshiva here under the leadership of the Rabbi Gamaliel, a member of the Sanhedrin (Acts 5:34-40). Here a ancient Roman bridge crosses the Elah River. Paul would have crossed this bridge each time he made the trip to Jerusalem. The bridge carried traffic between Yavne and Jerusalem, until it was bypassed and closed in 2010, to preserve the Roman bridge.

The Roman bridge at Yavne, over the Elah River, was the bridge often used by the Apostle Paul en route to Jerusalem.

View toward the Mediterranean Sea over Philistia and the Shephelah

Southern Coastal Plain

PHILISTINE PENTAPOLIS

The Philistines arrived in the Land of Canaan about the time that Israel was in God's "Desert School". They came from the Aegean Islands, including Caphtor, as part of a great migratory upheaval of the Sea People in the 13-12th centuries BC. They were one of Israel's most formidable foes (Judg. 13:1).

The Philistines allowed Israel little peace. They constantly encroached on the tribal borders of Dan and Judah. During King Saul's reign they controlled cities as far inland as the Valley of Jezreel. Their home base, however, was the Southern Maritime Plain. Since they were a seagoing people, they fought many marine battles with the Egyptians, especially against Ramses III.

Tel Gath is one of the city-states of the Philistine Pentapolis.

Gath (winepress) was a walled city which was not taken by Joshua or by David (I Chron. 18:1). Here Goliath lived with other giants (II Sam. 21:18-22). David feigned madness and lived briefly in Gath, in order to escape Saul's wrath (I Sam. 21:10, 17:2). This Philistine city was frequently captured by Israel, and was often considered an Israelite city.

Ekron (migration) was the second city of the Philistines. It was located inland near the **Valley of Sorek**. Joshua conquered the city (Josh. 13:3), but it was allotted to Judah and later given to Dan (Josh. 15:11, 19:43).

Israel took the **Ark of the Covenant** into the battle at Apehk, hoping it would bring victory over the Philistines. Instead, it was captured and taken into Philistia. First, it was placed in the Temple of Dagon in Ashdod. But their god Dagon fell before the presence of God (represented by the Ark) and was destroyed. The Philistines immediately sent it to Gath, with a similar outcome. In desperation they sent it to Ekron, their seat of worship for Baalzebub, the god of Philistia. After much suffering in the cities of Philistia, it was miraculously returned to Israel through the Valley of Sorek (I Sam. 5:10, 6:16).

Sunset over the excavation at Tel Ashdod 1959

Ashdod/Azotus (stronghold/fortress) was the home of some *"Anakim giants"* when Joshua attacked (Josh. 11:22). The city-state of Ashdod proved to be too well fortified, and too strong for Israel to conquer. The area was assigned to Judah's tribe, but was not possessed by Israel.

In Samuel's day, the Ark was brought from the battle of Aphek to Ashdod. It was placed in the house of their god, Dagon (I Sam. 5:1-2; Amos 1:8; Jer.25:20, Zeph.2:4; Zech.9:6). All these prophesied against Ashdod and predicted its ruin.

Jews intermarried with these Philistines after their return from Babylonian exile (Neh.13:23). The Maccabees took control of Ashdod between the Old and New Testament periods and destroyed the idols. Rome's Emperor Augustus restored the city and gave it to Salome, Herod the Great's sister.

The Greeks called the city Azotus, and according to *Acts,* Philip was here for a brief visitafter he baptized the Ethiopian eunuch (Acts 8:26-40).

Ashkelon (scallion, leek) is one of the oldest Canaanite cities in the world (2000 BC). It was the only Philistine city built on the coast, and their only harbor. Herod the Great, because of his love for Ashkelon, embellished the city.

In earlier history, Israel took the city for the tribe of Judah (Josh.13:3, Judges 1:18). David's lament over Saul was not to be mentioned in the city (II Sam. 1:20).

In the Old Testament, Ashkelon was the center of Philistine culture, and a stronghold of anti-Israel sentiment. The city revolted against Ramses of Egypt, but as a result, came under Assyrian rule. It was located on the Via Maris, as were Gaza and Ashdod. These three cities were of strategic economic importance to the ancient world. Ashkelon fell into Muslim hands in 1187 AD under Saladin. Afterwards, Richard the Lionhearted took it briefly for the Crusaders. At the end of that conflict Saladin won the city back to Muslim control.

The ancient seaport of Ashkelon dates back to the Neolithic Age. In the course of its history, it has been ruled by the Canaanites, the Philistines, the Egyptians, the Israelites, the Assyrians, the Babylonians, the Greeks, the Phoenicians, the Hasmoneans, the Romans, the Persians, the Arabs and the Crusaders, until it was destroyed by the Mamluks in 1270.

Gaza (azzah, stronghold in the Philistine language) was the fifth city in the Philistine Pentapolis. Today it is an Arab town under the elected control of the radical Hamas.

Gaza is the oldest and most important of the Philistine cities, and is located 40 miles south of Joppa. Joshua never conquered the city, but it was taken by Judah (Josh. 15:47; Judg. 1:18). Samson carried the

When Samson's strength returned, he destroyed the Temple of Dagon and pagan worshipers in Gaza. (Judges 16)

city gates to Hebron, some 40 miles away. Later, he was imprisoned, blinded and died in Gaza (Judges 16). After being controlled by Egypt and Assyria, Gaza was captured by Alexander the Great in 332 BC. Alexander killed the men of the city and sold the women and children into slavery.

Philip spent time in the area after he baptized the Ethiopian eunuch (Acts 8:26-27). Early in the New Testament period, many Christians were killed in Gaza.

During World War I, Gaza was a base for the Turks. The British lost 10,000 men while taking the city. In 1967 many Israelis died taking the city. With the Oslo agreement, Gaza was turned over to the PLO, but in May of 2007 it was taken over by Hamas. The U.S. pressured Israel to pull out of Gaza in 2005. Amidst much hardship, Israel responded, and since Gaza has become an armed terrorist camp, with Hamas terrorists in charge. Israel's tight border control has virtually eliminated infiltration. Still, it is tough to have "neighbors who are dying to kill you".

Due the political situation, tours do not go to Gaza, which is under the control of Hamas.

Gezer (portion) was a Canaanite stronghold that withstood Joshua's attacks. It later became one of Solomon's fortified cities, along with Megiddo and Hazor (I Kings 9:16). The Gezer Calendar (10th Century BC–Saul and David's time), inscribed in limestone, was found here. It was the agricultural calendar showing crops and seasons. Cultic pillars found here were likely referred to in Micah 5:13.

Memorial to Mordechaj Anielewicz next to the destroyed Water tower at kibbutz Yad Mordechai

Yad Mordechai is a small Israeli kibbutz south of Askelon. In 1948 the men and women of the kibbutz bravely held off an Egyptian armored division. They were equipped with only a few rifles, small hand guns, barbed wire, and courage. The young warriors laid down their lives to give the city of Tel Aviv enough time to prepare for battle, thus saving the nation. The name Yad Mordechai has become a symbol of bravery to all Israel.

The awesome Wilderness of Zin is referenced in the Torah, and was also called "Wilderness of Kadesh".

Kadesh-Barnea was located in this wilderness.

The Negev

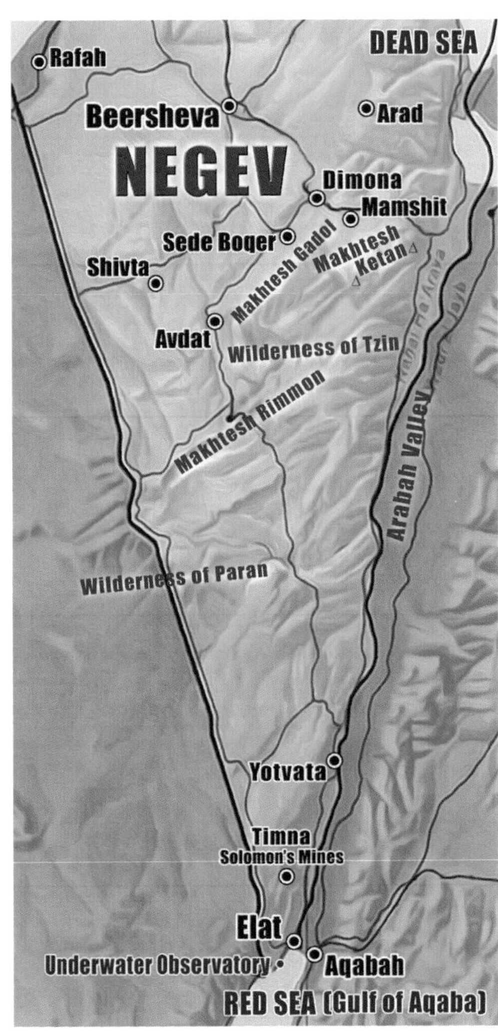

The Negev is a dry, scrub brushland stretching from southern Judea and Philistia to Beersheva. South of Beersheva there is only desert, "*...a land of hardship and distress*" (Isaiah 30:6). Hagar was driven from Beersheva into the Wilderness of Paran (Gen. 21:21). Ishmael was raised and lived in this desert of sand and rock. The Amalekites, Old Testament enemies of Israel, inhabited this wilderness (Num. 13:29).

The Wilderness of Zin marked the southern edge of Israel's territory (Num. 34:3), and it is the northern part of the Wilderness of Paran. Israel camped in the Wilderness of Paran. Moses sent the spies from Kadesh Barnea to spy on Canaan (Num. 12:16). Miriam died and was buried here (Num.20:1). Here Moses disobeyed God and struck the rock twice in his anger toward Israel. For this action he was not allowed to enter the Promised Land (Numbers 20:8-11), dying instead on Mt. Nebo (located in Jordan today).

Beersheva (well of the oath or well of seven) is on the northern edge of the Negev. It is still considered the Capital of the Negev. It was given to the tribe of Judah, and later, to Simeon. Beersheva was the center of patriarchal life, and was Israel's southern boundary during the most of the Old Testament period (Judges 20:1, I Kings 4:25).

Beersheva was first connected with Abraham, when Sara drove

Hagar, her handmaid, into the wilderness with Ishmael, Abraham's first son (Gen. 21:14-19). Abraham dug a 180′ well here, after which a dispute ensued with Abimelech. The name of the city was taken from the oath between them over water rights (Gen. 21:22-33). Abraham returned here after his journey to Mount Moriah to sacrifice Isaac. (Interestingly, Sara is not mentioned as living with Abraham after his return). His grandson Jacob also stopped in Beersheva, during the famine, to sacrifice to God before going to Egypt .An ancient well is located near the city gate which dates back to Abraham's time.

Beersheva means seven wells, the number Abraham dug before he was allowed to use one in ancient Beesheva. One of Abraham's wells is shown above.

Arad (fugitive) is located 20 miles east of Beersheva on the road from Judea to Edom. It was a large city in the Early Bronze Period (until Abraham's time). An ancient temple has been found there which is the size and shape of Solomon's Temple, which was built later. The King of Arad attacked Israel during their desert wanderings.

Sede Boker (field of the rancher) is the famous kibbutz where Israel's first prime minister, David Ben-Gurion, lived as an Israeli "cowboy". He moved to this desert kibbutz two years after its founding in 1952. Here he founded the first desert university in the world.

Avdat was a large Nabataean city in the central Negev desert. It was the most important city on the Incense Route after Petra, was later inhabited by the Romans and Byzantines.

The Nabateans were a nomadic pagan people of Arab origin. Their caravans transported perfumes and spices from Arabia to the Mediterranean Sea via Trans-Jordan and the Negev. Their desert kingdom lasted from the 4th Century BC until the Arab conquest in the 7th Century AD, except for a period when they were annexed by Rome. The Nabatean capital was the rose colored city of Petra in Trans-Jordan. The "way stations" along their caravan routes soon became flourishing cities of the Negev (south country).

By the 4th Century AD the Nabateans had adopted Christianity, and blended into the Byzantine Empire. They built beautiful and lavish desert churches, with baptismal founts.

They introduced farming to that area by driving flint rock around their plants to attract the heavy dew (over 300 of the 365 nights). They built an incredible network of dams and irrigation channels to direct their stored "lake" water from their wadi reservoirs to their lush green desert crops. They left behind elaborate cisterns for drinking water. Many hold water today, after nearly 2000 years.

Their tels/cities are Avdat, Shivta, Rehovot, Nitzana and Mamshit. (Most pictures shown are from Mamshit.) These ancient tels have revealed Nabatean, Roman and Byzantine ruins and artifacts. These amazing desert cities speak of their rich culture and past.

Palestina Limitus was the eastern limit of the Roman Empire. A small hilltop fortress south of the Dead Sea marks the spot. For over 500 years the Romans ruled over God's Land (Galilee, Israel and Judah). When the Roman General Titus conquered Jerusalem in 70 AD, his Tenth Legion led the conquest. The Tenth returned to Rome after Masada fell in 72. In 135 AD Hadrian completed the final conquest of the Jews. He led an angry Tenth Legion, which had to march across Europe four times to conquer the Jewish homeland.

From Israel (the eastern end of the empire) they marched through Syria, Cappadocia, Galatia, Macedonia, the Roman province of Dacia, Europe, Belgica, crossed the Channel to Britannica and on to northern Scotland (the western extent of the empire).

Left: The Wilderness of Palestina Limitus, showing the area

Right: Roman fortress at Palestina Limitus

Map shows the vast extent of the Roman Empire from east (Dead Sea)to west (Scotland).

This map shows a straight-line flight today from the farthest point east to the farthest point west in the Empire. It would take just over five hours by jet. That was an incredible journey for any Roman legion in hobnail sandals – four trips for the Tenth Legion across the continent. They were not the same soldiers, but it was bad enough to make them very angry with the Jews. Many Europeans seem to still hold the same anger. Wow!

Makhtesh Gadol is the largest in Israel.

Makhtesh/Mitspe Gadol (large) and **Makhtesh Ketan** (small) lie in the central Negev, and are enormous depressions in the earth's crust. Gadol, the largest, has a crater 20 miles long and 5 miles wide. They reveal volcanic-type geological formations with rare fossils dating to the Triassic period. The Tanystropheus, a 16′ lizard-like reptile, has been discovered here.

Brooks (Wadis) of Paran and **Tzin** cut wide and deep channels across the Negev floor. These perennial streams are very dangerous during flooding, and many drowned when the rain fell 50-70 miles away. Such desert storms sent flood waters sweeping everything in their path, and crushing two ton boulders. Armies camping in such wadis have been totally destroyed, swept by raging waters to their death in the desert. Israel passed through both wadis in route to Canaan. From the Wilderness of Sin, Moses sent the spies into the land (Num. 13:1-3).

The Wilderness of Paran is where Israel was led by God in the desert.

Arabah/Arava is the name of the depression from Mt. Hermon in the north to the Gulf of Aqabah in the south. This rift (earthquake zone) runs from the heart of Africa north into Israel. Today, Arava indicates the valley between the Dead Sea and the Red Sea, about 20 miles wide and 110 miles long. The Israelites traversed the Rift Valley in route to **Kadesh-Barnea.** When they returned, they detoured through Edom, of Trans-Jordan (Num. 20:21, 21:4; Deut. 2:8).

When the water levels rise in the Wadis, the flood waters fill natural "pocket" pools in the walls of the wadi. Wise shepherds find these water storage "pockets" and supply their sheep with drinking water, even when the area is barren and dry in the hot summers. *"Water from the rock"* can today be illustrated by shepherds grazing their sheep near these wadis.

These enormous pillars stand out from the surrounding mountain range. Solomon obtained copper from the Egyptian slave mining operations here at Timna. These pillars are near the Egyptian temple to Hathor, but are called *"Soloman's Pillars"*.

Timna (copper mines and smelters) lies 16 miles north of the Red Sea and Eliat. Copper mines here have been worked for over 3000 years, from the time of the Pharaohs. American archaeologist Nelson Glueck of Hebrew Union University in Cincinnati, Ohio, found the mines, furnaces, slag heaps, copper ore and work camps from the Egyptian Period. **"Solomon's Pillars"** (5 amazing russet colored rock projections) are located near the mines. Solomon obtained copper from the Egyptians for nearly 40 years. In 1948 a copper mining plant was established by Israelis in this desert. Today it is operated by a Chinese company. The Israelites passed through this area traveling to Canaan (Num. 33:35; Deut. 2:8). A model of Israel's desert **Tabernacle** can be viewed at **Timna Park**.

Eilat/Elath, Biblical **Ezion-Geber**, where the desert meets the **Red Sea** at the **Gulf of Eilat**, is one of the most beautiful cities in the world. This gateway to Africa and the Far East was conquered by Israeli forces in March 1949, as was the last military operation in the War of Liberation. Not a shot was fired as Israel returned to its ancient port on the Red Sea, after 2000 years.

In the Torah, Eilat is mentioned when the tribes of Israel passed from Egypt to Canaan (Deut. 2:8). The ancient harbor was located near where Aquaba stands today, and was the marine gateway for King Solomon, who brought gold from Ophir. King Hiram of Lebanon supplied Solomon with knowledge of the sea and sailors (I Kings 9:26-28).

Both divers and snorkelers are thrilled by the incredible beauty of the Red Sea at Eilat.

An Angel fish swims among the coral of the Red Sea.

When King Jehoshophat tried to do the same, his ships were *"broken"* and lost, at ancient Ezion-geber, (I Kings 22:48)

It is a 4-hour desert drive from Beersheva to Eliat. Today's city port offers towering hotels, white sand beaches, wonderful museums, an underwater observatory, scuba shops, quaint coffee shops, and jewelry factories. Quaint shops selling the "Eilat stone", which is a beautiful green turquoise. The Jordanian port of **Aqaba** is located in northeast corner of Gulf of Eilat.

The reefs of the **Red Sea** rival any reefs of the Caribbean for underwater coral, colorful fish, sea fans and sponges. The **Eilat Maritime Museum** is one of the most interesting in the world.

Boats are moored, south of Eilat, in a cove/"fjord", where the desert meets the sea.

Photo by Dr. Richard Cleave

The Petra Exception

With few exceptions, ***Discover Israel*** only visits sites within Israel. But, Petra in **Jordan** is so popular with tourists visiting Israel, I felt compelled to include information to assist with such visits, since Petra is the ***Seventh Wonder of the New World.*** It is necessary to plan well your border crossing into Jordan.

Petra (rock-Gr.) **Sela** (rock-Heb.) with her beautiful sandstone cliffs, is reachable only through a natural cut in the mountains called the *Siq*. It is over a mile long, and sometimes only 10′ wide, and the cut is 200′ deep into **Wadi Musa** (Valley of Moses). The Nabateans dammed up the desert rainfall, and channeled it to the city. The channel supplied the beautiful artificial oasis with an over abundance of water.

This incredible passage leads to the **"Rose Colored City"** of Petra. One's first glimpse of Petra reveals the beautiful sandstone carved facade of the **Treasury** (120′ tall), which was likely an early temple for worship. The *Nabatean* residents of Petra exchanged their nomadic life-style for one of prosperous city dweller. The population, at its zenith, was 20,000. They possessed incredible skills as architects, engineers, stonemasons, potters and artists. With their harnessed water supply, they developed ingenious agriculture in the desert. They carved their city and their homes from the beautiful sandstone cliffs. Their prominent buildings were; the awesome Treasury, an amphitheater (seating 8,000 people), the "monastery" and an incredible network of tombs.

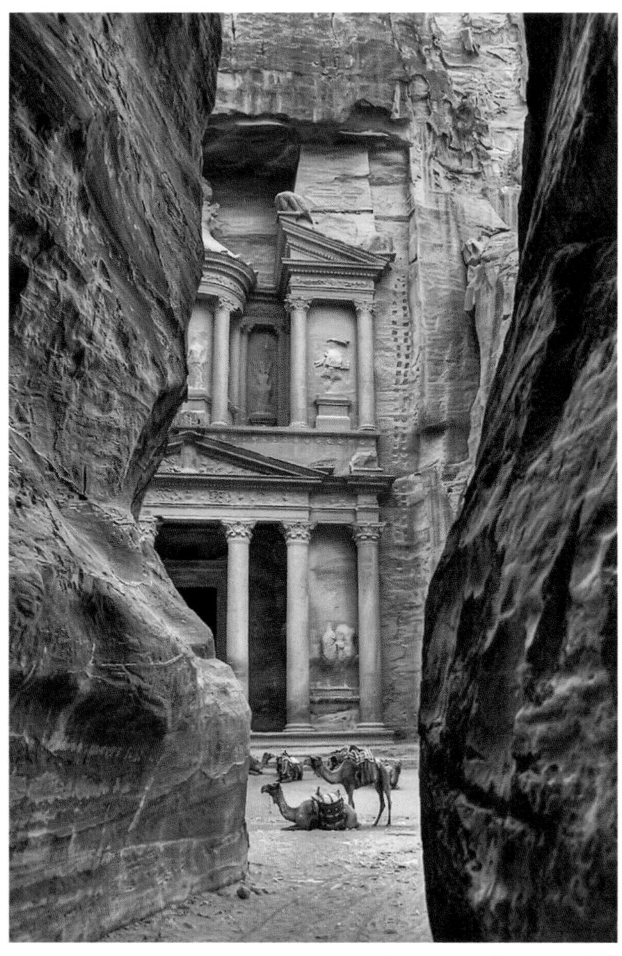

Petra was the capital of the Nabatean kingdom in southern Jordan, famous for its rock-cut architecture and water conduit system.

In their earliest history, the *Nabateans* pillaged the passing caravans on the nearby trade routes. Later, they offered protection and lodging to the travelers while exacting heavy taxes. Some caravans on these routes had as many as 2500 camels carrying textiles, spices, precious metals, ivory and incense of frankincense and myrrh.

In Jesus' day the *Nabatean Empire* controlled the Arabian incense trade. In Paul's day, some suggest that one branch of the *Nabataeans* controlled Damascus. Petra played a dominant role in Middle East history from the 6th century BC.

The vision of the prophet Obadiah is recorded as follows, *"Thus says the Lord God concerning Edom... 'I will make you small among the nations; you are greatly despised. The arrogance of your heart has deceived you, You who live in the clefts of the rock, in the loftiness of your dwelling place, Who say in your heart, 'Who will bring me down to earth?' Though you build high like the eagle, though you set your nest among the stars. From there I will bring you down', declares the Lord...Esau will be ransacked, and his hidden treasures searched out!"* (Obadiah 1:1-4, 6). The fulfillment of this prophesy can be seen at Petra.

The Romans conquered Petra in 106 AD. An earthquake destroyed the city and water system in 363 AD. Many believe the *Nabataeans* turned to Christianity under the influence of the Byzantine monk, Barsauma, a hermit who ministered there in 423 AD. Legend has it that when *Barsauma* came to Petra, the city was part Christian and part pagan. At that time, they were experiencing a terrible drought. God answered his prayer for rain, and a life-saving downpour of ensued. When that happened, they were amazed, and the entire city converted to Christianity. Later, in the 12th century, the Crusaders conquered the city, and built a citadel there.

The narrow passage (Siq) that leads to Petra

In 1812 Petra was discovered. More recently, she was made popular by the movie *Indiana Jones and the The Last Crusade*. Today many believe that Christians will flee to Petra for protection from the Antichrist in the *"end times"*.

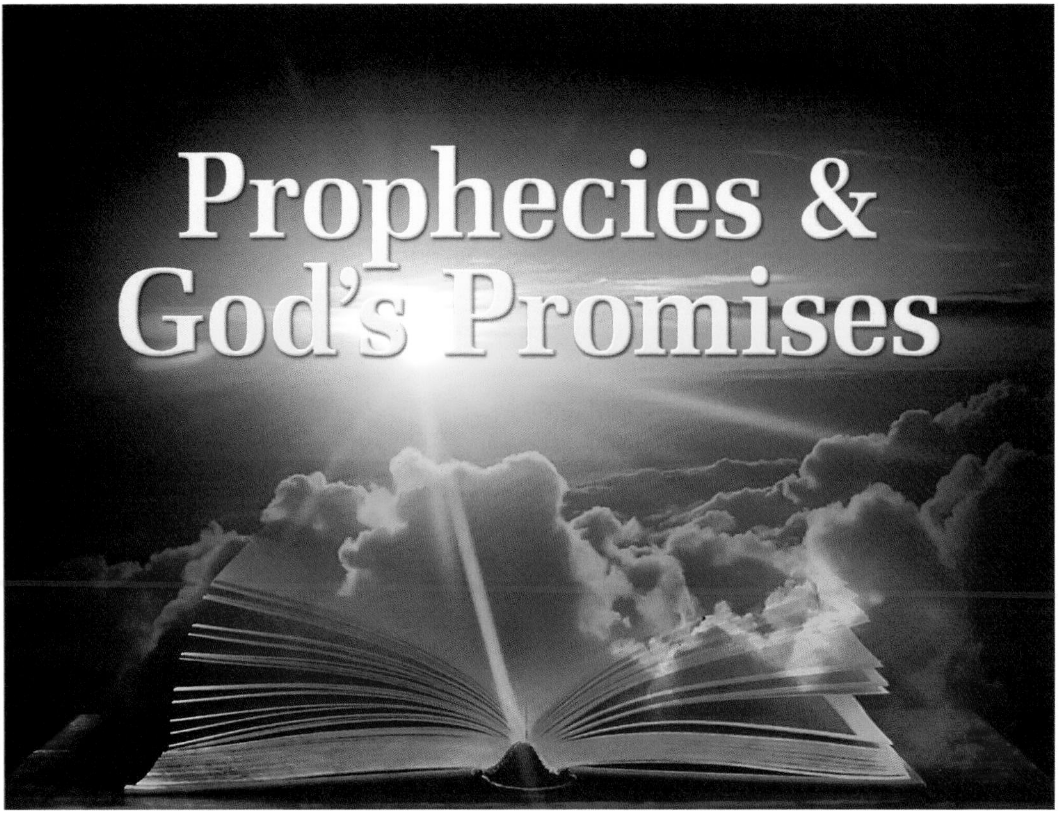

What God Promises He Does and Will Do.
Therefore, Prophecy Is History Before It Happens.

God has not listed His promises in the Scripture in chronological order, nor has He given them by subject matter. Usually His prophecies are tucked away in His revelation. Those who love and study God's Word will discover His promises.

Unfortunately, many try to *relate God's prophecies to current events.* Often Christians try to make *prophecies fit their own interpretation of the Scriptures.* Many in our day abuse prophecies in this way. Some go to the *opposite extreme and dismiss all prophecy*, and in so doing *"throw out the baby with the bath water"*. These approaches do not lead to reliable interpretations of God's prophecies. God wants us to know what He has planned and is accomplishing in our world.

We believe that Israel is God's timetable for what He is doing in these days. If you want to understand the "end times", then keep your eyes on Israel. Hundreds of God's promises are being fulfilled today with Israel and her neighbors. Often these are as plain as the nose on your face.

Most secular Israelis do not realize that they are being used by God to bring His promises to fruition. With typical Israeli pride, most feel that they have accomplished the rebuilding of Israel. The reality is... **God is fulfilling His promises! It is His work!**

Without God's intervention there would have been no return. Israel would not have been reborn, nor would Israel exist today.

I believe that when God said "Israel" He meant Israel. And when God said "Gentiles" or "World", He meant Gentiles or World (non-Jews). God's promises to Israel are not to the Church, and vice versa. God meant what He said and said what He meant!

Prophecies and Promises Fulfilled

Experience God's Faithfulness!
His Promises are being fulfilled daily.

We have simply listed God's prophecies and promises with few comments. The accompanying photographs help illustrate God's faithfulness to His people. Many of these were photographed by the author with the following prophecies in mind.

It is my hope that this study will cause you to more deeply love and trust our Faithful God. This study will help you to better understand what God has planned for His people, and the nation of Israel, in these *"end times"*.

The following Scripture selections are presented chronologically by their subject. All Scriptures are presented in *italics*. I have used ***Bold Italics*** to give emphasis to fulfilled prophecies and promises.

GOD'S PROMISES TO ABRAHAM AND HIS DESCENDANTS

God *said to Abraham,* ***"Go…to The Land which I will show you, and I will make you a great nation…I will bless you…I will bless those who bless you, and the ones who curse you I will curse …to your descendants I will give this Land"*** (Gen. 12:3,7 selected).

"To your descendants I have given this Land, *from the river of Egypt as far as the great river, the river Euphrates"* (Gen. 15:18).

BEFORE ISRAEL ENTERED THE LAND GOD PROMISED...

*"**The Lord your God is bringing you into a good Land**, a **Land** of brooks of water, of fountains and springs, flowing forth in valleys and hills;*

*A **Land** of wheat and barley, of vines and fig trees...*

*Pomegranates, and a **Land** of olive oil and honey;*
*A **Land** where you shall eat food without scarcity...*
***You will not lack for anything**; a **Land** whose stones are iron,*
And out of whose hills you can dig copper" (Deut. 8:7-9).

Southern end of the Sea of Galilee

"You shall therefore keep every commandment which
I am commanding you today,
So that you may be strong and go in and possess The Land...
A Land flowing with milk and honey...
Of hills and valleys
That drinks water from the rain of Heaven,
A Land for which the Lord your God cares;
The eyes of The Lord your God are always on it,
From the beginning even to the end of the year."

(Deuteronomy 11:8-12 selected)

Wheat fields with Mt. Hermon in the background

ISRAEL DWELT IN SECURITY

"The fountain of Jacob is secluded, in a **Land** *of grain and new wine, His Heavens also, drop down dew.* ***Blessed are you, O Israel! Who is like you O Israel... A people saved by The Lord!"*** (Deut. 33:28).

ISRAEL REBELLED AND SINNED AGAINST GOD

God said, *"****You have...become guilty*** *by the blood you have shed, and defiled by the idols you have made..."* not cared for parents...wronged aliens and the fatherless...*"despised Holy things and profaned My Sabbaths...committed acts of lewdness...committed abomination with your neighbor's wife...have taken bribes and taken interest and profits...injured neighbors for gain by oppression and you have forgotten Me, declares The Lord God. Thus,* ***you have brought your day near and have come to the fulfillment of your years...You will profane yourself in the sight of the Nations"*** (Ezek. 22:4-16, selected).

Sign, "Work Makes Free", welcomed Jews to a Nazi death camp at Auschwitz.

With a broken heart God continued, ***"I searched for a man among them who would build up the wall and stand in the gap before Me for The Land, so that I would not destroy it, but I found no one...thus, I have poured out My indignation on them...I have consumed them with the fire of My wrath; their way I have brought upon their heads, declares The Lord God"*** (Ezek. 22:30-31).

Nazi gas chamber where millions of Jews died

THUS, GOD SCATTERED ISRAEL FOR A SEASON

"My God will cast them away because they have not listened to Him; they will be wanderers among the Nations" (Hosea 9:17).

"Son of Man, ***these bones are the whole house of Israel****; behold they say, '****Our bones are dried up and our hope has perished. We are completely cut off****'"* (Ezek. 37:11).

*"Thus says The Lord God, '****Though I had removed them far away among the Nations, and though I had scattered them among the countries, yet I was a sanctuary for them*** *a little while in the countries where they had gone..."* (Ezek. 11:16)

. **(Refers to the Diaspora)**

Exiled Jews return home to their Promised Land.

HOPE IN GOD'S LOVINGKINDNESS

"...Thus says The ***Lord God, 'I will gather you from the peoples*** *and* ***assemble you out of the countries*** *among which you have been scattered, and* ***I will give you The Land of Israel'"*** (Ezek. 11:17).

JESUS FORETOLD THE END TIMES

Tender branches of the fig tree

Jesus said, *"Now learn the parable of the fig tree* **(representing Israel)**; *when its branch has become tender, and puts forth its leaves, you know that **summer is near**; even so, when you see all these things, recognize that **He is near, right at the door**"* (Matt. 24: 32, 33).

*"For **nation will rise up against nation**, and **kingdom against kingdom**, and in various places there will be **famines and earthquakes**"* (Matt. 24:7).

(Began with World War I)

"Then they will deliver you **(the Jews***)* ***to tribulation, and will kill you****, and* ***you will be hated by all Nations on account of My Name****. And at that time* ***many will fall away…and many false prophets will arise****, and will* ***mislead many…****"* (Matt. 24:9-11).

Jewish man dies on barbwire fence in a death camp.

*"And this **Gospel of the Kingdom** shall be **preached in the whole world for a witness to the Nations, and then the end shall come**"* (Matt.24:14).

"This Generation/this One Birthed/ this Born One **(Israel)**, ***will not pass away until all these things take place"*** (Matt. 24:34).

GOD REMEMBERED ISRAEL

"Can a woman forget her nursing child and have no compassion on the son of her womb? *Even these may forget, but **I will not forget you**. Behold, **I have inscribed you, Zion, on the palms of My hands**; your walls are continually before Me"* (Isa. 49:15-17).

"Thus says The Lord, Who gives the sun for light *by day and the fixed order of the **moon** and the **stars** for light by night, **Who stirs up the sea** so that its waves roar, **The Lord of Hosts is His Name: 'If the fixed order departs from before Me…then, the offspring of Israel also shall cease from being a nation before Me forever.'** Thus says The Lord, **'If the Heavens above can be measured and the foundations of the earth searched out below, then I will cast off all the offspring of Israel for all they have done, declares The Lord**"* (Jer. 31:36,37).

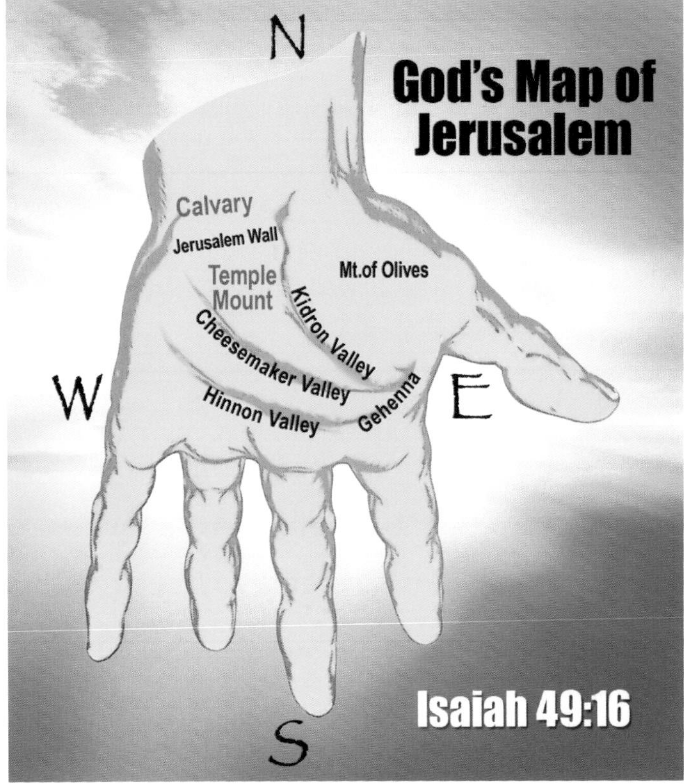

Springtime at the southern end of the Sea of Galilee

GOD RETURNED ISRAEL TO HIS LAND

"Thus says The Lord GOD, ...'I will gather you from the peoples and assemble you out of the countries among which you have been scattered, and I will give you The Land of Israel'" (Ezek. 11:16-17).

"The days are coming, declares ***The Lord, "'I will restore the fortunes of My People Israel and Judah...I will bring them back to The Land that I gave to their forefathers and they shall possess it...*"** (Jer.30:3-7b).

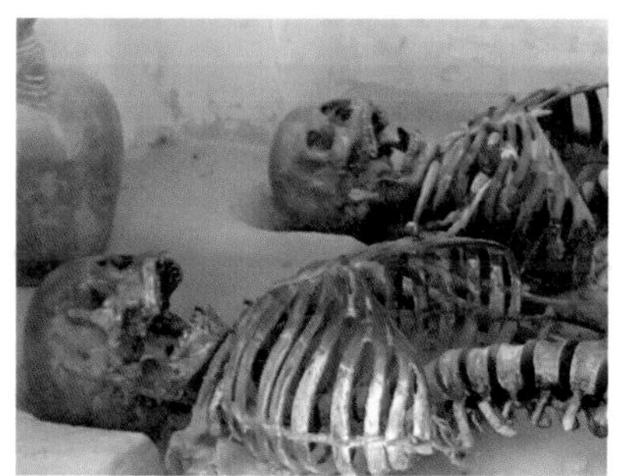

Our bones are dried up...

VALLEY OF DRY BONES

"...These bones are the whole house of Israel; behold they say, 'Our bones are dried up and our hope has perished. We are completely cut off.' Say to them, Thus says The Lord God, 'I will open your graves and cause you to come up out of the graves, My People; and I will bring you into The Land of Israel. I will put My Spirit within you and you will come to life, and I will place you on your own Land, then you will know that I The Lord have spoken and have done it'" (Ezek. 37:11, 12, 14).

"Behold, I will take the sons of Israel from among the Nations where they have gone, and I will gather them from every side and bring them into their own Land; and I will make them One Nation in The Land, on the Mountains of Israel...and one king will be king for all of them; and they will no longer be two nations and no longer be divided into two kingdoms...they will be My People, and I will be their God" (Ezek. 37: 21-23, selected).

Valley of Dry Bones... Skulls from a Nazi death camp of World War II

GOD BRINGS HIS PEOPLE HOME

"Behold, ***I am bringing them*** *from the* ***north*** *country, and* ***I will gather them from the remotest parts of the earth...they shall return here*** **(Israel)*...I will lead them*** *and make them walk by streams of water...****for I AM a Father to Israel****"* (Jer. 31:8-9).

"Ho there! ***Flee from the land of the North****", to which I dispersed you as the four winds of Heaven. Ho Zion!* ***Escape, you who are living with the daughter of Babylon...****"* (Zech. 2:6-7).

Israelis atop Mt. Masada

"The Lord will recover a second time with His hand the remnant of His People, *who will remain...from Assyria, Egypt...and from the islands of the sea. And, He will lift up* ***a standard*** *for the nations and will* ***gather the banished ones of Israel****, and will* ***gather the dispersed of Judah*** *from the four corners of the earth"* (Isa. 11:11-12).

"...I will bring your offspring from the ***East****, and gather you from the* ***West.*** *I will say to the* ***North, 'Give them up!' And to the South, 'Do not hold them back.' Bring My sons from afar and My daughters from the ends of the earth****"* (Isaiah 43:5-6).

"I Myself shall gather the remnant of My flock out of all the countries where I have driven them and shall bring them back to their pasture** and **they will be fruitful and multiply. I will raise up shepherds over them; and they will not be afraid any longer**...As The Lord lives, who brought you up and led back the descendants of the household of Israel, from the northland and from all the countries where I had driven them. Then, **they will live on their own soil" (Jer. 23:3, 4, 8).

Sheep graze in Shephelah

"Fear not, O Jacob, my servant, declares The Lord, and do not be dismayed O Israel...I will save you from afar, and your offspring from the land of your captivity... Jacob...*(not Esau), *will return and shall be at quiet and at ease, and no one shall make them afraid. I am with you to save you. I will destroy completely all the Nations where I have scattered you..." (Jer. 30:10-11, selected).

*"Thus says **The Lord, 'Behold, I will restore the fortunes of the tents of Jacob** and **have compassion on his dwelling places; the city will be rebuilt on its ruin,** and **the palace will stand on its rightful place"*** (Jer. 30: 18).

Jewish rabbi reads from the Torah at the Wailing Wall.

"...I will multiply them and they shall not be diminished; I will honor them and they shall not be insignificant...their congregation shall be established before Me; and I will punish all their oppressors...They shall be My People and I will be their God" (Jer. 30:19-22, selected).

"I will gather them out of all the lands to which I have driven them in My anger, in my wrath and in great indignation; and I will bring them back to this place and make them to dwell in safety...they shall be My people and I will be their God...I will make an Everlasting Covenant with them, that I will not turn away from them, to do them good...I will rejoice over them to do them good and will faithfully plant them in this Land with all my heart and with all My soul...Just as I brought all this great disaster on this people, so I am going to bring on them all the good that I am promising them" (Jer. 32:37, 38, 40-42, selected).

The sun rises over the Sea of Galilee.

"I will take you from the Nations and gather you from all the lands and bring you into your own Land...You will live in The Land that I gave to your forefathers...and you will be My People and I will be your God" (Ezek. 36:24, 28).

*"...**The Lord will have compassion on Jacob and again choose Israel,** and **will settle them in their own Land,** then strangers will join them"...* (Isa. 14:1).

"The Lord builds up Jerusalem; He gathers the outcasts of Israel. He heals the brokenhearted, and binds up their wounds" (Psa. 147: 2,3).

Bar Mitzvah is celebrated with dance at the Wailing Wall.

"And the ransomed of The Lord will return and come with joyful shouting to Zion, with everlasting joy upon their heads. They will find gladness and joy, and sorrow and sighing will flee away" (Isa. 35:10).

If you can't come to town, please telephone 4607
Lighting, Heating, Cooking, Refrigeration
CARL MARX

THE PALESTINE POST

JERUSALEM

THE PALESTINE POST
THE SUBSCRIPTION DEPARTMENT

STATE OF ISRAEL IS BORN

The first independent Jewish State in 19 centuries was born in Tel Aviv as the British Mandate over Palestine came to an end at midnight on Friday, and it was immediately subjected to the test of fire. As "Medinat Yisrael" (State of Israel) was proclaimed, the battle for Jerusalem raged, with most of the city falling to the Jews. At the same time, President Truman announced that the United States would accord recognition to the new State. A few hours later, Palestine was invaded by Moslem armies from the south, east and north, and Tel Aviv was raided from the air. On Friday the United Nations Special Assembly adjourned after adopting a resolution to appoint a mediator but without taking any action on the Partition Resolution of November 29.

Yesterday the battle for the Jerusalem-Tel Aviv road was still under way, and two Arab villages were taken. In the north, Acre town was captured, and the Jewish Army consolidated its positions in Western Galilee.

Most Crowded Hours in Palestine's History

JEWS TAKE OVER SECURITY ZONES

Egyptian Air Force Spitfires Bomb Tel Aviv; One Shot Down

U.S. RECOGNIZES JEWISH STATE

Proclamation by Head Of Government

2 Columns Cross Southern Border

Etzion Settlers Taken P.O.W.

Special Assembly Adjourns

THE REBIRTH OF ISRAEL

*"Who has heard of such a thing? Who has seen such things? **Can a Land be born in a day? Can a nation be brought forth all at once?** As soon **as Zion travailed, she brought forth her sons.** 'Shall I bring to the point of birth and not give delivery?' Says your God… 'Or, shall I give delivery and shut up the womb?' **Be joyful with Jerusalem and rejoice with her, all you who love her, be exceedingly glad with her, all you who mourn for her**"* (Isa. 66:8-10).

Hebrew is once again the language of God's chosen nation.

HEBREW WOULD BE SPOKEN AGAIN IN ISRAEL

"Once again they will speak this word/speech **(Hebrew)** ***in The Land of Judah and in all its cities when I restore their fortunes"*** (Jer. 31:23).

PROPHECIES FULFILLED CONCERNING WARS WITH ISRAEL, 1948, 1956, 1967, 1973

"O God, do not remain quiet...do not be still. Behold, Thine enemies make a uproar; and those who hate Thee have exalted themselves. They make shrewd plans against Thy People, and conspire together against thy treasured ones. They have said, 'Come, and let us wipe them out as a nation, that the name of Israel be remembered no more'...who said, 'let us possess for ourselves the pastures of God'" (Psa. 83:1-4, 12, Selected).

Israel's enemies stated, *"Make a tumult...crafty counsel... Let us cut them off from being a nation..."*

"All your adversaries, every one of them, will go into captivity; and those who plunder you will be for plunder, and all who prey upon you I will give for prey... I will heal you..." (Jer. 30: 16-17).

"I am going to make Jerusalem a cup that causes reeling to all the peoples around. I will make Jerusalem a heavy stone for all the people; all who lift it will be severely injured. And all nations of the earth will be gathered against it...and I will watch over Judah" (Zech. 12:2-4).

"...he who touches Israel, touches the apple of God's eye. For behold, I will wave My hand over them, so that they will be plundered..." (Zech. 2:8-9).

Israeli pilots ready for action in 1967

"They (Israel) will swoop down on the slopes of the Philistines on the west; together they will plunder the sons of the East; They will possess Edom and Moab; and the sons of Ammon will be subject to them" (Isa. 11:14).

"As flying birds, so the Lord of Hosts will protect Jerusalem..."

In that day "I will make Judah like a firepot among pieces of wood and a flaming torch among sheaves, so they will consume on the right and on the left all the surrounding peoples, while the inhabitants of Jerusalem again dwell on their own sites in Jerusalem...And in that day I will set about to destroy all the nations that come against Jerusalem." (Zech. 12:6, 8, 9).

(The Six Day War, June, 1967.)

"Like flying birds...The Lord of Hosts will protect Jerusalem. He will protect and deliver it; He will pass over and rescue it..." (Isa. 31:5).

PROMISES CONCERNING JERUSALEM

Jerusalem's Hadassah Hospital in West Jerusalem

"Jerusalem will be inhabited without walls...'For I', declares The Lord, 'will be a wall of fire around her and I will be the Glory in her midst'" (Zech.2: 4-5, selected).

Thus says The Lord of Hosts, "I am exceedingly jealous for Zion, yes, with great wrath I am jealous for her...I will return to Zion and will dwell in the midst of Jerusalem" (Zech. 8:2-3).

"Thus says The Lord of Hosts, 'Behold, I am going to save My People from the Land of the east and from the land of the west; and I will bring them back and they will live in the midst of Jerusalem, and they will be My People, and I will be their God...The vine will yield its fruit, and the land will yield its produce, and the Heavens will give their dew...I will save you so that you may become a blessing... many people and mighty nations will come to seek The Lord in Jerusalem and to entreat the favor of The Lord" (Zech. 8:7-8, 12, 13, 22).

Jerusalem's Jewish Quarter

GOD INSTRUCTED ISRAEL AND US

"Walk about Zion and go around her; count her towers; consider her ramparts; go through her palaces, that you may tell it to the next generation" (Ps. 48:12-13).

"Our feet are standing within your gates, O Jerusalem, Jerusalem, that is built as a city that is compact together; to which the tribes go up, even the tribes of The Lord..." (Psa. 122:2-3).

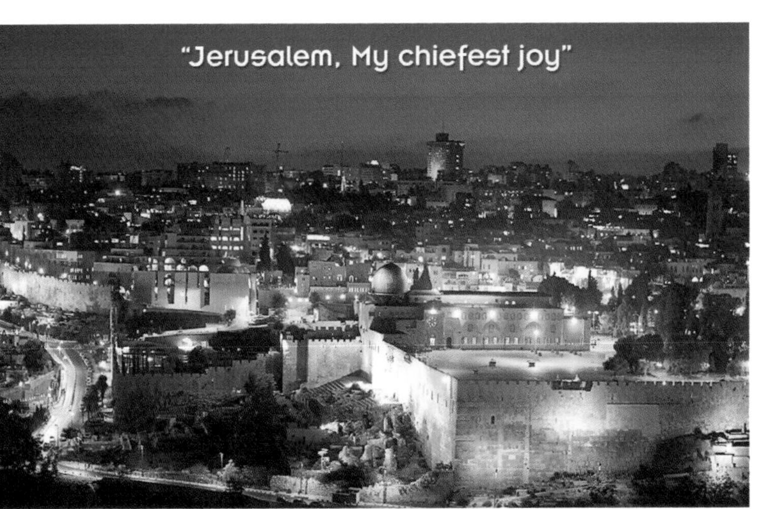

ISRAEL'S PRAYER DURING BABYLONIAN CAPTIVITY

"If I forget you, O Jerusalem, may my right hand forget her skill. May my tongue cling to the roof of my mouth if I do not remember you, if I do not exalt Jerusalem above My chief joy" (Psa. 137:5-6).

Many nations will join together in The Lord and become His people.

As Jaffa oranges are being picked in the Plain of Sharon, the tree is blooming for the next crop.

A Shepherd and his young goat at Nazareth Village

GOD'S BLESSINGS ON ISRAEL

"I shall give you The Land of Israel" (Ezek. 11:17).

"Sing for joy and be glad, O daughter of Zion; 'For behold I am coming and I will dwell in your midst', declares The Lord. 'Many nations will join themselves to The Lord in that day and will become My People. Then I will dwell in your midst, and you will know that The Lord of Host has sent me to you...The Lord will possess Judah as His portion in The Holy Land, and will again choose Jerusalem. Be silent, all flesh, before The Lord; for He is aroused from His Holy habitation" (Zech. 2:10-13).

"...As you were a curse among the Nations, O house of Judah and house of Israel, so I will save you and you may become a blessing*...let your hands be strong...* ***I have again purposed in these days to do good to Jerusalem...do not fear!"*** (Zech. 8:13, 15).

"Again ***I will build you and you will be rebuilt, O virgin of Israel!*** *Again you will take up your tambourines, and go forth to the dances of the merrymakers.* ***Again you will plant vineyards on the hills of Samaria;*** *the planters will plant and enjoy them"* (Jer. 31:4, 5).

"...I will watch over them to build and to plant" (Jer. 31:28b).

"Then they will rebuild the ancient ruins, they will raise up the former devastations; and they will repair the ruined cities, the desolation of many generations. Strangers will stand and pasture your flocks, and foreigners will be your farmers and your vinedressers...You will eat the wealth of nations, *and in their riches you will boast...instead of shame you will have a double portion, and instead of humiliation,* ***they will shout for joy over their portion...everlasting joy will be theirs...I The Lord will faithfully give them their recompense and make an everlasting covenant with them. Then their offspring will be known among the Nations and their descendants will be in the midst of the peoples...because they are the offspring whom The Lord has blessed"*** (Isa. 61:4-9 selected).

Almond trees bloom in February

"I will multiply the fruit of the tree and the produce of the field...the desolate land will be cultivated, *instead of being a desolation in the sight of everyone who passed by. They will say,* ***'This desolate land has become like the garden of Eden;*** *and the waste, desolate and* ***ruined cities are fortified and inhabited...I The Lord have spoken and will do it...I am The Lord"*** (Ezek. 36:30-38 selected).

GOD SPEAKS TO THE *"MOUNTAINS OF ISRAEL"*

"But you, O Mountains of Israel, *will* ***put forth your branches and bear fruit for My People Israel; for they will soon come...you will be cultivated and sown and I will multiply men on you, all the House of Israel, all of it;*** *and the* ***cities will be inhabited and waste places will be rebuilt...****I will treat you better than at first.* ***Thus you will know that I am The Lord...My people Israel will walk on you and possess you,*** *so that* ***you will become their inheritance..."*** (Ezek. 36: 8-12, selected).

Present day "***Mountains of Israel***", near Jerusalem

David hid from King Saul in a cave at En Gedi; perhaps behind the veil of the falls.

En Gedi (Spring of the Young Goat–center picture), or (Rocks of the Wild Goats/Hinds/Gazelle)

"The wilderness and the desert will be glad, *and* ***the Arabah will rejoice and blossom;*** *like a crocus it will blossom profusely and* ***rejoice with rejoicing and shouts of joy. The glory of Lebanon will be given to it, the majesty of Carmel and Sharon. They will see the Glory of The Lord, the majesty of our God...your God will save you...****the eyes of the blind will be opened...the Lame will leap like a deer...* ***waters will break forth in the wilderness and streams in the Arabah. The scorched land will become a pool*** *and the* ***thirsty ground springs of water;*** *In the haunts of jackals...grass becomes as reeds and rushes.* ***A highway will be there...called the Highway of Holiness"*** (Isa. 35:1-8, selected).

"I will open rivers on the bare heights and springs in the midst of the valleys; I will make the wilderness a pool of water and the dry land fountains of water. I will put the cedar in the wilderness, the acacia and the myrtle...and the olive tree; That they may see and recognize...that the hand of The Lord has done this...The Holy One of Israel has created it" (Isa. 41:18-20).

The acacia tree - The Ark of the Tabernacle was built from this wood.

Israeli tour guide prepares a traditional Jewish meal.

ISRAEL IS GOD'S ETERNAL POSSESSION!

"*'**They will possess The Land forever,**'* declares The Lord" (Isa.60: 21).

*"**I will make them one nation in The Land, on the Mountains of Israel...I will make a covenant of peace with them, and it will be an everlasting covenant** with them. And **I will set my sanctuary in their midst forever**"* (Ezek. 37:22).

*"**I will restore** the captivity of **My People Israel,** and **they will rebuild the ruined cities and live in them;** They **will also plant the vineyards** and **drink their wine,** and **make gardens** and **eat their fruit. I will plant them on their Land, and they will not again be rooted out from their Land which I have given them, says The Lord**"* (Amos 9:14-15).

*Pray for the peace of Jerusalem: "**May they prosper who love you. 'May peace be within your walls, and prosperity within your palaces'.** For the sake of my brothers and friends, I will now say, '**May peace be within you.**' For the sake of the house of The Lord our God, I will seek your good"* (Psa. 122:6-9).

North shore of the Sea of Galilee

JOSHUA II
499
They that wait upon the LORD shall renew their strength;
they shall mount up with wings as eagles;
they shall run, and not be weary;
and they shall walk, and not faint. Isaiah 40:31 KJV

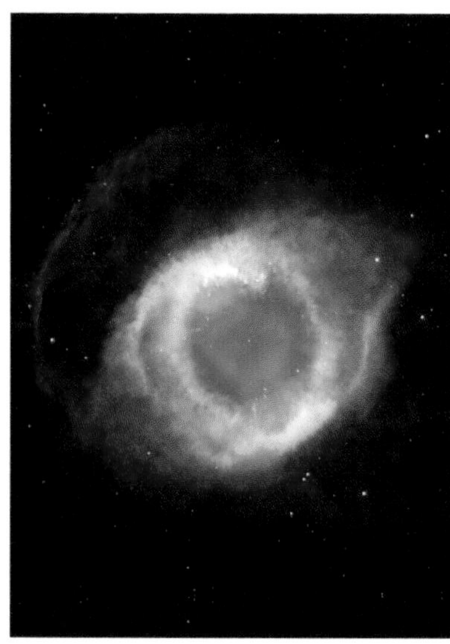

The Eye of God / Helix Nebula
"The eyes of the Lord are in every place, watching the evil and the good". **Proverbs 15:3**
"For the Word of God is living and active and sharper than any two-edged sword and piercing as far as the division of soul and of spirit, of both joints and of marrow, and able to judge the thoughts and intentions of the heart. No creature is hidden from his sight, all things are open and laid bear to the eyes of Him with whom we must give account". **Hebrews 4: 12-13**

Israel's Mediterranean coastline

Joshua II

SECTION 1

***God "makes nations great and He destroys them; He enlarges nations, and He leads them away"* (Job 12:23).**

GOD IS FAITHFUL TO FULFILL ALL HE HAS PROMISED TO ISRAEL

The facts of Arab-Israeli conflicts have not changed across the years. God, who led Israel in victory, is still on His throne. Studying these wars is like reading the book of *Joshua* again. This first section is presented in detail, but the sections which follow are in outline form. Please study the accompanying maps.

WHOSE LAND? GOD'S PROMISES AND "THE MOUNTAINS OF ISRAEL"

It is extremely difficult to keep a clear picture of what is happening in the Middle East. Most western news reporting any Arab-Israeli conflict is incomplete, slanted, with an agenda, and often inaccurate. The events are interpreted and reported by people who do not believe the Word of God, nor do they have an understanding of the 4000-year-old conflict.

Today's media report the news like geese who get up every morning to a new day–much noise, much wandering in circles, and much concern–but only about what is happening in their immediate vicinity. They act as though there is no historical background to be considered in their reporting. Yet, without historical background, daily reports are out of context, having little or no meaning.

To understand what God is accomplishing one must examine the historical context of events. Only then will an accurate picture come to light.

God, who has promised us *"Everlasting Life"*, is the same God who promised Abraham an *"Everlasting Covenant"*. God is the Promise Keeper of the ages. He has never broken a promise since He created planet earth. God will accomplish everything He has ever promised! The most vivid example of His faithfulness is present day Israel.

Middle East events are not easy to understand. They require research to accurately interpret them. Yet these events are very important to an understanding of God's plan for the future. Christians and Jews who love God and His Word should wisely prepare for these *"end days"*.

PROMISES FROM THE HEART OF GOD

God's covenant with Abraham takes us back to *Genesis 15-17.* That covenant was unconditional and eternal.

Unlike the covenant with Moses, God's Covenant with Abraham was NOT dependent on Israel's performance.

God told Abraham, *"Arise, walk in the land...I give it to you"* (Gen. 13:17).

"To your descendants I have given this Land, from the River of Egypt to the great River Euphrates" (Gen. 15:18). Before the birth of Isaac, Abraham begged God to give a blessing to Ishmael (father of the Arabs). But God had other plans, and told Abraham, in no uncertain terms, *"I will establish My covenant with Isaac for an everlasting covenant, and with his descendants"* (Gen. 17:19). Isaac sired Jacob and God said to him, *"The land on which you lie I will give to you and your descendants"* (Gen. 28:13). Then the Lord changed Jacob's name to Israel.

Under Joshua, the sons and descendants of Jacob became the Tribes of Israel. And God gave each of them a portion of the land (Josh. 14-19). Judah was given the area of Judea, including Jerusalem, Hebron, Bethlehem and Gaza. Today the tribes of Israel have become *one,* and they are called Israel/Jews. Jew is an English word for Judah. Today's Jews, and the Biblical *Children of Israel,* are from the same blood line and lineage, contrary to Arab propaganda.

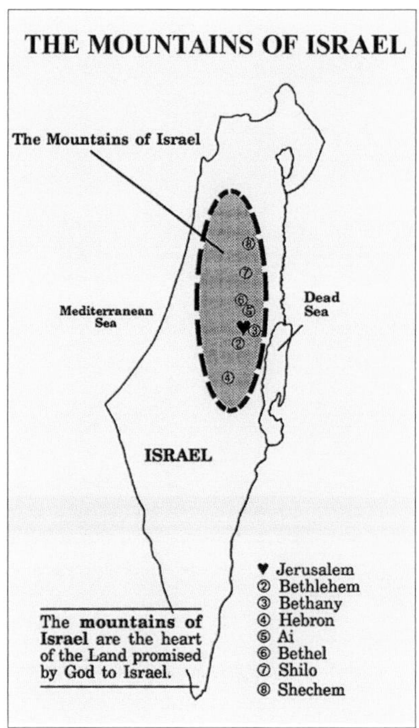

Abraham was near Bethel, north of Jerusalem, when God promised him the Land.

Now, let's back up. Where was Abraham in the land when the covenant was made? He was in the *"Mountains of Israel".*

Remember, the *"Mountains of Israel"* are the very heart of Israel. In *Ezekiel 36* we read what God promised to the *"Mountains of Israel".* Why is this area so much in question today? What has happened? This is the area of the patriarchs, the very heart of Jewish life and worship under King David, Solomon and the kings of Israel and Judah. This is the area of the Holy City of Jerusalem, where the Jewish Temple stood for centuries. This is where Jesus taught and ministered, died and arose. Here He called out His church. How did the name get changed from Samaria, Israel and Judah to the "West Bank"? The Arabs claim that Israel has grabbed their land. Is this accurate? No! Absolutely not!

1. ***God deeded The Land to Israel.***
2. ***Israel won The Land by conquest under Joshua.***
3. ***Israel occupied The Land for 1,380 years.***
4. ***Israel purchased The Land from the Turks.***

The Arabs claim that the land always belonged to them and Israel has stolen it from them. Their propaganda screams this daily through the world media. But it is not so!

The Northern Kingdom of Israel sinned grievously against God. And God said, *"...when the house of Israel was living in their own Land, they defiled it by their ways and their deeds...Therefore I will pour out My wrath on them…I scattered them among the nations, and they were dispersed throughout the lands; I judged them according to their ways and deeds"* (Ezek. 36:17-19 selected). But God promised, *"When they are in the land of their enemies, I will not reject them to destroy them, breaking my covenant with them; for **I Am the Lord their God. I will remember The Covenant with their ancestors,** whom I brought out of the land of Egypt in the sight of the nations, that I might be their God. I AM the Lord"* (Lev. 26:44-45).

The Northern Kingdom of Israel was conquered by Sennacherib of Assyria in 722 BC.

God loves His people Israel. ***"Thus says the Lord who gives the sun for light by day and fixed order of the moon and the stars for light by night, who stirs up the***

Bust of Emperor Hadrian

sea so that its waves roar; the Lord of Hosts is His name: if this fixed order departs from before Me,' declares the Lord, 'then the offspring of Israel also will cease from being a nation before Me forever...If the heavens above can be measured and the foundations of the earth below, then I will also cast off all the offspring of Israel...' declares the Lord" (Jer. 31: 35-37).

In 70AD the Temple and Jerusalem were destroyed by the Romans, just as Jesus had prophesied in *Matthew 14:1-6.* Three years later, Masada fell to Rome. That Jewish rebellion cost the lives of some 500,000, and about 100,000 were taken into slavery (Zech. 7:11, 12, 14).

In 135AD the last Jewish rebellion was squelched by Hadrian. He built a pagan temple over the site of God's temple in Jerusalem. Approximately 580,000 men were killed in Judea alone, and starvation and disease took an equal number. The Jews were dispersed to all parts of the world. The Romans ruled over God's Land, which they renamed "Palestine".

The name "Palestine" came from the name Philistine, Israel's sworn enemy in the Old Testament. The name was given by the Romans to degrade Israel and Judah and to erase the memory of the Jews from the land. God calls His Land Israel! Only the enemies of God have ever tried to change that. Today, the Arabs are trying to resurrect the name, and call themselves the Palestinians, led by the Palestinian Liberation Organization (PLO). Thus, they lay claim to a land that never really belonged to them. The Philistines were destroyed before the close of the Old Testament. Moreover, the Arabs of the Arabian Peninsula have never had any genealogical link with the Greek Philistines. Thus, the *"ancient hatred, and lust for the Land"* raises its ugly head. The psalmist prophesied, *"O God, the Nations have invaded Your inheritance; they have defiled Your Holy Temple; They have laid Jerusalem in ruins"* (Psa.79:1).

The Dome of the Rock in Jerusalem

During the Muslim period, 640 to 1099AD, Mohammed united the scattered nomadic tribes of the Arabian Peninsula and North Africa and sought to conquer the world by force. The Arabs in control cut off all contact with the West. The Muslim Dome of the Rock was built on the Temple Mount, and they claimed Jerusalem as the third most holy site to Muslims, after Mecca and Medina. The Arab rule over "Palestine" lasted for 459 years.

The Crusaders conquered the Muslims and took control of Jerusalem from 1099-1250AD. Their control was short-lived.

1250-1517AD – the Mamaluks under Saladin took Jerusalem for the Turks. Note that the Turks are mostly Muslim, but they are *not* Arabs. During this turbulent period, lasting 267 years, there were 47 different Muslim rulers over Palestine.

1517-1917AD – the Ottoman Turks terrified all of Europe and ruled the Mediterranean and all of North Africa. For 300 years they ruled Palestine. In 1566 they rebuilt the present walls of Jerusalem.

Christmas 1917, General Allenby dismounted his horse at the Jaffa Gate and entered Jerusalem to accept the Turkish surrender.

On Christmas Day, 1917, the British, under General Edmund Allenby, took the Holy City in a bloodless surrender from the Turks.

From the days of Joshua, when the land was taken from the Canaanites by God's chosen people, Israel possessed the land for 1,380 years. The Turks controlled it for 567 years, and the Muslim Arabs for 459 years.

From 70AD until 1917, there have always been small communities of Jews in God's Land. The Land has never been without Jews, and often they have been in the majority. In 1917, approximately 40% of the inhabitants were Jews, numbering about 125,000.

During the Diaspora, under kings and dictators, Jews survived genocide, purges, massacres, relocations and deportations. Under Hitler an estimated 6 million died in the gas chambers of Europe. Yet they still survived as a race and a religion, and have even maintained their national identity. In all of history, no other people have survived as an ethnic group outside their homeland for more than 500 years. Jews have survived more than 1,900 years, thanks to God's protection.

As the chosen people of God, Jews have survived against all odds, and established themselves in their homeland. The Land was virtually uninhabited and desolate through the 1800's. Ezek. 6:2, 6, 8, 14 states, *"When you are scattered through the countries...I will...make the Land...more desolate than a wilderness"* (Ezek. 6:2, 6, 8, 14).

In 1874 Samuel Manning wrote, "The Land is left void and desolate and without inhabitants." He told us that it was difficult to find even one tree for shade from the blistering sun. Sand smothered the coastal plains, and behind them were swamps with alligators. The mountains were simply piles of rocks. The Turks had destroyed the land. Their laws taxed the land according to how many trees a person owned. The population simply cut down all their trees, refusing to pay the land taxes. The land was left as desolate as God foretold.

Death Camps of Europe

GOD ALWAYS KEEPS HIS PROMISES

Baron Rothschild started an agricultural kibbutz for European Jews in Palestine in 1861. Then faithful Jews started to look to The Land as a possible national homeland. At every Passover they had said for centuries, "Next year in Jerusalem!" In 1897 Theodore Hertzel held the first Zionist Congress in Switzerland, with the purpose of creating a home in Palestine for the Jewish people.

The years of 1917 to 1948 were the period of the British Mandate over Palestine. After World War I, the British were placed in charge of the "peace" in Palestine.

Jew working the land 1900

In 1917, Britain approved the Balfour Declaration, which "viewed with favor the establishment in Palestine of a national home for the Jewish people." Jewish immigrants started to return.

The Land belongs to Israel through purchases of enormous sections of land from the Arabs and Turks. These transactions often involved valleys and swamp land. The sellers considered these sections of land worthless, since they were mosquito-infested. The Arabs and Turks thought the Jews would die from malaria, and the land would then revert back to them as the sellers. Instead, the Jewish settlers drained the swamp areas, and planted fields for the first time since they were driven from the land by the Romans. They planted eucalyptus trees, indigenous to Australia, to drink up the swampy water, and the cultivated land began to blossom and produce bountifully.

Arab nomad tents

For thousands of years Arabs roamed the millions of square miles of the Middle East and Africa. They were unhindered by any borders. Bedouin followed the grass to pasture their flocks. By the mid-1800's, the land was 99% empty. The Jews improved The Land, and created jobs, generating the strongest economy in the Middle East. Arabs from Jordan, Syria and Saudi Arabia left their goat herding tents seeking work and income in Jewish territory. No one would have considered these migrant workers to have been owners of that land.

A census of Jerusalem in 1934 showed that the Arab population of Palestine was born in 39 different countries; few were born in Palestine. Most were immigrants and peasants from other Arab countries. These common laborers from surrounding countries poured in to do the labor, for the highest prices paid in the Middle East.

These migrant workers can be compared with the U.S./Mexico situation of today. Unfortunately, most of the families who came as migrants to Palestine claimed that the land had always been their land and that their families had possessed it for centuries. Most of these workers fled during the War of Liberation in 1948, when the going got tough. The reality was, they were not willing to stay and die for land that was not their land. The nations from which they came would not allow them to return, and placed them in refugee camps. Over the course of 60 years these camps have been, and still are, supported by the United States and the United Nations. In the words of Paul Harvey, "and now you know the rest of the story."

After WWI England occupied Palestine under the British Mandate. They promised the Jewish people a homeland. In 1920 the League of Nations agreed to the creation of a Jewish Homeland in Palestine

In 1929, jealous and fearful Arabs started nightly terrorist attacks on small Jewish communal settlements (kibbutzim). The Jews organized the Hagganah, the Underground, to protect these settlements. In spite of the attacks, Jewish immigration accelerated as Europe became more hostile to the Jews. As Jewish immigrants flowed into Palestine, the Arabs became more fearful. As the situation escalated, the British were in the middle, trying to keep the peace under their Mandate.

God promised Abraham, *"I will bless those who bless you and I will curse those who curse you"* (Num. 24:9). In 1939, under Arab pressure, England reversed her stand on Jewish immigration policies and approved the White Paper. Britain, favoring the Arabs, tried to halt Jewish immigration into Palestine.

In those years it was said, "The sun never sets on the British Empire." Within only a few years, England fell from being the leader of the world to 39th in rank among the world powers. Today, the sun can set on the British Empire in a matter of minutes.

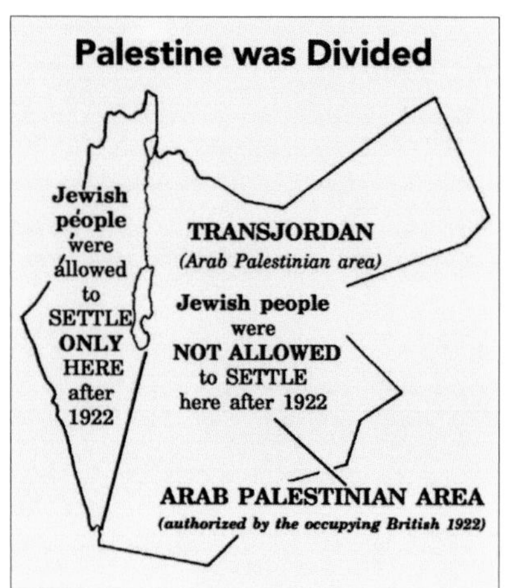

GOD IS THE PROMISE KEEPER!

God is serious about nations who stand with or against His people, Israel. He is in charge of nations. *"He makes nations great and He destroys them: He enlarges nations, and He leads them away"* (Job 12:23).

Germany surrendered in 1945, ending World War II in Europe, and the Allied Forces liberated the Jews of Europe from prison and death camps. The world was in shock over the Holocaust, and allowed more immigrants to relocate to Palestine. This inflamed the Arabs even more.

In 1945, the Arab League was formed to unite all Muslim Arabs against the Jews. For the first time Egypt, Syria, Lebanon, Iraq, Saudi Arabia, Yemen and Trans-Jordan found a cause that brought them together. At that time the land was called "Palestine" and was then the exact area of modern Israel and Jordan.

In 1946, Trans-Jordan, under King Abdullah, obtained full independence from the British Mandate, and annexed the so-called "West Bank."

In 1947 Abdullah rushed as many Arabs as possible to populate the West Bank. Most were considered second-class citizens, and they were not wanted in the new Jordan anyway. The exact area the Arabs call the West Bank God calls the *"Mountains of Israel"*.

God returns His people to Israel and Israel became a nation once again.

Today the PLO, Hamas, Hezbollah and other Muslim terrorist groups claim that they are the rightful owners of the Land. But most are descendants of Arabia, Moab, Ammon or Edom (Jordan), and they have no historical links to ancient Israel. They are mentioned in the Scriptures. *"Because you have said, 'These two nations* [Israel and Judah] *and these two countries shall be mine, and we shall possess them'"*(Ezekiel 35:10). But God said, *"Behold, I am against you Mount Seir"* (Ezek. 35:3). And in Ezekiel 36:5 we read *"The fire of My wrath...is against all Edom, who appropriated My Land for themselves as a possession..."*

In 1947, the United Nations sought to partition The Land. The Jews accepted the partition, but the Arabs rejected any possible nation of Israel. If they had accepted the partition, a Palestinian state would be well over a half century old. But because of their hatred, they have nothing.

Fearing a civil war in the West Bank, 300,000 Arabs fled. Since most of them were immigrants or squatters in The Land, why would they give their lives to keep The Land? The nations from which they had come (most were from Jordan) would not allow them to return. Therefore, they became refugees.

Then came May 14, 1948, which we believe to be the most important date on God's calendar in modern history.

The British ended their Mandate in Jerusalem and raised the Red Cross flag over their central command center at King David Hotel in Jerusalem.

MAY 14, 1948
ISRAEL DECLARES STATEHOOD!

What a day! What a miracle! What a faithful God! Our Faithful God did it all. Read Isaiah 66:7-10. Israel hoped only to possess the area given them in the U.N. partition. Nevertheless, the Arab world gathered for war. Seventeen Arab countries, with a combined population of over 200 million, were committed to wiping out the new nation of Israel. The 713,000 Jews in the new nation were still trying to care for newly arrived men, women and children from the Nazi concentration camps of Europe. The Arab League had armed the Arab military camp to the hilt with their oil money from the West. Israel had little more to fight with than a desire for a homeland after 1,900 years.

Israel had finally come back home to the only place they had on earth, The Land of Israel. God promised it would happen. Prophecy is history written before it happens. Whenever God speaks on a subject, it will happen with 100% accuracy!

Declaration of Statehood by David ben Gurion

When President Harry S. Truman took office, he made clear that his sympathies were with the Jews, and that he accepted the Balfour Declaration. He stood for Israel in 1948 when Israel became a nation, assuring Israel they would have a Democratic partner standing by there side. It is the author's opinion that God placed Truman in office for that specific reason.

ISRAEL BECAME A NATION- IT WAS GOD'S MIRACLE!

It was a miracle that the population grew from 125,000 in the 1800's to 650,000 in 1948 (especially since 6 million people were slaughtered in Europe in that same decade).

George Marshall, U.S. Secretary of State, said of the 1948 situation, "You are surrounded by Arabs. Your backs are to the sea. How can you withstand the assault? You are on the coast and the Arabs are in the mountains. You have but a few arms, and the Arabs have standing armies, well trained with heavy equipment. How can you hold out?" He forgot the God factor.

It was a miracle that Israel ever declared statehood. For Israel to survive the odds of 280 Arabs to 1 Israeli was definitely a miracle. God led Israel from one victory to another. The Lord of Hosts is once again in charge of the battles. It reminds us of the conquests in the book of *Joshua* 3400 years ago – with new names, old places, old enemies but the *same God*.

Twenty years later, in 1967, Israel was the third strongest military power in the World. HOW? ONE ANSWER: GOD! Israel is God's miracle today.

GOD IS THE PROMISE KEEPER!

"I will take you [Israel] *from the nations, and gather you out of all the lands and bring you into your own Land"* (Ezek. 36:24). God promised Israel The Land as an everlasting covenant. The Land belongs to Israel!

Joshua II

SECTION 2

ARAB'S "Lust for The Land"

1. God's Promises and the Father's Blessings

To Abraham	Gen. 13:14-15, 15:18, 17:1-8, 19, 21
To Isaac	Gen. 17:19, 26:2-4, 27:28-29
To Jacob	Gen. 28:13-15, 35:10-12

Jacob's name was changed to Israel (Prince of God). Thus, God's promises are to his descendants. Jacob's sons and his descendants became the 12 Tribes of Israel.

To Ishmael	Gen. 16:12, 17:20
And his Descendants	East of Israel (Arabs)
To Esau	Gen. 27:39-41 *"Esau bore a grudge against Jacob"*
And his Descendants	Edom (Arabs)
Lot's Descendants	Moab (Arabs)

Abraham and his family entering God's Land

2. Animosity Builds

The passing of the Israelites through Edom was denied. Later, Edom, Ammon and Moab (Arabs) came to conquer Jerusalem during the days of King Jehoshaphat.

3. God Charged Edom

With a *"lust for the land"* and *"an ancient hatred"* Arabs have historically hated Israel (See Ezekiel 35:5).
They shed Israel's blood (v.5).
They wanted Israel's land (v.10).
They spoke blasphemy against God and boasted against God (vs.12-13).
These charges are very accurate in our day! God said, *"Edom, I am against you!"* (Ezek. 35:3, 5).

Mohammed's militant faith intensified the *"ancient hatred"*. Muslims conquered God's Land. Yet, from the beginning of the Muslim reign, The Land became desolate, as God had promised (Ezek. 6:2, 6, 8).

Israel had been *"scattered"* since the diaspora of 70 and 135AD. Only a few Jews were in The Land. Life was difficult in God's Promised Land.

4. The Arabs and Israel

The Arabs have been nomads for nearly 3000 years. In the late 1800's the Jews began to return and rebuild the land of their forefathers. Arabs came to this area for work opportunities, and settled in Israel. Only a few Arabs were actual natives of Palestine. A census from that period shows that well over half of the "native-born population" was Jews.

In May, 1948 (Jewish War of Independence), the Jordanian Royal Army held control of the "West Bank". Historically, this was Old Testament Samaria and

God returned His people to Israel in 1948. Israel becomes a nation again on May 14.

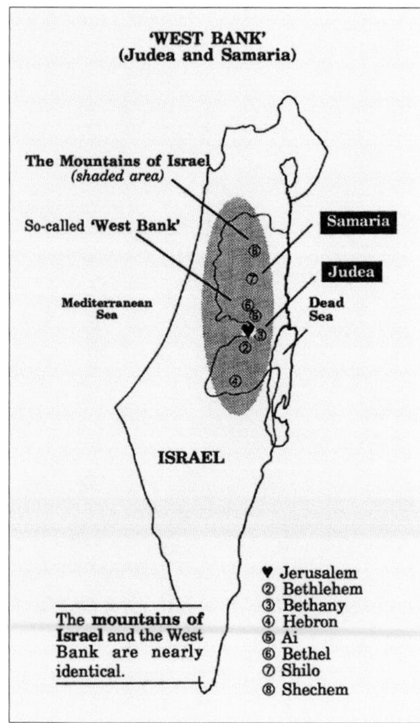

Judea. Jordan, in a political move, renamed the Old Testament "Mountains of Israel" the "West Bank" of Jordan. Arab propaganda sought to convince the world that the Arabs had lived there, and that the land had been Palestinian across the ages. It simply is not so! But, if you tell a lie often enough some people will believe you. In this case, the United Nations was gullible. As a result of the Six Day War in June, 1967, Judea and Samaria were returned to the rightful owner, Israel. This is what God's Word indicates!

5. What Do the Arabs Want?

The Arabs already have 500 times more land in the Middle East than does Israel. In 1947 Jordan engineered a "land grab" of 77% of British Palestine (when 50% had been intended for Israel). In 1982, Israel gave the Sinai Peninsula to Egypt, third time in recent history. At that time the Sinai was 68% of all the land Israel owned, and had enough developed oil resources to supply Israel well into the future. The United States, in the negotiations, promised Israel they would have plenty of oil for their future.

The PLO and Hamas are now demanding another 27% of Israel, that is, the entire "West Bank". We think it is amazing that the Arab's have such an intense desire to possess such a small piece of land. The reality is, they are not so much interested in the Land, but want to annihilate Israel.

End the Unjust Jewish Occupation of Muslim Land!

The Arab Nations now own 99.4% of the Middle East. Israel's *next door neighbors* are seven Muslim nations; Lebanon, Syria, Jordan and Egypt – with Iraq, Iran and Saudi Arabia nearby.

Israel possesses less than 4/1000ths of the Middle East, yet these Arab nations are *dying* to control Israel's .0037%. The Muslim desire for Israel's destruction is insane, as they fight to their death against God's promises to Israel.

Begin-Sadat Peace agreement between Israel and Egypt brokered by President Carter. Israel gave the entire Sinai to Egypt, but they refused to place their embassy in the Jewish capitol of Jerusalem.

6. God's Land – God's Decisions

The Land belongs to God! Thus, no nation can decide what to do with The Land, not even Israel. God said, *"The Land shall not be sold permanently, for the Land is Mine. You* (Israel) *are but aliens and sojourners with Me"* (Lev. 25:23).

How then can Israel give away land, in any *peace agreement,* that God has given to them? The nations of our world see the problems of the Middle East as top priority, and are searching for a solution. As a result, they constantly pressure Israel to *"give back"* The Land that God has given to them, supposedly for "peace". The United States continues to pressure Israel to "return" the land to the Palestinians when, in reality, it never belonged to them. The Palestinians have never had a country, a capital, or a president or king. They have never been a nation. They were "squatters" on some of Israel's land for a brief time. But they act like The Land has been theirs from time immemorial.

Those who support *"Land for Peace"*, whether they are from Israel or any other nation, are in reality striving against God. God is serious about His Land, and He has not changed His mind! The litmus test for the Nations, when they stand before God, will be their relationship to Israel. After all, God said, *"I will bless those who bless you, and the one who curses you I will curse"* (Gen 12: 3).

Could the political stance towards Israel taken by Rabin, Sadat, Arafat and Sharon have led to their downfall? These leaders preferred *the approval of men,* rather than *obedience to God.* (Read all of Ezekiel 36, with emphasis on verses 1-12. Then read Jer. 31:5).

The Israeli flag was raised over Eliat without firing a shot. In the Arab invasion of 1948 the Arab nations surrounding Israel sought to end all Jewish immigration and destroy the newly declared Jewish State of Israel. In the Armistice Agreement of 1949, the Arabs demanded, after their defeat, what they could have had before the invasion without firing a shot!

7. Israel Became a Nation on May 14, 1948 - as God Promised.

The nations of the Arab League gathered to annihilate the new nation. The odds were 280 Arab fighters to every Israeli. Israel not only survived but won the War of Independence (Isaiah 66:7-10).

However, Israel did not gain the *"Mountains of Samaria"* in 1948. God only gave Israel The Land they needed, and He knew what they could handle. Then, in June of 1967 God enlarged Israel's borders.

God has harsh warnings for the Arabs, and any other nation that fights against His people Israel. If the Nations would listen to God, it would save them much bloodshed. Muslims seem to be guided by *"another god"*. Their god "Allah" leads them from one destructive action or war to another. "Allah" of the Koran is *not* the God of Israel or the Bible. The more the Muslims fight Israel, the more Land they will forfeit to Israel. Fiftynine times in *Ezekiel alone,* God says, ***"Then you will know I Am The Lord!"***

Rabin and Arafat shake hands at the Oslo Conference.

God demonstrates His faithfulness through His promises to Israel.

8. Men and Nations Against Israel and God

The historic Rabin-Peres-Arafat-Clinton *Peace Process* was little more than a political sham. The *Oslo Agreement* has been virtually impossible to implement. It has splintered the "West Bank" into ridiculous fragments (see map on page 169). The bottom line is this – how is it possible to have *peace with a neighbor who is dying to kill you?* The PLO and Hamas charters refuse to recognize the legitimate existence of Israel and call for the total annihilation of the Jewish nation.

Ariel Sharon bowed to U.S. pressure to remove Israeli's who had lived and worked in Gaza for over 40 years. He give all of Gaza to the Palestinians. How tragic! What did that accomplish? Today Gaza is an armed terrorist training camp, sponsored by an "elected" Hamas. This U.S. decision has led to rocket bombardment across Israel's border from Hamas, and to Israel's invasion, "Protective Edge"– thus, the 2014 Gaza War.

What do U.S. leaders and the State Department want of Israel? If the U.S. pressures Israel to give up the "West Bank" in any "Land for Peace" agreement, it will make Israel's borders impossible to defend. That could lead to the annihilation of Israel.

Arab leaders in the Middle East use terrorism to accomplish their military goals. Exchanging "Land for Peace" on the "West Bank" would lead to an Arab military build-up of Hamas, Hezbollah, the Muslim Brotherhood or *ISIS (Islamic States of Iraq and Syria)* militants.

From the "West Bank" to Haifa is 21 miles, 9 miles to Netanya and only 11 miles to Tel Aviv. Jerusalem would be physically divided by any proposed borders. It is impossible to defend against rocket attacks from such short distances. From the "West Bank" to Ashdod is 22 miles, with Beersheba only 10 miles away. Today, Ashkelon is only 7 miles from Gaza.

Additionally, Israel has never had a genuine "peace partner" at any "negotiation" table. Both Arafat and Abbas chose terrorist activities to peaceful negotiations. Their stripes never change. As God said, they have *"a lust for the Land"* and *"an ancient hatred"* against Israel.

God has blessed America for her support of Israel.

However, today the use of the term ISL, by US or international leaders, is a "code word" to Middle East Muslims, that they are referring to a Middle East without Israel.

Since the birth of Israel in May of 1948, America's relationship with Israel has been strong, committed and blessed by God. Recently, that relationship has taken a dramatic turn. Support for Israel has wavered, yet the U.S. has consistently given financial and military aid to Israel's enemies. (Still, *Israel is America's only democratic friend in the Middle East).* One example is America's financial support of Gaza. The U.S. is sending millions into that "terrorist camp", while Hamas is building more tunnels in order to attack and kill Israeli citizens. Hamas is more committed to destroying Israel than caring for their own citizens and building Gaza's infrastructure.

In recent years Israel's Arab neighbors have struggled for existence, as civil wars have shredded Lebanon, Iraq, Egypt and Syria. A new name (ISIS) for an old player (Muslim Brotherhood) is seeking to take over the Arab world and remove all the "arbitrarily imposed post-WWI Middle Eastern boundaries";

including Syria, Jordan, Lebanon and Iran. They want to return the Muslim borders to those of the Turkish Ottoman Empire. The new Arab world (ISL, without Israel) would be ruled by radical terrorists, under a caliphate, and controlled by Shite sharia law, spiritually led by the returning 12th Imam.

Under this ISL banner the radical Muslims plan to first eliminate Israel (the "little Satan"), and next "Muslim-ize" the control of all Europe. Lastly, the radical Muslims will isolate and conquer (the "big Satan") America. Without a strong Israel, moderate Jordan and Saudi Arabia have no *friend* in the neighborhood. Without Israel, non-Muslims in the Middle East would have little defense against these radical Islamists (ISIS, Hamas, Hezbollah and Al Qaeda), who are committing atrocities against "infidels" daily. Without Israel, the rest of the civilized world would have no *force* to stand against this imminent ISIS tsunami!

The one goal that unites Muslim nations is their desire to eliminate the "little Satan" Israel. But Psalm 83, penned some 3000 years ago, is more accurate than the morning news, *"They say, 'Come, let us wipe them out as a nation, that the name of Israel be remembered no more...Let us possess for ourselves The pastures of God'"*(Ps. 83:4,12). But God promised Abraham, *"I will bless those who bless you and, I will curse those who curse you"* (Gen. 12:3).

If only the Arabs could learn to live in peace with their Jewish cousin, they would save so much Arab bloodshed. So far, the Muslim nations have lost eight major wars fighting Israel. And God moves Israel closer to her promised borders in the "end days". Unfortunately, the Muslim "spirit of war" and their "culture of death" is an imminent danger to every nation on earth. But nothing compares with their hatred for Israel and her "supporter", the United States.

Unfortunately, it is becoming more difficult for Israel to trust the U.S., due to our "vacillating" foreign policy and broken promises. Most Israelis fear that America would not come to her aid in a crisis. Rather, they are concerned that the administration would "throw them under the bus". As a matter of fact, today Israel's leaders expect only changing *political rhetoric* from the U.S. administration. Israelis deeply love and appreciate America, and most Americans love and support Israel (especially Evangelicals and Conservatives). Fortunately, the U.S. Congress continue to show strong support for Israel.

Meanwhile, God has not changed His mind concerning Israel. He will judge the nations which refuse to support Israel. His promises to Abraham and his descendants are true. ***"I will bless those who bless you, and those who curse you I will curse"***. God who said this is, ***"the same yesterday, today and always"***.

No peace has ever, or will ever come, from *"Land for Peace"* proposals. The concept has not worked since 1967. Israel is finally standing up to the E.U., the U.S., the U.N. and the world. They are shouting, *"Enough is enough"!* Israel has no "Peace Partner" among the Muslim nations in the Middle East, so why negotiate?

The time has come when Israel must obey God, rather than please men.

Hamas has turned Gaza into an Islamic terrorist base and training camp.

Territory held by Israel before and after the Six Day War. The Straits of Tiran, between the Gulf of Aqaba to the north, and the Red Sea to the south, are circled.

Joshua II

SECTION 3

God's Faithfulness to Israel

The Land was promised to Abraham by God, and thus, the Nation of Israel–through Isaac and Jacob–and Jacob's sons and descendants (Gen. 12:2-7, selected, 15:18).

The Beautiful Details of God's Promises Concerning The Land

- Moses told Israel (Deut. 8:7-10)
- Joshua told Israel (Deut. 11:11-17)
- God told Israel (Deut. 33:28-29a)

An Overview of Israel's History

- God directed Israel's conquest of Canaan. He gave them The Land. Unfortunately Israel worshiped other gods.
- The First Exile to Babylon lasted 70 years.
- The Israelites returned and built the second temple under Ezra and Nehemiah.
- Roman Rule - Jesus' birth, life and ministry.
- Jerusalem fell to Rome in 70 AD and 135 AD.
- Jewish Diaspora – Israel was scattered all over the world, and endured 1900 years of exile from their land.

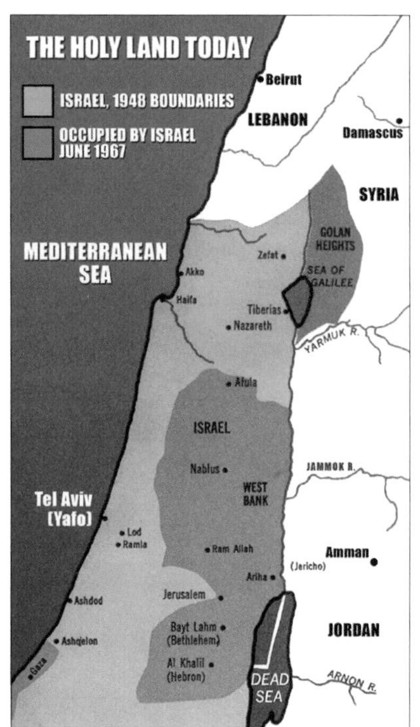

God Remembers and Is Faithful to Israel – Jer. 31:35-37; Isa. 49:15f.
God Brings Israel Back to the Land – Ezek. 11:16-17, 21, 28, 36:24, 37:1-14; Isa. 11:11-12, 14:1, 35:10, 43:5-6; Jer. 18-22 23:4f, 28, 30:10, 31:8-9, 32:37f; Zech. 2:6-7, Psa. 126.
God Blesses Israel – Jer. 31:4-5; Zech. 2:10-13.
The Birth of Israel – May 14, 1948 – (Isa. 66:7f) Jesus taught His disciples on the Mount of Olives about Israel and the end times. He gave a timetable in Matthiew 24:32f.
Blessings on Israel – Isa. 61:49, 60:21; Ezek. 36:8f, 36:30-38; Isa. 35:1-8, 41:18-20
Blessings on Jerusalem – Psa. 48:12-13, 122:2-3, 147, 137:5-6; Zech. 8:4-5, 7-8, 12, 22, 8:2-5.
Hebrew would be spoken when Israel returned – Jer. 31:23.
Israel will bless others – Zech. 8:13.
Israel's Conflicts and Wars – Psa. 83:2-5; Zech. 2:8-9, 12:6; Isa. 31:5, 11:14.
Jerusalem will be a *heavy stone* – Zech. 12:2-4.
Israel is God's eternal possession – Amos 9:14-15.
Pray for the *Peace of Jerusalem!* – Psa. 122:6-9.
"Zion, I have inscribed you on the palm of My Hand" – Isa. 49:16.

Joshua II

SECTION 4

"A Spirit of War" and an *"Ancient Hatred"* Against God and Israel

Isaiah 66:6-10, 12b-16.

1. War of Jewish Independence, 1948

Israel was attacked by five Arab nations. These enemies intended this to be "the war of extermination". The Arab League and the world did not expect the new nation of Israel to survive. However, against all odds, Israel won its independence, and God tells us why in *Ezekiel 35:2-15.* The events of this conflict remind us of those in the book of *Joshua*. The formation of Israel in 1948 was truly a miracle of God. Evidence of the Hand of God in these events include; Israel's night attack on the unified Arab camp; the Valley of Hinnon Rifleman; Eliat taken without a shot; and the taking of Lod/Lydda.

Arab leaders encouraged the Arab population to flee Palestinian territory until they could conquer the Jews. At the request of the Arab leaders some 700,000 fled, but they were not allowed to return to the Arab nations from which they had come. The resulting refugee problem was left in the hands of the United Nations. The Arabs refused to contribute to the financial needs of the refugees, and used the situation for propaganda. During this time approximately the same number of Jews were driven from their homes in Arab countries, and forced to leave all their possessions behind. Israel resettled all of them quickly and efficiently, and has never had a refugee problem. Jordan annexed the "West Bank" while Egypt occupied Gaza.

The armistice came in January, 1949. Israel lost the areas of Judea and Samaria to Jordan, but the young nation was saved as God had promised. For the next 13 years Israel was *"nursed at the breast of Gentile nations" (Isaiah 60:16)*. By age 13, the age of Bar Mitzvah, Israel had paid back every debt owed. Israel became a ***man*** and was accepted by the United Nations. The details of how Golda Meir arranged Israel's acceptance is amazing.

In the Arab invasion of 1948, the Arab nations surrounding Israel sought to end all Jewish immigration and destroy the newly declared Jewish State of Israel.

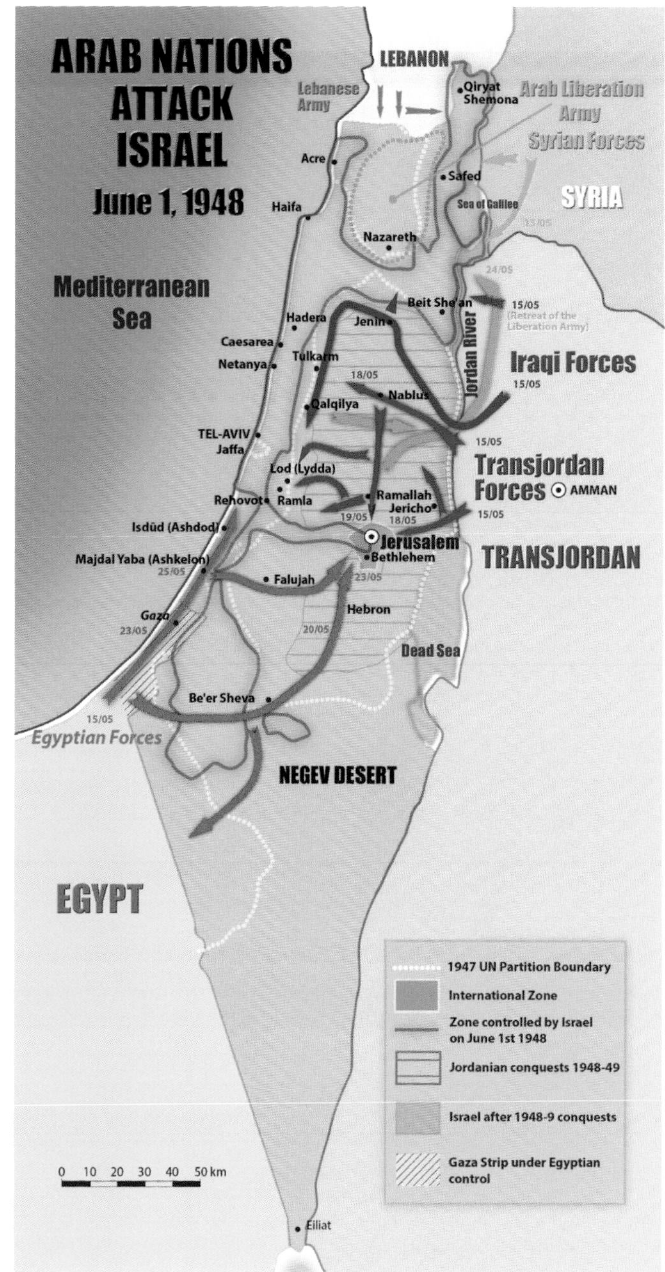

Israeli Commander Moshe Dayan in the Suez Canal region during the 1956 war.

2. The "100 Hour War" – July, 1956

Terrorism and border disputes with Egypt forced Israel into military action. Israel drove Egypt out of the Sinai and secured her borders. The victory came in a brief 100 hours. The United Nations and the United States demanded Israel return the Sinai, which they had won, to Egypt. Because the U.S. was courting the Arabs for oil, Israel was forced to withdraw from the Sinai. There was an uneasy border treaty, with little protection from the U.N. Nine years of difficulty followed, as the U.N. forces acquiesced to Arab demands.

3. The "Six Day War" – June, 1967

Israel became a *"man of war"* (Num.1:3). Egypt's leader, Gamal Abdel Nasser, united several Arab nations. Egypt then demanded that the UN leave the Suez. They left immediately with no questions asked.

Hatred for Israel finally united the Arab nations. Egypt announced,"This time we will exterminate Israel." Iraq said, "Our goal is clear; we will wipe out Israel." Libya: "Israel will cease to exist". The PLO said, "The struggle is not about Israel's borders, it is about Israel's existence."

God said, ***"Mt. Seir (Arabs), I am against you and I will stretch out My hand against you...because you have an ancient hatred"*** (Ezek. 35:3,5).

"I will destroy all nations that come against Jerusalem" (Zech. 12:6).

"He who touches Israel, touches the apple of God's eye. Behold, I will wave My Hand over them, so that they will be plunder" (Zech. 2:8-9).

It is unhealthy for any nation to boast against God and Israel! The Arab nations don't seem to learn this lesson. The more the Arabs war against Israel, the more God gives Israel their lands. He has promised these lands to Israel in the "end days".

Israel is the apple of God's eye Zech. 2:8.

In 1967, Russia armed the Arabs to the hilt. Nasser closed the Straits of Tiran, which cut off shipping to Israel's second largest port. *This was an act of war.* Israel had two options: they could wait for a slow death from economic strangulation, or they could attack! The Arabs started the war, but Israel attacked first.

June 1967 tank battle - Israel cut off the Mifla Pass coming in to Israel and captured an entire division of Egyptian tanks.

Arab Troops and Arms

- **Egypt** - 240,000 men of war poised for the fight
- **Algeria** - 60,000 soldiers in the Sinai and Gaza with 1,200 tanks plus several missile bases in the Sinai
- **Russia** - prepared to direct the war activities from the eastern Mediterranean. As the main supplier of arms, Russia had great interest in the 1967 war
- **Syrians** - 50,000 troops in the Golan Heights with many tanks
- **Iraq** - 1,000 Russian-made tanks in the Golan ready to strike
- **Jordan** - 50,000 troops well prepared to defend Jerusalem and the "West Bank"
- **Saudi Arabia** - 50,000 troops

Total Arab Troops at the beginning of the war - 520,000

Israeli Troops and Arms

- 70,000 regular army troops plus every adult male in their reserves
- Israel hitch-hiked to the battlefront or took public buses

Israel Was Outnumbered

- Manpower: 8 to 1
- Jets: 3 to 1
- Tanks: 3 to 1

  Israel attacked Egypt in an early pre-dawn air strike and wiped out their aerial capabilities.

Israeli fighters fly en route to their preemptive strike on the Egyptian Air Force during the morning of June 5, 1967.

The Results

- **Air Power, Fighter Jets**
- Israel annihilated all Egyptian air bases within 2 to 3 hours.
- The Arabs lost 441 fighter jets while Israel lost only 21 (1:21 ratio).

A wounded Egyptian tank commander sits depressed, an Israeli prisoner of war. He was one of thousands taken captive; returned to Egypt at the close of the Six Day War.

Israel blocked the Mifla Pass, which leads from the Suez Plateau into the heart of the Sinai. Arabs fled their tanks by the thousands. They were rounded up, placed in temporary corrals, fed and cared for. Israel moved a paint shop to the pass, painted the Star of David on the Egyptian tanks, and drove them back to the Suez Canal.
They crossed the canal on their prefabricated bridges and headed for Cairo. The Arab League immediately petitioned the United Nations for a cease-fire.

Arab Casualties

- Syria – 2,000; Jordan – 8,000; Egypt – 20,000; 50,000 – Wounded.

Israeli Casualties

- **679 warriors (45:1 ratio);** 2563 Wounded

Arab and Russian Weapon Loss

- Israel captured all Sinai missile bases intact – ready for immediate action.
- Israel captured 1,000+ field guns, 70,000 tons of ammo, 10,000 trucks and vehicles – ready for use. Israel has enough supplies to equip 7 Egyptian divisions.

The Financial Losses

- Israel's war cost was $100 million.
- The Arab war cost was $1,500,000,000.
- Egypt's debt to Russia was $2 billion for military hardware, which was a small price to pay if they had annihilated Israel. Egypt's entire cotton crop was wiped out by insects during the war. It was like the Book of Joshua.
- Israel's economy was hardly disrupted.

War Stories Worth Researching

- Israel's attack on the Arab air bases
- Capture of Egyptian tanks at Mifla Pass in the Sinai
- Israel's victory of the Golan Heights
- The incredible Golani Brigade.

Israel Gained

Sinai, Gaza, the Golan Heights, the West Bank, Judea, Samaria – and the most prized of all, Jerusalem! This was ***"the end of the age of the Gentiles..."*** (Lk. 21:24).

Amazing Victory! God did it!

"O God, do not remain quiet; Do not be silent and, O God, do not be still. For behold, Your enemies make an uproar, And those who hate You have exalted themselves. They make shrewd plans against Your people, And conspire together against Your treasured ones. They have said, 'Come, and let us wipe them out as a nation, That the name of Israel be remembered no more.' For they have conspired together with one mind; Against You they make a covenant: Who said, 'Let us possess for ourselves The pastures of God.'

O my God, make them like the whirling dust, Like chaff before the wind. Like fire that burns the forest And like a flame that sets the mountains on fire, So pursue them with Your tempest And terrify them with Your storm. Fill their faces with dishonor, That they may seek Your name, O LORD. Let them be ashamed and dismayed forever, And let them be humiliated and perish, That they may know that You alone, whose name is the LORD, Are the Most High over all the earth" (Psa. 83:1-5, 12-18).

Arab League Rejected Israel's Offer

Israel offered to return the captured land in exchange for peace, recognition and negotiations. This offer was rejected "hands down" by the Arab League.

"Then I saw in the right hand of him who was seated on the throne a scroll written within and on the back, sealed with seven seals. And I saw a strong angel proclaiming with a loud voice, "Who is worthy to open the scroll and break its seals?" And no one in heaven or on earth or under the earth was able to open the scroll or to look into it, and I began to weep loudly because no one was found worthy to open the scroll or to look into it. And one of the elders said to me, "Weep no more; behold, the Lion of the tribe of Judah, the Root of David, has conquered, so that he can open the scroll and its seven seals" (Rev. 5:1-14 NAS).

The Lion of Judah is the symbol of the tribe of Judah. Judah, the fourth son of Jacob, was the tribe's founder. The association between Judah and the lion can first be found in the blessing given by Jacob to Judah in Gen. 49:8-10. Both King David and Jesus are from the tribe of Judah. The phrase "Lion of Judah" is used in Revelation to represent Jesus.

"One of the elders said to me, "Stop weeping; behold, the Lion that is from the tribe of Judah, the Root of David, has overcome so as to open the book and its seven seals" (Rev. 5:5 NAS).

GOD IS FAITHFUL

God keeps every promise He has ever made.
He blesses nations who bless Israel and, He curses nations who curse Israel.

PRAY FOR THE PEACE OF JERUSALEM

QUESTION: TO WHOM DOES THE LAND BELONG?

Five Ways God Gave HIS LAND to the Jews:

1. **By Deed: God promised The Land to Abraham, Isaac, Jacob, and their descendants.**
2. **By Conquest: Joshua conquered The Land under God's leadership.**
3. **By Occupation: Israel occupied The Land for 1,380 years.**
4. **By Purchase: Israel bought The Land from the Turks and Arabs.**
5. **By Defense: Israel has won every conflict, including the wars in 1948, 1956, 1967, 1973 and 1982.**

These wars were started by the surrounding Arab nations, which wanted to annihilate Israel.

Hamas terrorist with shoulder rocket

It seems that God has allowed the Arab nations to have a "spirit of war". The more the Arab world attacks Israel, the more God moves Israel toward the End-Time borders He has promised to them.

Since the Arabs have lost every war they have fought with Israel, they have today turned to diplomatic intrigue to accomplish their purpose of gaining the land. This is what the Peace Process, or "Land for Peace", is all about! Others have turned to terrorism.

The flawed concept of "Land for Peace" is based on the premise that the land of "Palestine" all belonged to the Arabs across the centuries. This is revisionist history at its worst, but is convenient for the Muslim cause.

Many Arab families have lived in the land of Palestine for generations. However, most Arabs in Israel today came more recently from Jordan, Saudi Arabia, Syria and other Arab countries. They came to Palestine in the late 1800's and early 1900's for economic reasons (best compared to the Mexicans who flow into the U.S. today for work). Most true Palestinian Arabs who lived in Israel for generations chose to remain as Israeli citizens after the war in 1948. Today they are better off than any of their middle eastern Arab counterparts.

Others, unfortunately, fled into nearby Arab countries, and rather than being accepted and settled in those countries, were forced into refugee camps. Most remain in those camps today. All who live in these camps claim that Israel belongs to them and to their families, and that they have the Right of Return.

Israeli soldier argues with a member of the PLO.

The Land of Israel was never promised to the Arab people by God. Their promises from God lie to the East (Gen. 16:11, 12, 17:20). The Koran and Bible are in total disagreement on this subject. The Koran says that Ishmael, the first-born of Abraham, was the heir of God's promises. The Bible plainly ascribes God's promise of the Land to Isaac (Gen. 17:2-8, 18, 19, 21).

According to the Koran, both Jews and Christians are enemies of Islam. There are early statements in the Koran that "bless" both Jews and Christians. However, these are statements made by Mohammed early in his life. Later writings by the prophet and others (in the Hadith) state that all infidels must convert to Islam, or die. Once in power, Mohammed proclaimed that what he taught earlier was no longer valid for the Muslim faith. Then he had all killed who disagreed with him. We see this same spirit in many of his followers today – all over our world.

Arab Wars with Israel and Jews Relationships from 1964

PLO demonstration

In 1964 Yasser Arafat (a native-born Egyptian) founded the Palestinian Liberation Organization. With funds from the World Bank, U.N. and many other nations, he assisted the PLO and padded his personal bank accounts in Switzerland. Arafat never spoke publicly to "his people" as he could not speak with their Arabic dialect.

Since the War of Liberation and the rebirth of Israel, Egypt continually fought Israel on her Negev borders. Infiltrators poured into Israel nightly, attacking the towns and kibbutzim. Finally, after many warnings to its southern neighbor, Israel fought an all-out campaign in Egypt's Sinai. The trigger: Nasser nationalized the Suez Canal to prevent Israel's use of the passage.

By the end of October the Israelis occupied all of the Sinai Peninsula. When Israel started to march toward Cairo, Nasser suddenly decided he wanted a peace treaty. After the "peace" was agreed upon, world opinion put pressure on Israel, and the Arabs forced Israel to withdraw to the 1949 armistice lines.

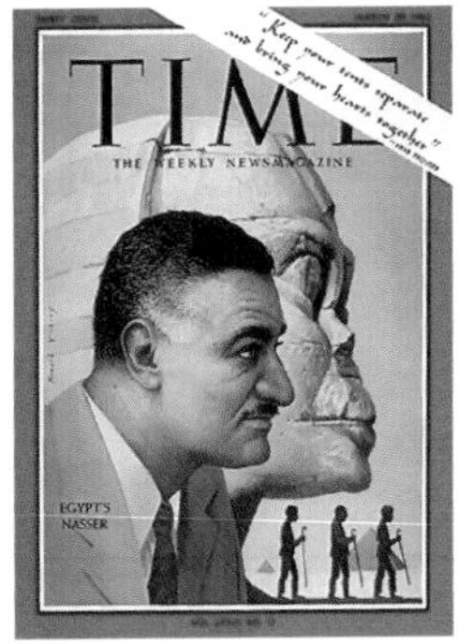

Abdul Nasser committed an act of war.

Then United Nations troops were stationed along the Israeli-Egyptian border. But, Egypt continued to attack Israel. And when Nasser wanted the U.N. troops to leave the Suez in May of 1967, they obliged immediately, as if they had been anxious to leave at any point.

When Egypt closed the Straits of Tiran into the Gulf of Aqaba on May 23, 1967, Israel was cut off from their second most important port, Eliat. Nasser had presented Israel with an act of war. The U.N. was nowhere to be found in the Sinai. Appropriately, at that time they got a new name from the Israelis: "United Nothing."

June 1967-1995 Highlights and Lowlights.

Golda

1969: Golda Meir became Israel's fourth Prime Minister. Moshe Dayan was commander of the IDF (Israeli Defense Forces).

1970: Israel fought the War of Attrition in the Jordan Valley against the Jordanians on the holiest day of the Jewish year, Yom Kippur (Day of Atonement).

1973: The Yom Kippur War began in October, when Israel was attacked by four nations, including Syria and Egypt. Israel was not expecting this attack, nor were they prepared for another war. (From that point on, Israelis blamed Prime Minister Golda Meir and General Moshe Dayan for their lack of preparedness). Israel came closer to losing that war than any fought in their history. God protected Israel over and over again. Israel held the land gained in 1967, but not without loss of life and limb by young Israelis.

1979: On March 26th, Egyptian President Anwar Sadat and Israeli Prime Minister Menachem Begin signed a peace treaty in Washington DC. Sadat received the Nobel Peace Prize, and a bullet from a Muslim fundamentalist on Cairo's military parade grounds. Israel gave up the entire Sinai, including beautiful resorts they had built, as well as oil wells with enough oil to have sustained them for years. In return, they got another embassy in Tel Aviv and lots of promises and lies. Peace promises from the Arab world have been "much ado about nothing", and that is not changing.

Sadat and Begin

1982: In response to ongoing missile attacks from Lebanon, and in a desperate attempt to save Christian Lebanese from systematic genocide at the hands of Arabs, Israel entered Lebanon on June 5. Two days later, they were in Beirut. They destroyed all the Russian anti-aircraft missile bases in the Bekaa Valley with highly advanced weaponry, and took the country by kicking Arafat all the way to North Africa. They saved the Lebanese government from certain collapse and returned to Israel after establishing a security belt between Israel and southern Lebanon. And guess who the world insisted on to patrol the borders? The U.N. – United Nothing!

1986: The first Arab Muslim Intifada broke out; Israel started a campaign of containment.

Yassir Arafat

1994: Israel agreed to give up "land for peace" and entered into an agreement with Yassir Arafat and his PLO to give them Gaza and Jericho. You know how much "peace" has come out of that agreement. Arafat, the world-renowned terrorist, got a Nobel Peace Prize. Gaza would, within the next decade, become an armed terrorist camp, led first by the PLO, and then in 2005 by the radical Hamas.

1995: When Israel started negotiations with Syria to return the Golan Heights, Israelis rose up en-mass against their government. On Nov. 4, Prime Minister Yitzhak Rabin was assassinated in Tel Aviv by an Israeli Jew. This did not stop the process of giving control of Bethlehem and Nablus to the PLO in December. The city where Jesus was born was 85% Christian when it was turned over to the PLO. Today, only about 12% remain. Remaining Christians live under constant Muslim threats. Nablus is a Muslim extremist stronghold.

2000-2010: At Camp David the Palestinians rejected Israel's offer to return 90% of the West Bank and Gaza. The PLO made no counter-proposal. Instead, they initiated the Second Intifada, forcing Israel to rethink her relationship with the Palestinians. Following a series of suicide bombings and attacks, the Israeli army launched Operation Defensive Shield. It was the largest military operation conducted by Israel since the Six Day War. As violence between the Israeli army and Palestinian militants intensified, Israel expanded its security apparatus around the West Bank. Israel established a complex system of roadblocks and checkpoints around major Palestinian areas to deter violence and protect Israeli settlements. Since 2008 the IDF has slowly transferred some of this authority to the Palestinian security forces.

Ariel Sharon

2003: Israeli Prime Minister Ariel Sharon began a policy of unilateral withdrawal from the Gaza Strip. This policy was fully implemented in August 2005. Sharon's announcement to disengage from Gaza came as a tremendous shock to his critics, both on the left and on the right. A year previously he had commented that the fates of the most far-flung settlements in Gaza, Netzararem and Kefar Darom were regarded in the same light as that of Tel Aviv. The formal announcements to evacuate seventeen Gaza settlements and another four in the West Bank in February, 2004, represented the first reversal for the settler movement since 1968. This divided his party, but was strongly supported by Trade and Industry Minister Ehud Olmert and Tzipi Livni, the Minister for Immigration and Absorption. But Foreign Minister Silvan Shalom and Finance Minister Benjamin Netanyahu strongly condemned it.

2005: Israel withdrew from Gaza after 38 years of living and working there. Two years later, radical Hamas replaced the PLO, and forced those they did not kill to retreat to Nablus in the West Bank.

2006: In June 2006, Hamas militants infiltrated an army post near the Israeli side of the Gaza Strip and abducted Israeli soldier Gilad Shalit. Two IDF soldiers were killed in the attack, and Shalit was wounded after his tank was hit with an RPG. Three days later Israel launched Operation Summer Rains to secure the release of Shalit. He was held hostage by Hamas, who barred the International Red Cross from seeing him until October 18, 2011, when he was exchanged for 1500 Palestinian prisoners.

In response to border kidnappings of their soldiers, Israel invaded both Gaza and Lebanon in May and June. Unfortunately, this was done without proper planning and forethought, and the government paid a high political price. During the conflict, rockets hit northern Galilee, but there was no invasion of Israel. Strong border security with Lebanon, Jordan and Gaza prevented infiltration into Israel.

In July, Hezbollah fighters crossed the border from Lebanon into Israel, attacked and killed eight Israeli soldiers, and took two more hostage, setting off the 2006 Lebanon War, which resulted in much destruction in Lebanon. A U.N. sponsored ceasefire went into effect on August 14, 2006, officially ending the conflict. Over a

Gilad Shalit was released from Gaza in exchange for 1500 militant Muslim prisoners from Israeli prisons.

Hezbollah parade in Beirut, Lebanon

thousand people were killed as a result of this conflict, mostly Lebanese civilians. Much of Lebanon's infrastructure was destroyed, displacing approximately one million Lebanese and some 300,000–500,000 Israelis – although most were able to return to their homes. After the ceasefire, some parts of Southern Lebanon remained uninhabitable due to unexploded Israeli cluster bomblets.

2007: In the aftermath of the Battle of Gaza, where Hamas seized control of the Gaza Strip in a violent civil war with rival Fatah, Israel placed restrictions on its border with Gaza, and ended economic cooperation with the Palestinian leadership based there. Israel and Egypt imposed a blockade on the Gaza Strip in 2007. Israel maintained the blockade, for it was necessary to limit Palestinian rocket attacks from Gaza, and to prevent Hamas from smuggling in advanced rockets and weapons capable of hitting its cities.

On September 6, in Operation Orchard, Israel bombed an eastern Syrian complex, which was a nuclear reactor being built with assistance from North Korea. (Israel bombed a Syrian nuclear reactor in 2003).

2008: In April, Syrian President Bashar Al Assad told a Qatari newspaper that Syria and Israel had been discussing a peace treaty for a year with, Turkey as a go-between. This was confirmed in May 2008 by a spokesman for Prime Minister Ehud Olmert. Along with a peace treaty, the future of the Golan Heights was being discussed. President Assad said "there would be no direct negotiations with Israel until a new U.S. president took office".

A fragile six-month truce between Hamas and Israel expired on December 19th, 2008. Attempts at extending the truce failed, amid accusations of breaches from both sides. Following the expiration of the truce, Israel launched a raid on a tunnel suspected of being used to kidnap Israeli soldiers. As a result, several Hamas fighters were killed.

Following these events, Hamas resumed rocket and mortar attacks on Israeli cities, most notably firing over 60 rockets on December 24th. On December 27th, Israel launched Operation Cast Lead against Hamas. Numerous human rights organizations accused Israel and Hamas of committing war crimes. In 2009 Israel placed a 10 month settlement freeze on the West Bank. Hillary Clinton praised the freeze as an "unprecedented" gesture that could "help revive Middle East talks".

Hamas terrorists prepare to fire home-made rockets into civilian cities in Israel.

2010: In May, 2010, a raid was carried out by Israeli naval forces on six ships of the Gaza Freedom Flotilla after the ships refused to dock at Port Ashdod. On the MV Mavi Marmara, activists clashed with the Israeli boarding party. During the fighting nine activists were killed by Israeli Special Forces. Several dozen other passengers and seven Israeli soldiers were injured.

Wars and Violent Events Over Six Decades

In the past 66 years 23,169 soldiers of the Israel Defense Forces, Security Forces and pre-state underground fighters have lost their lives serving the small nation. Plus, another 2,495 civilians have been killed by terrorists.

After six decades Israel still faces the neighborhood challenges. Israel has a population of 8.2 million, and they are surrounded by 400 million Arabs who are "dying to kill them". The UN brokered cease-fire of 1949 never ended anything. The fighting continues to this day.

1948-49 Israeli War of Independence

1951-55 **Crossborder attacks by the Egyptians and Jordanian supported "Fedayeen" terrorists...Retribution Operations by Israel**

1956 **The** Sinai Campaign **and** Suez War **stopped the Fedayeen attacks and removed the Egyptian blockade of Eliat.**

1967 June **The** Six Day War **against Egypt, Jordan, and Syria**

1967-1970 War of Attrition **against Jordan and Egypt**

1973 Yom Kippur War **against Egypt, Syria, Jordan and Lebanon**

1978 "Operation Litani" **against the PLO in Lebanon, to help prevent the annihilation of Christian communities in Lebanon**

1982 First Lebanon War **- Operation Peace in Galilee against PLO**

1987-1993 First Palestinian Intifada

2000-2004 Second Palestinian Intifada

2006 Second Lebanon War

2008 **Gaza** "Operation Cast Lead" **against Hamas**

2012 **Gaza** "Operation Pillar of Defense" **against Hamas & Islamic Jihad**

2014 **Hamas indiscriminately launched 4000 rockets with the purpose of killing innocent Israeli civilians (14% hit in Gaza, 69% hit in Israel in unpopulated areas, and 17% over urban areas were intercepted by the "Iron Dome"). Israel retaliated with** "Operation Protective Edge" **(July-August), with targeted strikes against Hamas. Unfortunately there were civilian casualties, as Hamas used women and children as "human shields". Israel destroyed the Hamas' rockets and tunnels.**

Hamas uses private home, mosques, hospitals and schools to store their rockets and weapons.

Mahmoud Ahmadinejad was the President of Iran (2005 to 2013). He constantly threatened Israel while building Iran's nuclear capabilities. Iran's present leaders continue to follow the same path. Israel is the only nation willing to stand against Iran, thereby protecting Europe and the U.S. Unfortunately, Israel may have to fight this battle alone.

U.S. brokered peace talks were a total failure; Arabs refused to continue. Fatah leader Tawfik Tirawi stated, "The two-state solution does not exist." Then he called for Israel's destruction. He continued, "Palestine is Gaza, the West Bank, Haifa, Jaffa, Acre...and all of Israel is Palestine."

Hamas leader Moussa Abu Marzouk stated that Hamas would never recognize Israel, and they won't abide by previous agreements (agreements when the U.S. insisted that Israel completely withdrawal from Gaza). Today (2014), Gaza is an armed terrorist base under Hamas leadership.

Israel's only peaceful neighbors have been Egypt and Jordan. For a time, Egypt honored the Sinai withdrawal agreements. When The Muslim Brotherhood took control of Egypt, they nullified all treaties with Israel and ceased all trade and cultural ties with the "Zionist" state. In both Jordan and Egypt, Hamas leaders and the Muslim Brotherhood object to all "peace treaties" with Israel.

Iran's Shiite Muslim leaders are Israel's most dangerous enemy, as they continue to develop nuclear weapons at a rapid pace. (This is the sole *purpose* of their thousands of centrifuges). These bombs are first intended to annihilate Israel and moderate Arab countries. Europe and the United States will follow. With Arab civil wars and ISIS distractions in the Middle East, Israel is the only nation that keeps their focus on the real danger, taking Iran's threats seriously.

The U.S. on the other hand, has enlisted Iran in their fight against ISIS (Sunni Moslems, who are supposed "moderates" compared to Muslim Shiites). ISIS is sweeping Iraq and Syria, with their sights on control of the Arab world. Then they plan to destroy Israel (the Little Satan) in their campaign to control the world.

Iran is glad to the join the U.S. in the fight against ISIS (since ISIS is their enemy), and any "alliance" will remove sanctions levied against them, and allow them to continue nuclear development and their march toward world control. So, does the U.S. see Iran as an ally, when Iran's goal is destroy and dominate the Big Satan, the United States?

Prior to Yom Kippur, early October 2014 (5775 on the Jewish calendar), Israel's Prime Minister, Binyamin Netanyahu said, "Militant Islam wants to take us back to the early Medieval Period, where women were chattel and minorities were subjugated, and where all 'infidels' (non Muslims) were given the choice to convert or die. That is insane! But when you couple this insanity with weapons of mass destruction, the road leads to a world wide catastrophe."

Two Texas friends of Israel pray at the Wailing Wall.

Israel is strong, vibrant and determined to fulfill the 2000 year dream of her people. They will continue to thrive and expand medical, scientific and technological boundaries...being a light to the nations.

Israel has to live with their "swords" drawn. The IDF is stronger technologically than her Arab neighbors. Her security depends on her advanced military and defense technology. Israel will continue to be safe, secure and prosperous. This is God's promise.

The information above has been gleaned from an article by former Lieutenant Colonel Gil Elan, of the IDF. Gil is widely regarded as an expert on Israel, and is the President and CEO of the Southwest Jewish Congress. He presents monthly briefings in North Dallas, updating people about events in Israel and the Middle East.

PRAY FOR THE PEACE OF ISRAEL

IDF Soldiers write out prayers and pray at the Wailing Wall prior to going into battle.

History of "Land for Peace" Attempts between Israel and Palestinians

Sept. 1978- *The Camp David Accord* was signed by Menachem Begin (Israel), Jimmy Carter (USA) and Anwar Sadat (Egypt). *Result:* Israel gave the Sinai to Egypt with all the developed oil and hotels intact. Israel got an Egyptian ambassador in Tel Aviv (refused to have the embassy in Jerusalem) Sadat was hated and killed in Egypt by radical Muslims.

Sept. 1993- *The Oslo Peace Accords* led to the establishment of the Palestinian authority over Gaza and the West Bank. *Result:* Autonomy for the Palestinians, or self-rule on interior matters like roads, education, health. Palestinians agreed to remove all incitement from their school curriculum. That never happened.

Sept. 1994- *The Peace Agreement with Jordan - Israeli-Palestinian Interim Agreement* on the West Bank and Gaza Strip. *Result:* A move from Palestinian autonomy to a self-rule, non-militarized state. Much low tech industry moved to Jordan, many jobs were lost in Israel.

Oct. 1998- *The Wye River Memorandum* between Ehud Barak (Israel) and Yasser Arafat (PLO), hosted by Bill Clinton. *Result:* Gave self-rule to the Palestinians in heavily populated Palestinian areas. 22% of the "West Bank" was given to the Palestinians, *Sector A* (including Bethlehem, Ramallah, Jericho, Bethany, Nablus, and half of Hebron). Artificial political borders and difficult administration of the "West Bank".

Oct. 2000- *The Clinton Peace Plan. Result:* Areas populated by Jews would remain Jewish, areas populated by Arabs would be under Palestinian rule. Rejected by Arafat. He insisted on Israel's return to their 1967 pre-war border. All was rejected by East Jerusalem Arabs with Israeli citizenship.

Oct. 2003- ***The Israeli/Palestinian Geneva Accord.*** *Result:* Intention to move from autonomy to a two state solution.

Aug. 2005- ***Sharon Disengagement from Gaza.*** *Result:* 8,000 Israelis were forcefully dragged from their homes (many families lived and worked there for over 40 years). Since that time, the PLO has turned control of the Gaza Strip over to Hamas, who in turn have turned it into an armed Muslim terrorist camp.

Nov. 2007- ***Annapolis Conference*** involving Prime Minister Ehud Olmert (Israel), President Mahmud Abbas (PLO), President George Bush (U.S.) and Prime Minister Tony Blair (U.K.). *Result:* There was no agreement because Abbas insisted on all of Jerusalem and Israel's return to her pre-1967 borders.

2009- President Abbas of the PA rejected a proposal of 97% of the West Bank with compensatory land swaps. *Result:* None

July 2013- ***President Obama's Peace Plan,*** submitted by John Kerry, set a deadline of April 29, 2014 to compose "preconditions" for negotiations. *Result:* After much shuttling and high hopes for peace on Kerry's part, he could not even get an agreement on "preconditions" for the discussions.

Overall Results - Thirty six years of *"Land for Peace agreements"* and dialogue between Israel and the Palestinians have done little to bring *peace* to the Middle East. Israel has not yet had a true *Peace Partner* with whom they can negotiate. None have recognized Israel's right to exist. Instead, the Muslim world is intent on annihilating Israel.

The U.S. State Department administration insist on negotiating toward an Israel-Palestinian *"Two State Solution"* (with the two nations side by side). Seventy percent of the US citizens disagree, and feel that a Palestinian Arab State would remain hostile toward Israel. Ninety-two percent of Israelis feel that there can never be a lasting *Peace Accord.* And sixty-two percent of Israeli Arabs agree. So much for learning from mistakes.

In June 2014, the PLO merged with Hamas (an internationally recognized terrorist organization). Yet the U.S. continued to fund this terrorist organization that hates both Israel and the US. There is little doubt that the July 2014 rocket fire into Israel was "supported" by US funding, though designated for other causes.

After enduring constant rocket attacks from Gaza, in mid-July, 2014, Israel organized a sustained attack and ground offensive to take out Hamas, and to destroy rocket launchers and tunnels in Gaza. During the invasion, Israel continued to supply the life-sustaining food (60-70 truck loads per day), gas, electricity, medical supplies, and water for Gaza residents. Palestinian rockets crippled the power lines from Ashkelon, which brought electricity to Gaza. Under fire, Israel repaired the damaged power lines and restored electricity to her enemies. Israel set up a field hospital in Gaza to provide for the wounded Palestinians, and provided blood for those who needed it.

Israel destroys Hamas' Gaza headquarters and ammunition depot.

Israel provides for and protects her citizens at any cost. Israel respects all life. The IDF dropped

leaflets to warn the Palestinian civilians to get out of particular neighborhoods before the bomb attacks.

On the other hand, Hamas hid rockets, launchers and ammunition in kindergartens, schools, hospitals, mosques and homes. They used Palestinian children as human shields, to hinder any Israeli attack. They then warned Arab civilian families, at gunpoint, to stay in homes which Israel had already targeted for destruction.

Every terrorist who kills an Israeli, or dies as a martyr, he or his family receives $9,000 per month. These funds are supplied through Hamas, from monies that have been given by the U.N., E.U., and U.S. Such martyrs become Gaza's national heroes.

Israel captured and destroyed over 40 tunnels, built by Hammas, to infiltrate Israel and kill innocent civilians.

Palestinian Authority's (PA's) Preconditions for Peace (Negotiation Sticking Points)

Israel must return to the pre-1967 cease-fire lines and East Jerusalem must become the PA's Capital, with the Temple Mount under their control. If that were to happen, no Jew would be allowed to live in East Jerusalem, or in the West Bank – unless they carried a PA identity card. Today (2014) approximately 680,000 Jews live in the West Bank and East Jerusalem. Would all these Israeli residents be relocated?

The PA will never recognize Israel as a Jewish State. The PA demands the "Right of Return" for an "unknown number" of Palestinian "refugees", whose ancestors (less than 200,000) fled from Israel during the 1948 War. Today these Arabs number in the millions. Surrounding Arab nations refused to assimilate these "refugees". They forced them into endless refugee camps, using them as political pawns.

Israel's Major Conditions for Peace

The Palestinians must recognize Israel as a Jewish State before negotiations can begin.

Jerusalem is out of any negations, period!*

Arab refugees will not be allowed to return to Israel, and Israel must approve any individuals who do return to the West Bank.

Israel will always control the airport and any seaports bordering Palestine. Palestine must be demilitarized, certainly with no air force. The IAF must be allowed to fly over the West Bank.

*East Jerusalem and the West Bank were conquered by Israel in June 1967 (Six Day War). Israel will never give up the Wailing Wall or East Jerusalem. For 2,000 years, while in the Diaspora, Jews have prayed toward the Temple Mount. Unfortunately, Moshe Dyan after that war gave the Temple Mount to the Muslim Waqf for their administration – even though Israel was in charge East Jerusalem.

Israel's Prime Minister Benyamin Netanyahu insists, "Jerusalem was unified 47 years ago, and it will never again be divided." How can Israel be expected to absorb 9 million refugees under the Arab proposal of "the Right of Return"? Immediately six million Jewish citizens would be out-numbered, making a Jewish democracy impossible. Over 1.3 million Palestinians live in Israel today with full citizen's rights, including seats in the congress. They live far better than Arabs in any part of the Middle East. ***"Land for Peace"*** **is totally impossible and absolutely against God's Word.**

Israel's Prime Minister Benyamin Netanyahu speaks to the United Nations.

"As birds hovering, so will Jehovah of hosts protect Jerusalem; he will protect and deliver it , he will pass over and preserve it".
Isaiah 31:5

The Camp David Agreement of 1995 divided the West Bank into three "sectors"

Sector A: *Palestinian administration, Palestinian security* - presently active, in all heavily populated Arab cities and villages.

Sector B: *Palestinian administration, Israeli security* - resulting in mixed Jewish / Arab settlement areas with Arab areas.

Sector C: *Israeli administration, Israeli security* - Includes the Jordan Valley, all roads in the West Bank leading to Jerusalem or Eliat. (i.e. All the major roadways through the West Bank.

Jerusalem is out of any negotiations!

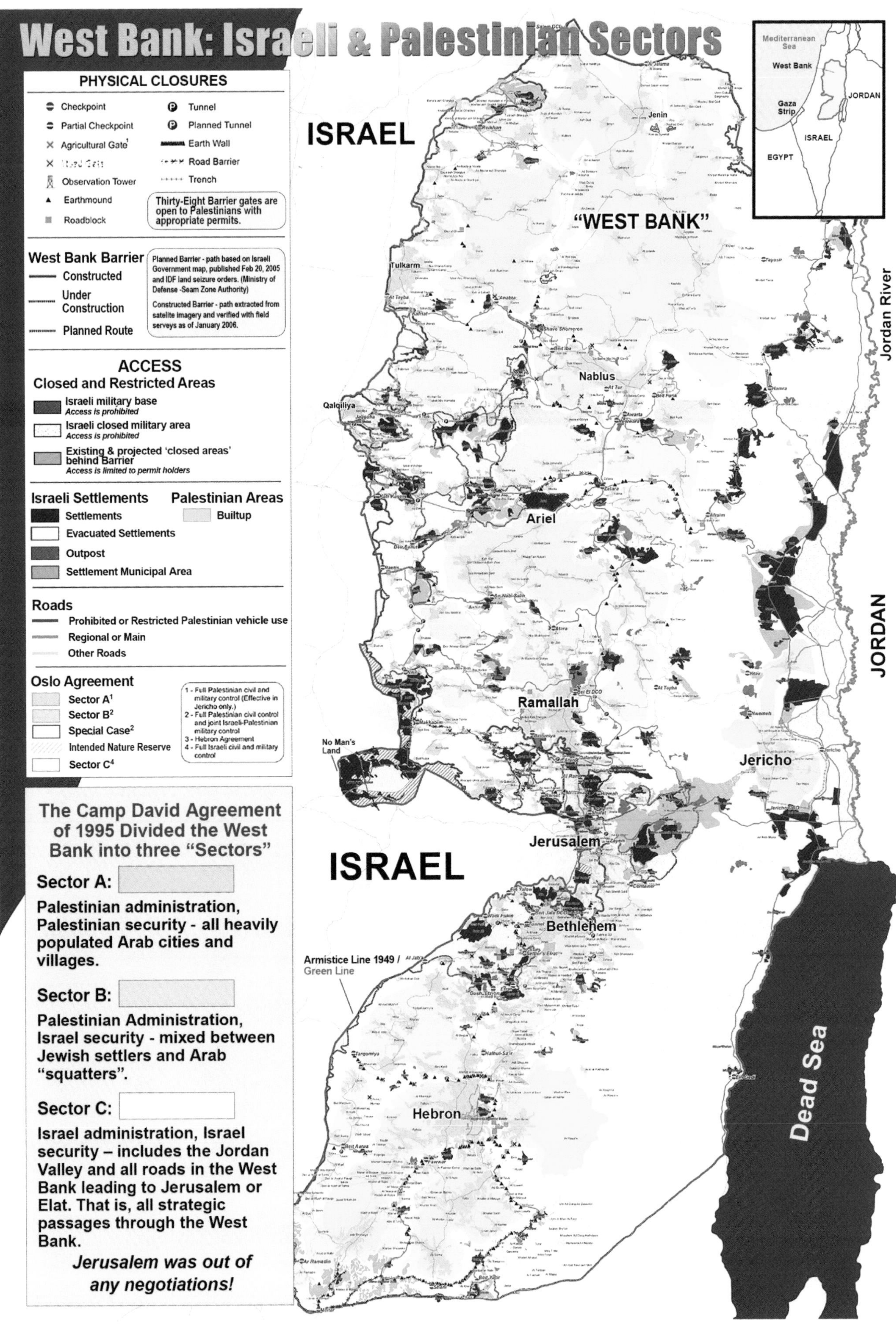
West Bank: Israeli & Palestinian Sectors
PHYSICAL CLOSURES
Checkpoint
Partial Checkpoint
Agricultural Gate[1]
Observation Tower
Earthmound
Roadblock
Tunnel
Planned Tunnel
Earth Wall
Road Barrier
Trench
Thirty-Eight Barrier gates are open to Palestinians with appropriate permits.
West Bank Barrier
Constructed
Under Construction
Planned Route
Planned Barrier - path based on Israeli Government map, published Feb 20, 2005 and IDF land seizure orders. (Ministry of Defense -Seam Zone Authority)
Constructed Barrier - path extracted from satelite imagery and verified with field serveys as of January 2006.
ACCESS
Closed and Restricted Areas
Israeli military base
Access is prohibited
Israeli closed military area
Access is prohibited
Existing & projected 'closed areas' behind Barrier
Access is limited to permit holders
Israeli Settlements
Settlements
Evacuated Settlements
Outpost
Settlement Municipal Area
Palestinian Areas
Builtup
Roads
Prohibited or Restricted Palestinian vehicle use
Regional or Main
Other Roads
Oslo Agreement
Sector A[1]
Sector B[2]
Special Case[2]
Intended Nature Reserve
Sector C[4]
1 - Full Palestinian civil and military control (Effective in Jericho only.)
2 - Full Palestinian civil control and joint Israeli-Palestinian military control
3 - Hebron Agreement
4 - Full Israeli civil and military control
The Camp David Agreement of 1995 Divided the West Bank into three "Sectors"
Sector A:
Palestinian administration, Palestinian security - all heavily populated Arab cities and villages.
Sector B:
Palestinian Administration, Israel security - mixed between Jewish settlers and Arab "squatters".
Sector C:
Israel administration, Israel security – includes the Jordan Valley and all roads in the West Bank leading to Jerusalem or Elat. That is, all strategic passages through the West Bank.
Jerusalem was out of any negotiations!
Mediterranean Sea
West Bank
Gaza Strip
JORDAN
ISRAEL
EGYPT
ISRAEL
"WEST BANK"
Jenin
Tulkarm
Nablus
Qalqiliya
Ariel
Ramallah
No Man's Land
Jericho
Jerusalem
ISRAEL
Bethlehem
Armistice Line 1949 / Green Line
Hebron
Jordan River
JORDAN
Dead Sea

Bob Ross has been an avid student of God's Word for over 50 years, and has dedicated his life to the study of Jesus, His ministry, and the Land of his Birth. Many seed thoughts sown in Bob's early years have grown in the crucible of this research and writing. *Discover Israel* and *The Jewishness of Jesus* have been his focus of study for the past five decades.

Fifty Years of Influences on *Discover Israel*

APPRECIATION and CREDITS

Georgetown College, Kentucky

Since my early college experiences, I have been a committed student of our Lord—His life, His ministry and His People. Many seed thoughts sown in my early years have grown in the crucible of my research and writing. The subject matter covered in Discover Israel and the Jewishness of Jesus has become my "favorite study" across the past five decades.

My initial inspiration came from our experiences of living in Israel in 1959-60. My learning experience related to Israel and Jesus' Jewishness has been fleshed out by over 50 years of diligent research and study. I have learned about Israel firsthand, having led 38 study tours to The Land of the Bible. For nearly 30 years I have taught Discover Israel Seminars in colleges, seminaries and churches. However, I confess that I am still just a "student of God's Word"... no more than that. The more I study, the more I wonder how "experts" and "scholars" get such titles. How does that happen? Who makes the determination? I choose to remain a *"disciple"* (student/learner) of our Lord.

It is with deep regret that I am unable to fully document all the influencing sources. I never expected to write these books. They simply grew in my heart and mind, and were penned out of that overflow. My life has been greatly influenced by many wonderful Bible teachers, from my college years until today. These include rabbis, pastors, professors and well-educated Israeli guides. Across the years we have discussed, dialogued, argued, researched and studied together. Our subjects have been God, Israel, the Jewish culture and the Word of God.

Hill Chapel
Georgetown College

Dr. H. Leo Eddleman influenced me to choose **Georgetown College**, in the heart of Kentucky's Bluegrass, for my under-graduate work. **Dr. George Redding**, professor and head of Georgetown's Bible Department, first whetted my appetite for the study of God's Land, His people, and Jesus' Jewish culture. I will never forget Dr. Redding's passionate teaching in his Bible Introduction course. God used his teaching, and his personal photographs of Israel, to pull my heartstrings toward God's Land.

Dr. George Harrison, Georgetown Bible Professor, worked hard to make me proficient in Hebrew, but sadly, his endeavor ended up as a lost cause. Today, however, I appreciate even more deeply his teaching and insights into the Hebrew language and culture.

Since Dr. Eddleman had served in Nazareth as a Southern Baptist Missionary (before becoming president at Georgetown), he arranged for Barb and me to spend a year in Israel during 1959-60, teaching at the **Kefar ha Baptistim** (Baptist Orphanage). We are indebted to him for our first son, Randy being born in Israel as a *sabra*. A *sabra* is the fruit of the prickly pear, representing a native born Israeli—*sweet on the inside but prickly on the outside.* Our *sabra* was born in Nazareth, hence he is also a *Nazarene.*

Soon after Barb and I returned from Israel, I attended **New Orleans Baptist Seminary**, 1961-64. Interestingly, during that period, our friend Dr. Eddleman served as president.

New Orleans Baptist Theological Seminary

Dr. Bob Lindsay
Missionary, translator and author

Bayou Baptist Church, Slidell LA

Highland Baptist Church, Waco TX

Prairie Creek Baptist Church, Plano TX

Two pastors greatly influenced my life in those days. The first was my mentor during college, **Dr. Fred Moffatt**, with whom I served as Minister of Education at **First Baptist Church** of Paris, Kentucky from 1957 until 1959 (prior to us going to Israel).

Then, after graduating from **New Orleans Seminary**, **Dr. Landrum Leavell** invited me to join him in ministry at **First Baptist Church** in Wichita Falls, Texas. I served with him as his Associate Pastor from 1964 until 1967. I look back fondly on the times of Bible discussions and dialogue with these two pastor-mentors. I am grateful to God for my training under these two godly pastors.

Dr. Bob Lindsay, our long-time friend and veteran missionary in Israel, was an exceptional Hebrew scholar. He spent much of his mission ministry as pastor of **Narkis St. Baptist Church** in Jerusalem. Weekly, he studied and researched with **Dr. David Flusser**, an Orthodox Jew and Professor of Early Christianity at the **Hebrew University** in Jerusalem. Dr. Flusser advised and collaborated with Dr. Lindsay, as Bob translated the Greek New Testament into modern Israeli Hebrew.

Dr. Lindsay organized and led **The Jerusalem School**, a symposium of several outstanding Christian scholars in Jerusalem. Their early studies focused on New Testament interpretation and the application of Jesus' Hebrew language to His life and ministry.

Later, I delved into publications by **Dr. Roy Blizzard**, Chairman of the Hebrew Department at the **University of Texas**. His teachings helped me tie up many "loose ends" regarding Jewish culture.

I must give credit and praise to the churches where I have served across the years. The deacons, church leaders and individuals in the pews all had an impact on my thoughts. Perhaps I need to ask their forgiveness for "testing the water" with several early concepts and interpretations. These wonderful friends have helped to purify many of the concepts presented in both ***Discover*** and ***Jewishness***.

Perhaps it is fortunate that my earliest pastorate at **Bayou Baptist Church** in Slidell LA was spared this early "persecution". I started teaching my earliest seminars on Israel at **First Baptist Church, Wichita Falls**, TX. Those Sunday evening studies laid the foundation for ***Discover Israel.***

Highland Baptist Church in Waco, Texas was a marvelous congregation, and an incredible joy, as we ministered to the community and the **Baylor University** students. Often, the Sunday evening college dialogue in our home would continue until midnight. Most Sunday evenings we would have 150-200 Baylor students in our home for food and dialogue. Through the **Fellowship of Christian Athletes** we shared Jesus from the football field to the basketball court. As a result of my work with the FCA, I became the **Chaplain of the Baylor Bears.** What a wonderful time in my life! In 1970, Highland Baptist encouraged me to return to New Orleans Seminary to complete my Master of Theology degree.

First Baptist Church in Hobbs, N.M. called me as pastor early in 1973. It was my privilege to serve there for two years. In Hobbs and Waco we preached and taught about the ***Jewish Jesus***. While in Hobbs, I took my first study tour to Israel.

The Church buildings (left) were built while Bob was pastor.

Randy Ross, author of Remarkable-thebook.com

Prairie Creek Baptist Church in Plano Texas called me as pastor in October of 1975. This became my pastorate for the next 29 years. Here, our children completed elementary and high school prior to attending Baylor University. Prairie Creek was a marvelous church in which to raise our family. The educational level and openness of our people led to challenging, exciting and stimulating dialogue. Prairie Creek encouraged me to host study tours to Israel and teach the Discover Israel Seminars in earnest. This in turn led to the writing of both ***Discover Israel*** and ***The Jewishness of Jesus***. I am so grateful for the wonderful people at Prairie Creek for their love and encouragement. I deeply thank them for being my *sounding board* for many ideas related to our publications. What a wonderful journey together!

I stepped down from the Prairie Creek pulpit in August of 2004 to "retire" and lead mission activity in the Yucatan of Mexico, Cuba, Romania, Bulgaria, Poland and Alaska. In my spare time, I have written and developed our seminars on ***The Jewishness of Jesus*** for colleges and seminaries. My ***Jewishness*** Power Point outlines have paved the way for the present two volume text. We have rejoiced to see the life changes of those who have walked with the *Jewish Jesus* and fallen deeper in love with Him—as they interpret His life through His Jewish roots and background.

The influences on my life and ***Discover Israel*** have been many, and have been scattered across more than half a century. My greatest encourager has been my wonderful wife and helpmate **Barbara Ross**. We have known and loved each other for over 60 years (married for 56 years, as of 2014). I am so grateful to God for Barbara, His precious and special gift to me.

"Better looking than my brother – My humble and accurate opinion" – Mike Ross

Randy Ross, our oldest son and "sabra", was born a *"Nazarene"*. He is an avid student of God's Word and His Land. Randy has returned to Israel five times. After pastoring for over 20 years, he has recently co-authored a bestseller, ***Remarkable***. Randy has been a valuable source of suggestions and recommendations related to the topics of Israel and the Jewish culture.

Mike Ross, our second son *(our New Orleans Cajun)* and his family are very involved in Christian music, mission activities and world-wide outreach. Mike serves on our ministry board.

Saturday mornings in Waco TX – 1971

Terri Pope and **Sherri Rapp**, our wonderful *Texas twins,* are involved, along with their families, in mission work in the US and abroad. Their work with the handicapped, the deaf and persons in need is a major part of their ministry.

All four of our children have blessed us by choosing **wonderful mates.** They have further blessed us with **10 incredible grandchildren**. Most of them are involved in church ministries and missions. Life is exciting!

Terri & Sherri – 1970

Yehuda and **Tzippy Hecht** from **Jerusalem, Israel**, are wonderful Jewish cheerleaders for our writing, teaching and ministry. Yehuda has been our tour guide for over 27 years. Our tour lectures are a *tag team effort*, both on the bus and at Biblical sites. Yehuda and I have mentored each other across all these years. We research, dialogue, discuss, debate and argue (Jewish d'rash) as we seek God's Truth in preparation for our teaching. No person challenges me more than my dear friend Yehuda. I am deeply grateful for his sharing and insights, especially in d'rash.

Dr. Harlan Capps presented Bob Ross with a doctorate in Jewish studies.

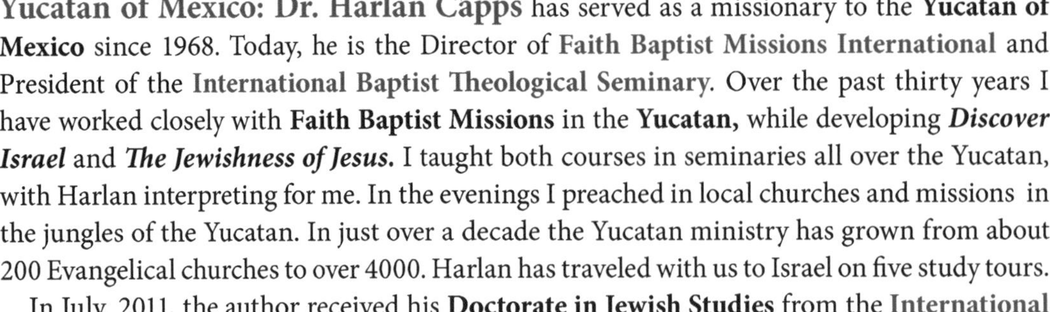

Yucatan of Mexico: Dr. Harlan Capps has served as a missionary to the **Yucatan of Mexico** since 1968. Today, he is the Director of **Faith Baptist Missions International** and President of the **International Baptist Theological Seminary**. Over the past thirty years I have worked closely with **Faith Baptist Missions** in the **Yucatan,** while developing ***Discover Israel*** and ***The Jewishness of Jesus.*** I taught both courses in seminaries all over the Yucatan, with Harlan interpreting for me. In the evenings I preached in local churches and missions in the jungles of the Yucatan. In just over a decade the Yucatan ministry has grown from about 200 Evangelical churches to over 4000. Harlan has traveled with us to Israel on five study tours.

In July, 2011, the author received his **Doctorate in Jewish Studies** from the **International Baptist Theological Seminary**.

Cuba: In the past decade our ministry has worked with **Miguel Romero**, our "Lead" in Cuba, with outreach and training for pastors and missionaries touching all 13 provinces of Cuba, and involving over 300 churches and missions. Today we link with Romero in training Cuban foreign missionaries for mission work in Latin America, South America, Africa and other parts of the world.

Bob Ross teaches the *Jewishness of Jesus* seminar in Havana, Cuba.

We were involved in the early stages of the **Cuban Evangelical Seminary**, led by **President Miguel Gonzales**. Our seminar on ***The Jewishness of Jesus*** has been taught to pastors and church leaders all over the island. In 2011 this Seminary honored me with a second doctorate.

Encouragers: When I resigned the Prairie Creek pulpit to continue mission activities, study tours to Israel, writing and publishing, a faithful group of prayer warriors and financial supporters joined us in ministry. Without these God given individuals we could not have fulfilled our calling. They are; **Ron Skaggs, Chuck Flint, Chuck Stephenson, Juan Cano, Brent Markham, Roger Hatton, Abe Azoulay, Larry Riordan, John Blake, Blaine Smith, David Knoles, Alan Nelson, Justo Gonzales, Roger Hudgins, Kenneth Ross,** and **Abe Sharp**. Many others have joined these supporters of our ministries and publications.

Carson-Myre Foundation in Paducah, KY is a strong supporter of our **Jewishness of Jesus** project. We are grateful to God for His provision through this benevolent foundation.

David Pickett at the Cove of the Parables

David Pickett is a strong supporter of our Israel ministry. His personal ministry, **Leaves of Gold**, reaches thousands of pastors and lay leaders each month in the Third World with sermon outlines, which are developed into sermons for thousands of churches throughout the world. David serves on our Board, and assists our ministry with water purification and mission outreach. **www.leavesofgold.com**

Eric Robishaw interned with us while he was at *Dallas Theological Seminary*. He too hopes to assist with our future tours. Eric and his family spent six months in Jerusalem in personal study.

Jerry R. Aris has assisted me on five study tours to Israel, and has advised and assisted in rewriting segments of the publications. Jerry plans to lead future tours and assist in our other ministries following the completion of his Th.M. at ***Dallas Theological Seminary.***

Gary Crossland, author of the *Merged Gospels*

Dr. Gary Crossland, author of the ***Merged Gospels,*** is a friend and a co-laborer with our publications. He has handled all of the video editing and website development for ***The Jewishness of Jesus.*** His ***Merged Gospels*** is a must for any serious student of the Gospels.

Bill Cadenhead has now been on six study tours, and has spent time in Israel traveling and researching after these tours with Yehuda Hecht and me. Bill helps our ministry with administration, and has assisted me with research concerning the timing of events during ***Jesus' "Passion Week".***

Proof-readers for these publications have been: **Rosemary Lee** (my secretary for 25 years) and **Nelda Sifford**, (Prairie Creek's church secretary and a Board member). Other proof readers have been: **Nita Cadenhead**- ***Discover Israel***, her daughter, **Laura Stewart** – on our ***Jewishness*** project, **Jerry R. Aris** and **Anne Alexander** – on ***Discover Israel*** and ***The Jewishness of Jesus.***

Craig G. Lundie – Creative Director at Adquest Creative

Craig G. Lundie has been involved since the beginning. He has directed all the creative and art production for ***Discover Israel*** and ***The Jewishness of Jesus.*** He has also designed and developed the logo branding, website, graphic design, digital imaging, illustrations and publication production for **Bob C. Ross Ministries**, ***Discover Israel*** and the ***The Jewishness of Jesus*** **Ministries.** Craig is the President and Creative Director at **Adquest Creative**, an advertising, graphic & web design agency. **www.adquest-creative.com**

PUBLICATION THOUGHTS

If I have quoted any writer or lecturer and failed to give proper credit, it is not intentional. I must confess, passing of time and the flow of information from so many different sources has made it impossible to accurately reference all material from which this book has grown. My heart's intent is to give proper credit to all contributors, but the way this publication has evolved, that has become impossible.

I am indebted to **Dr. Stephen Hedges**, director, professor and curriculum writer for the **Evangelical Seminary in Sofia, Bulgaria** (under the umbrella of the **United Church of God**). When I taught in Sofia in 2005, Stephen and I spent two weeks sharing about ***Jesus' Jewishness***. Because of his Jewish theological background, I invited Stephen to critique every session of my seminar. We openly and frankly discussed our agreements and disagreements into the wee hours of the morning. It was d'rash at its finest.

Stephen Hedges has encouraged Bob Ross to write and publish ***Discover Israel*** and ***Jewishness of Jesus.*** Stephen has recently written ***Jesus, the Torah and Messianic Judaism.***

Stephen encouraged me to write from the crucible of my studies, without being overly concerned about the lack of documentation for my work. He pointed out that my purpose was not to write a doctoral dissertation, but a study guide for the average Jew or Christian. Realizing that I could never supply all of the source documentation, I almost decided *not* to write ***Discover Israel*** or ***The Jewishness of Jesus***. If these studies bless you, thank my friend Stephen Hedges.

I have come to understand that most Jewish scholars and rabbis across the ages have recognized God as the Source of all knowledge, and have given that credit to Him. He is the One from whom all knowledge comes.

Jewish sages immersed their minds and hearts in the study of God's Word, and today they

Jewish rabbi teaches a young boy the Torah

are involved in intense Scriptural studies and Beit Midrash (d'rash/dialogue). Involving their students and peers, they ask questions and seek answers related to the Scriptures and context. Their approach is not to protect, or give men credit for any knowledge that God revealed or entrusted to them. Thus, the whole body of knowledge, and revealed truth, *belongs to God and to Him alone.* God created the mind of man and then revealed to him any knowledge he might possess.

Therefore, *God is the owner of all knowledge.* It all belongs to Him! Thus, copyrighting and documenting everything we publish seems a bit foolish. It is not our knowledge to copyright in the first place—it is on loan, and we are just passing through. We are to be good stewards of what God has loaned to us.

When we consider what God has revealed... it is God who should have the *copyright* on every book written, and it is not man's to claim. Anything we can add to the body of Jewish and Christian knowledge and literature is because God has entrusted it to us. His revelations have been given to us through life experiences, godly professors, teachers, peers, fellow students of God's Word and many other influences.

Therefore, to quote Stephen Hedges, "copyright ought to mean your right to copy". Now *copyright* is a fairly recent development, designed to prevent unscrupulous theft of printed and electronic materials. Unfortunately, in our unscrupulous society and publishing world, copyrighting has become a necessity. One can't publish without a *legal copyright.*

With all this said, my heart's desire is that you use what I share with you on these pages to bring Glory to God and advance of His Kingdom. My reason for this *copyright* on ***Discover Israel*** is to prevent unscrupulous use and misquotes of these materials.

To God Be the Glory!

Thank you for allowing me to be so informal as I have shared about those who are dear to my heart, and have influenced this book.

Thank you for studying Discover Israel with us.
We hope you have enjoyed the *"Tour"*

Panorama of Haifa and the bay, viewed from Mount Carmel

Appreciation and Credits Resources

Our author has used materials from the following Sources

THE BIBLE
The Living Word of God

Yehuda Hecht teaching a tour group

Yehuda Hecht, Israeli Guide - A vital influence

For the last 30 years Bob and his dear friend Yehuda (Jewish Scholar and Guide) have studied and traveled the length and breadth of The Land. They have led over 35 intensive Study Tours of Israel, and shared deeply the truths from God's Word.

Yehuda majored in New Testament studies at the Hebrew University and minored in the Crusades. His unique Jewish perspective, deep knowledge of his language and Land, and his experiences relating to his native Jerusalem all bring an irreplaceable viewpoint to our study tours. His firsthand knowledge of the conflicts and wars between Israel and her Arab neighbors has given every tour a unique perspective on the Middle East. Bob and Yehuda have united as partners, bringing together over 100 years of research and study to their tours and this book.

Dr. Gary Crossland, author of *The Merged Gospels*

The Merged Gospels by Gary Crossland

The Merged Gospels is a must for every student of the Gospels. Gary has accurately translated all four Gospels from the Greek, and merged them into *one* chronological and flowing narrative. All duplicated materials have been removed. It is far more than just another *harmony* of the Gospels, with every recorded word and event accurately presented. This book will become your number one study tool for the Gospels.

Contact **mergedgospels.com** to order your copy. You are in for a thrilling adventure.

Zev Vilnay's Publications

When all else fails (for discovering detailed information on Israel), go to ***The Guide To Israel*** by **Zev Vilnay**. It was first published in 1955, and by 1977 was in its 19th edition. Search for it; new or used, it will be worth the effort.

Zev Vilnay's The Guide to Israel

Roy Kreider – Sojourners in the Sacred Land

This is an outstanding guide book to Biblical events where they occurred. Roy was a dear friend and fellow student with us in Israel (1959-1960). This booklet may still be available in Israeli bookstores, or possibly as a "used" book. This book was published by Amir Publications of Tel Aviv.

Lamar C. Berrett – Discovering the World of the Bible

This book was first published in 1979 by Thomas Nelson of Nashville, TN. The book is an outstanding guide to the Middle East and a must for the library of any serious student on Israel. The last three books can be found on Amazon (as of 2014).

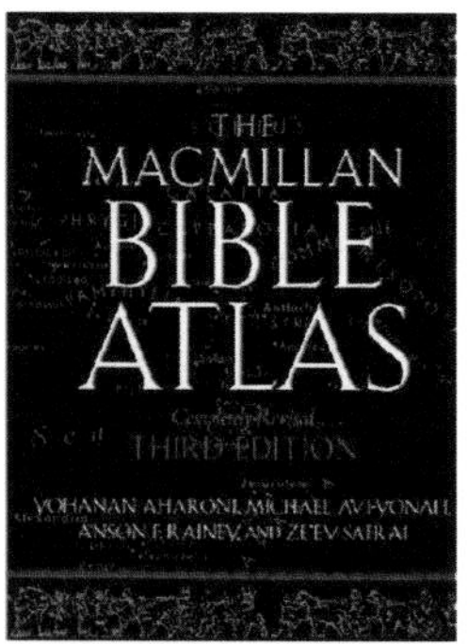

The Macmillan Bible Atlas
by Aharoni, Avi-Yonah, Rainey and Safrai

The Macmillan Bible Atlas is outstanding, and a "must" for any serious Bible Student.

Lance Lambert's Books on Middle East Studies

Lance writes on Israel's history and wars. He has carefully documented the personal experiences of many of those directly involved, and in each book he focuses on God's influence and action. We have related a few of these thrilling accounts in this manual. I encourage you to pick up every book you can find by Lance.

Statue from MGM's Jewish village in the *Exodus*. Arab Cana across valley.

Martin Gilbert – Historical Atlas Studies

Martin maps the development of the Jewish People and Israel across their years of history.

Suggested Videos and Movies on Israel

Exodus, based on the book by Leon Uris • ***Masada*** • ***Cast a Giant Shadow*** • ***Golda*** • ***Yentle*** ***Raid on Entebbe*** • ***Sword of Gideon*** • ***Saddat*** • ***Not Without My Daughter***

REMARKABLE – The Book
A Leadership Parable by Dr. Randy Ross & David Salyers

Randy is a continuing inspiration and wise advisor to Bob. Randy was born in Nazareth when Bob & Barb took their first trip to Israel. Since then, he has returned to his birthplace on five occasions. Prior to becoming an inspirational coach, Randy served as a pastor or associate pastor for over 25 years.

Remarkable means notably or conspicuously unusual; extraordinary; worthy of notice or attention. The ideas explored in this book have come from a lifetime of observing some extraordinary people and organizations as they live out their conspicuously unusual ideas, producing uncommon results. The effect is that those who work for and those who benefit from these people and organizations find themselves with an irrepressible desire to "remark about them!" What is it that these folks know that others seemingly do not? How does their view of the world lead them to think and behave differently than others? When faced with the same opportunities and challenges, how are their choices different... and why?

Discover and apply the principles contained within *Remarkable–the Book* and you too, can become Remarkable! www.remarkable-thebook.com

Remarkable-the book

A Word from Author Bob Ross

About *DISCOVER ISRAEL*

"***Discover Israel*** *is the result of nearly five decades of study and preparation. I have been influenced by hundreds of sources, and many cannot now be referenced. The information in this book has become a part of my life. Feel free to use* ***Discover Israel*** *for teaching, preaching or any related ministries".*

Have a Blessed "Journey" to Israel!

SATELITE MAP of ISRAEL and MIDDLE EAST
LEBANON
SYRIA
Mediterranean
Sea
WEST
BANK
ISRAEL
JORDAN
GAZA
EGYPT–SINAI
SAUDI ARABIA

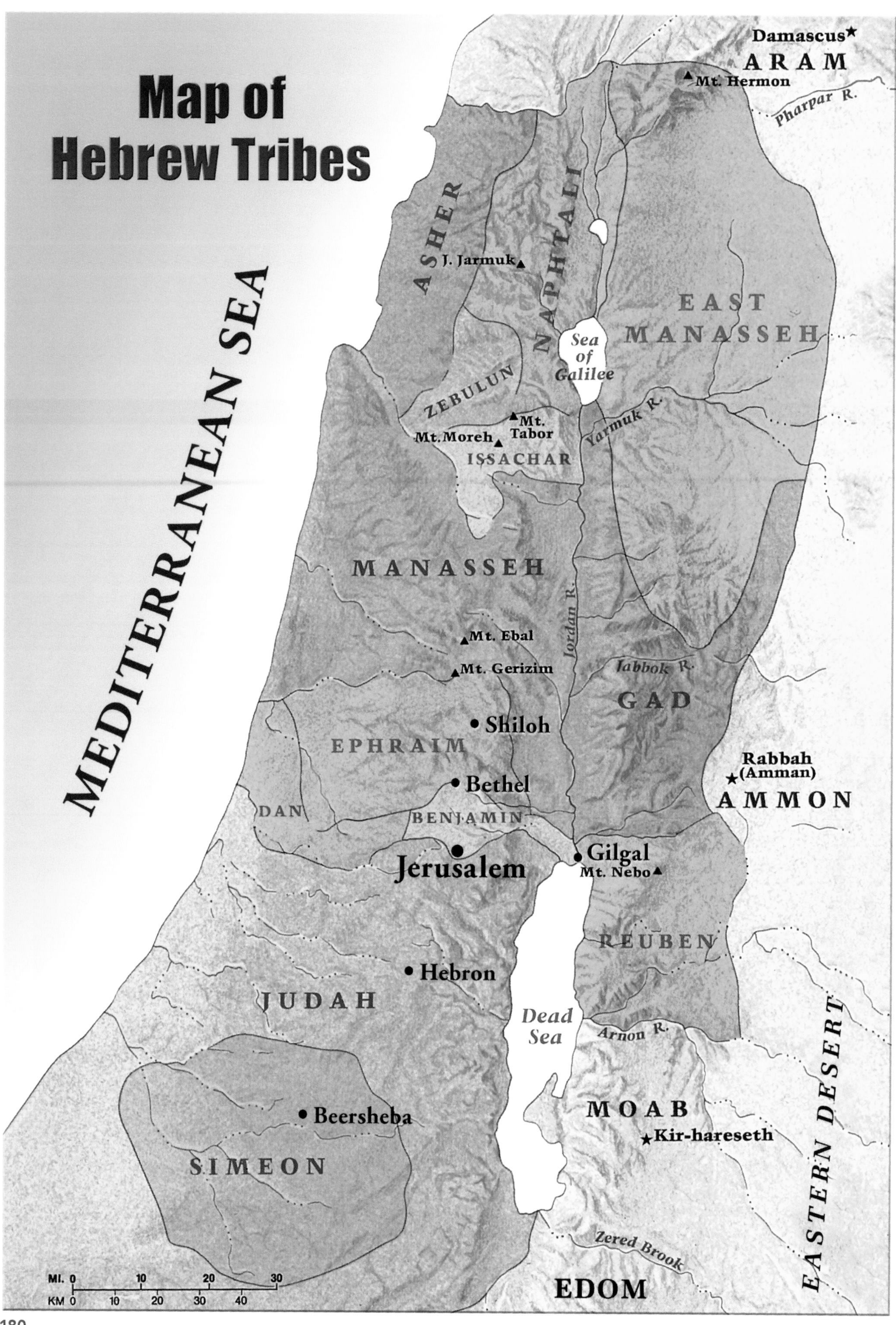

Map of Hebrew Tribes
MEDITERRANEAN SEA
Damascus
ARAM
Mt. Hermon
Pharpar R.
ASHER
NAPHTALI
J. Jarmuk
EAST MANASSEH
Sea of Galilee
ZEBULUN
Mt. Tabor
Mt. Moreh
ISSACHAR
Yarmuk R.
MANASSEH
Jordan R.
Mt. Ebal
Mt. Gerizim
Jabbok R.
GAD
Shiloh
EPHRAIM
Bethel
Rabbah (Amman)
AMMON
DAN
BENJAMIN
Jerusalem
Gilgal
Mt. Nebo
REUBEN
Hebron
JUDAH
Dead Sea
Arnon R.
EASTERN DESERT
MOAB
Beersheba
Kir-hareseth
SIMEON
Zered Brook
EDOM
MI. 0 10 20 30
KM 0 10 20 30 40

KINGDOM OF DAVID & SOLOMAN
Aleppo
Euphrates River
Orontes R.
HAMATH
Cyprus
Kadesh on the Orontes
Mediterranean Sea
PHOENICIA
Litani R.
Sidon
Damascus
Tyre
Dan
Hazor
Acco
Ramoth-gilead
Megiddo
Beth-shan
Jordan R.
Shechem
Joppa
Rabbah (Amman)
Gezer
PHILISTIA
Gibeah
Ashdod
Jerusalem
Gath
Gaza
Dead Sea
Beersheba
EASTERN DESERT
W. el-Arish
Brook of Egypt
Kadesh-barnea
Petra
SINAI
Ezion-geber
Gulf of Aqaba
In Genesis Chapter 2: a river flowed from the Garden of Eden and formed four rivers, two mentioned were the Euphrates and the Tigris.
Gen.15:18 God promised Abram, *"to your descendants I have given this Land from the River (Brook) of Egypt as far as the great river, the River Euphrates."*
To Moses in Deut. 1:7, the border of the Euphrates River was included in God's promises concerning His Land.
To Joshua in 1:4, God renewed His promise concerning the Euphrates River being the border of Israel.
For these promises to be fulfilled in the *"end days"*, Israel will come to control nearly all of Jordan, Gaza, most of Lebanon and all of Syria. The more the Arab nations attack Israel, the more land God gives to His People, Israel.
boundary of Solomon's Kingdom
Saul's Kingdom
territory conquered by David
area effectively under Solomon's economic control (1 Kgs 4:24)
MI 0 50 100
KM 0 50 100 150

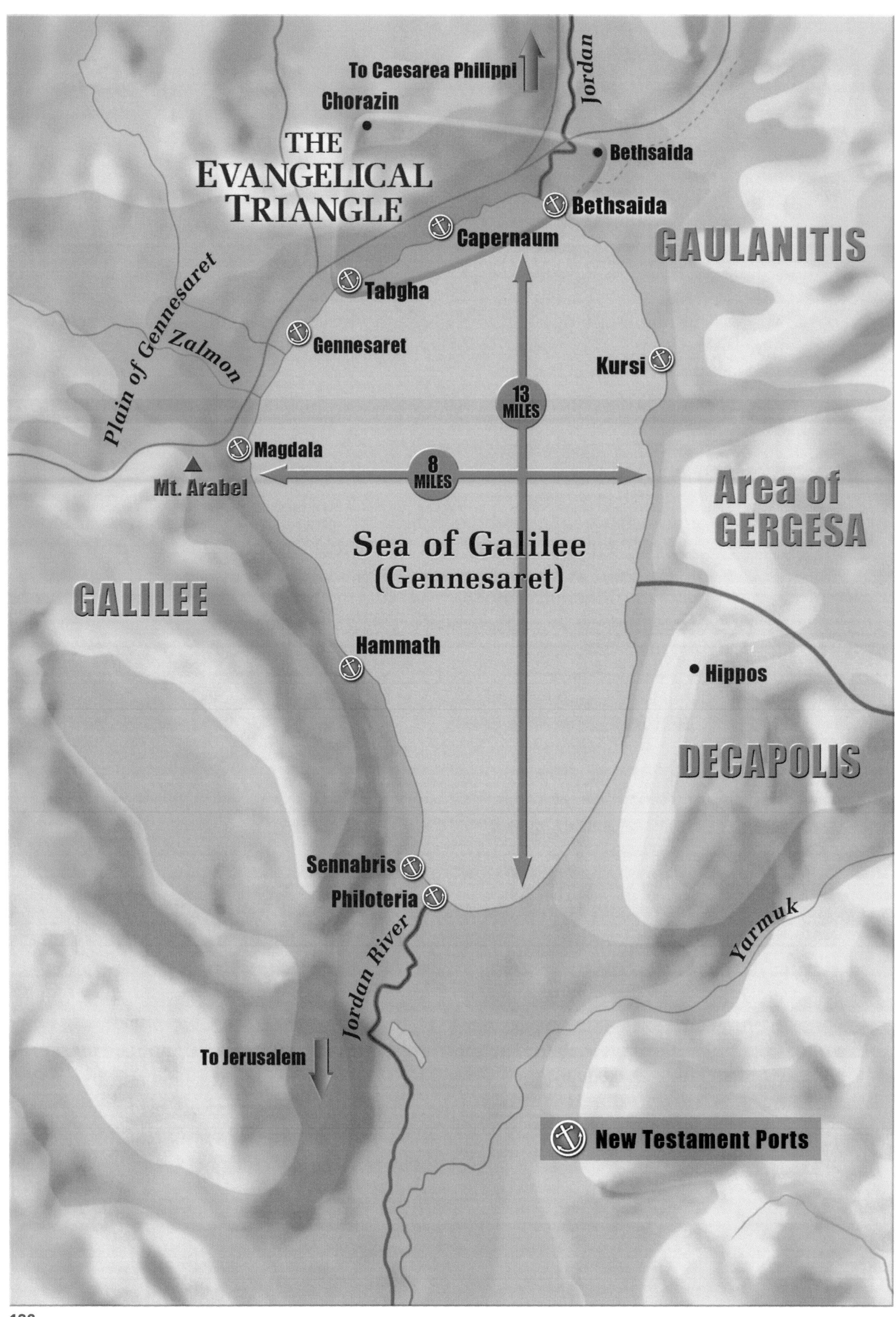

To Caesarea Philippi
Jordan
Chorazin
THE EVANGELICAL TRIANGLE
Bethsaida
Bethsaida
Capernaum
GAULANITIS
Plain of Gennesaret
Tabgha
Zalmon
Gennesaret
Kursi
13 MILES
Magdala
8 MILES
Mt. Arabel
Area of GERGESA
Sea of Galilee (Gennesaret)
GALILEE
Hammath
Hippos
DECAPOLIS
Sennabris
Philoteria
Jordan River
Yarmuk
To Jerusalem
New Testament Ports

HERODIAN DYNASTY

Herod the Great
37-4 BC

- King of Judea, Galilee, Samaria, Iturea and Traconitis
- Built Caesarea Maritina, the Herodian Temple & Masada

Herod Philip
4BC-AD34

- Tetrarch of Iturea Trachonitus and Gaulanitus
- Built Caesarea Philippi (Luke. 3:1)

Archelaus
4BC-AD6

- Governor of Judea, Idumea and Samaria
-Ruling when Jesus was "dedicated" in the Temple (Matt. 2:22-23, Luke 2:21-39)
- He was the reason Joseph and Mary settled in Nazareth (Luke 2:39)
- Deposed by Romans

Herod Antipas
4BC-AD39

- Tetrarch of Galilee & Perea
- Built the city of Tiberias
- Married his brother's wife
- Put John the Baptist to death
- Sent Jesus back to Pilate (Mark 6:14-29, Luke 3:1, 13:31-35, 23:7-12)

Herod Agrippa I
AD37-44

- King of All the Land
- Killed James, the brother of John. Imprisoned Peter (Acts 12:1-19)
- Struck down by God at Caesarea (Acts 12:1-24)

Herod Agrippa II
AD48-70

- King of Chalcis and Northern Territory
- Heard Paul's defense at Caesarea (Acts 25:13-26 – 26:32)

Key to Titles

King

 Tetrarch

 Governor

Observed Miracles from Our Lord's Ministry

Jesus' Miracles	Location	Matthew	Mark	Luke	John	Merged Gospels*
Changed Water into Wine	Cana of Galilee				2:1-11	25
Healed Nobleman's Son	Capernaum				4:46-54	32
Nets Filled with Fish	Sea of Galilee	4:18-22	1:16-20	5:1-11		40
Healed Man with Demonic Spirit	Capernaum		1:21-28	4:31-37		36
Healed Peter's Mother-in-Law	Capernaum	8:14-17	1:29-34	4:38-41		37
Healed a Leper Near	Capernaum	8:2-4	1:40-45	5:12-16		42
Healed a Paralytic	Capernaum	9:1-8	2:1-12	5:17-26		43
Healed a Lame Man	Jerusalem				5:1-47	95
Healed Man with a Withered Hand	Capernaum Synagogue	12:9-14	3:1-6	6:6-11		51
Healed Centurion's Servant	Capernaum	8:5-13		7:1-10		80
Raised Widow's Son from the Dead	Nain on Mt. Moreh			7:11-17		135
Healed a Demoniac, Blind, Dumb and	Village in Galilee	12:22-37				151
Quieted the Storm or Tsunami	Sea of Galilee	8:18, 23	4:35-41	8:22-25		93
Healed Demoniac in Gentile Area	Gerasa, "Other Side"	8:28-34	5:1-20	8:26-39		94
Healed Woman Who Touched His Talit	Capernaum	9:20-22	5:25-34	8:41-48		48
Raised Jairus' Daughter to Life	Capernaum	9:18-19	5:22-24	8:41,49f.		49
Healed Two Blind Men Near	Capernaum	9:27-31				96
Healed a Dumb Man with a Demon	Near Capernaum	9:32-34				97
Fed 5,000 Men, Women and Children	Desert near Bethsaida	14:13-21	6:30-44	9:10-17	6:1-13	101
Walked on the Stormy Sea, with Peter	Sea of Galilee	14:24-33	6:45-52		6:16-21	102
Healed Syro-Phoenician's Daughter	Gentile – Tyre & Sidon	15:21-28	7:24-30			108
Healed a Deaf and Dumb Man	Bethsiada		7:31-37			109
Healed the Lame, Blind, Dumb & Maimed	Bethsaida Area	15:30-31				109
Fed 4,000 Men Plus Women & Children	Near Bethsaida	15:32-38	8:1-9			110
Healed Blind Man	Bethsaida	16:5-12	8:13-26			112
Healed Boy with Demon	Caesarea Philippi	17:14-20	9:14-29	9:37-43		119
Fish w/ Temple Tax Shekel in It's Mouth	Capernaum	17:24-27				123
Jesus Is Transfigured	Mt. Hermon	17:1-8	9:2-10	9:28-36		117
Healed Man Born Blind at Pool of Siloam	Jerusalem				9:1-41	146
Healed Crippled Woman	Judean Synagogue			13:10-21		166
Healed Man with Dropsy on the Sabbath	Perea at Jordan River			13:22-35		177
Raised Lazarus from the Dead	Bethany				11:1-44	149
Healed Ten Lepers	Samaria or Galilee			17:11-37		199
Healed Blind Bartimaeus, Two Blind Men	Jericho	20:29-34	10:46-52	18:35-43		213
Cleansed the Temple of Money Changers	Jerusalem Temple	21:12-13	11:15-18	19:45-48		220
Healed Malachus' Ear	Garden of Gethsemane			22:49-51		266
Jesus Arose from the Dead	Garden Tomb	28:1-8	16:1-11	24:1-12	20:3-18	289-291
Risen Lord Instructs Disciples Fish Catch	Sea of Galilee				21:1-14	297

Jesus Performed Many Other Miracles...

Miracles that healed ...	Villages & Countryside	4:23		5:15		41,42
Diseases, Sicknesses, Demoniacs,	Markets, Synagogues,			6:18-19,		
Epileptics, Paralytics, Blind, Evil spirits				7:21-22		
and the Dead Raised...	Capernaum	9:25	5:41			49
	Nain			7;11-17		81

"Many other thing Jesus did... if they were all written down, I suppose... the world itself would not contain the books..." John 21:25

*Gary Crossland's Merged Gospels faithfully translates each Gospel and merges them into one column. Gary numbers each event and teaching for easy reference. Order this study at www.mergedgospels.com.

Jesus' Recorded Parables

Jesus' Parables	Location	Matthew	Mark	Luke	John	Merged Gospels*
Destroy This Temple	Jerusalem				2:19-22	26
The Physician	Nazareth			4:23f		33
The Speck and Beam	Mt. Beatitudes	7:3-5		6:41-42		72
Blind Guide	Mt. Beatitudes			6:39-40		107,235
Wise and Foolish Builders	Mt. Beatitudes	7:24-27		6:47-49		79
Children in the Market Place	Galilee	11:16-17		7:31-32		83
Two Debtors	Galilee			7:41-43		84
Return of the Unclean Spirit	Galilee	12:43-45				152
Sower and the Seed	Sea of Galilee	13:3-23	4:3-25	8:5-18		87
Why Did Jesus Teach in Parables?	Sea of Galilee	13:10-16				88
Seed Growing by Itself	Sea of Galilee		4:26-29			90
Tares...	Sea of Galilee	13:24-30				167
...Jesus Explains the Parable of the Tares	Capernaum	13:36-43				171
Mustard Seed	Sea of Galilee	13:31-32	4:30-32			168
Leaven	Sea of Galilee	13:33-34	4:33-34			169
"Without a Parable Jesus Spoke Nothing"	Sea of Galilee	13:34-35				170
Hidden Treasure	Sea of Galilee	13:34f				170
Pearl of Great Price	Sea of Galilee	13:45-46				173
Net	Sea of Galilee	13:47-50				174
Treasures New and Old	Sea of Galilee	13:51-53				175
Corban	Capernaum		7:11-13			107
Unmerciful Servant	Capernaum	18:23-35				196
Good Shepherd	Jerusalem				10:1-21	147
Persistent Friend	Judea			11:5-13		139
Rich Fool	Judea			17:17-21		199
Waiting Servants	Judea			12:37-40		161
Wise Servant	Judea			12:41-48		161
Barren Fig Tree	Mt. of Olives			13:6-9		165
Seats at Banquet/Feast	Perea			14:7-11		180
Feast for the Poor	Perea			14:12-14		180
Great Supper	Perea			14:16-24		181
Tower and the King	Perea			14:28-33		182
Lost Sheep	Perea			15:3-7		183
Lost Coin	Perea			15:8-10		184
Lost Son	Perea			15:11-32		185
Unrighteous Steward	Perea			16:1-8		186
Rich Man and Lazarus	Perea			16:19-31		190
Unprofitable Servants	Perea			16:7-10		187
Persistent Widow	Perea			18:1-8		201
Pharisee and the Publican	Perea			18:9-14		202
Laborers in the Vineyard	Perea	20:1-16				207
Pounds	Perea			19:11-27		212
Two Sons and Wicked Husbandmen	Jerusalem Temple	21:28-32	11:1-9	20:9-17		223
Rejected Stone	Jerusalem Temple	21:42f	11:10f	20:17f		225
Marriage Feasts and Garments	Jerusalem Temple	22:1-14				226
Fig Tree and End Times	Mt. of Olives	24:32-33	13:28-29	21:29-31		238
Porter	Mt. of Olives		13:33-37			239
Master and the Thief	Mt. of Olives	24:43-47				161
Wise Servant and the Evil Servant	Mt. of Olives	24:48-51				161
Ten Virgins	Mt. of Olives	25:1-13				240
Talents	Mt. of Olives	25:14-30				241
Sheep and the Goats, Final Judgment	Mt. of Olives	25:31-46				242

*Gary Crossland's Merged Gospels faithfully translates each Gospel and merges them into one column. Gary numbers each event and teaching for easy reference. Order this study at www.mergedgospels.com.

"Word Pictures" Taught by Jesus... Most of His Illustrations Were Drawn from Galilee and the Sea of Galilee

- "Cathedra" (chief seat) in Synagogue
- "Husks" that the Swine Eat
- "The Other Side" Gentile Galilee
- Village Judges
- Anchors, Weights & Hooks
- Animal Falling in a Well or Ditch
- Anointing Oil and Oil for Healing
- Armed Robbery
- Bad Eye/Stingy
- Bad Religious Leaders
- Barley Loaves
- Beit Midrash/Dialogue
- Children in the Market Place
- City Set on a Hill Can't Be Hidden
- Clean and Unclean/Mikvas
- Craftsman with Wood & Stone
- Shepherd's Care & Dangers to the Flock
- Demon Possession
- Disciple's Commitment
- Leaven in the Dough
- Eggs and Scorpions
- Family Disputes
- Fish and Snakes
- Fishing Boats, Care of Nets
- Fishing Methods
- Fishing Nets: Drag or Casting
- Forced Labor & Slavery
- Forgiveness in Action
- Foxes and Their Dens/Holes
- Funeral Practices
- Celebration...Going "Up to Jerusalem"
- Good & Useless Salt
- Kosher and Non-Kosher Fish
- Good and Bad Fruit Trees
- Good and Bad Managers
- Harvesting...Grain, Vine or Fruit
- Hens and her Chicks
- Hidden Treasure
- Highway Robbers
- Hospitality
- House Built on a Rock/Sand
- Jewish Feasts
- Jewish Torah & Tanakh
- Labor and Heavy Burdens
- Leavened & Unleavened Bread
- Lepers
- Lilies of the Field
- Lost Coin
- Marked Graves (Whitewashed)
- Mending & Drying Nets
- Military Personnel and Actions
- Millstones (Village and Home Stones)
- Mud and Thatch Roof
- Mustard Seed & Mature Mustard Plants
- Narrow Gate and Narrow Path
- Olives, Presses, and Oil
- A Steward Pays His Laborers Their Dues
- Pearl of Great Price
- Plowing and Planting
- Pruning Grape Vines
- Rabbis: Training & Ministry
- Reed Shaken in the Wind
- Rich and Poor
- Sawdust in the Eye
- Scribes and Scrolls
- Shepherd and His Sheep
- Sign from Heaven (God)
- Slave's Duty
- Small Fish (Sardines)
- Sparrows, Birds of the Air, & Their Nests
- Storms at Sea
- References to a Cross
- Tallit/Prayer & Prayer Shawl
- Tax Collecting and Collectors
- Thorns of the Field
- Tithe of Garden Herbs
- References to Horses, Camels & Donkeys
- Treasures
- Types of Soil – Old and New
- An Unjust Steward
- Village Ovens or Furnaces
- Washing Hands before Meals
- Weather Forecasting
- Wedding Traditions & Appropriate Dress
- Wheat and Tares
- Wine and Wineskins
- Large & Small Harvests
- References to the Language of Hebrew...

JERUSALEM
Chronological Events of Jesus' Last Week
April 29 AD

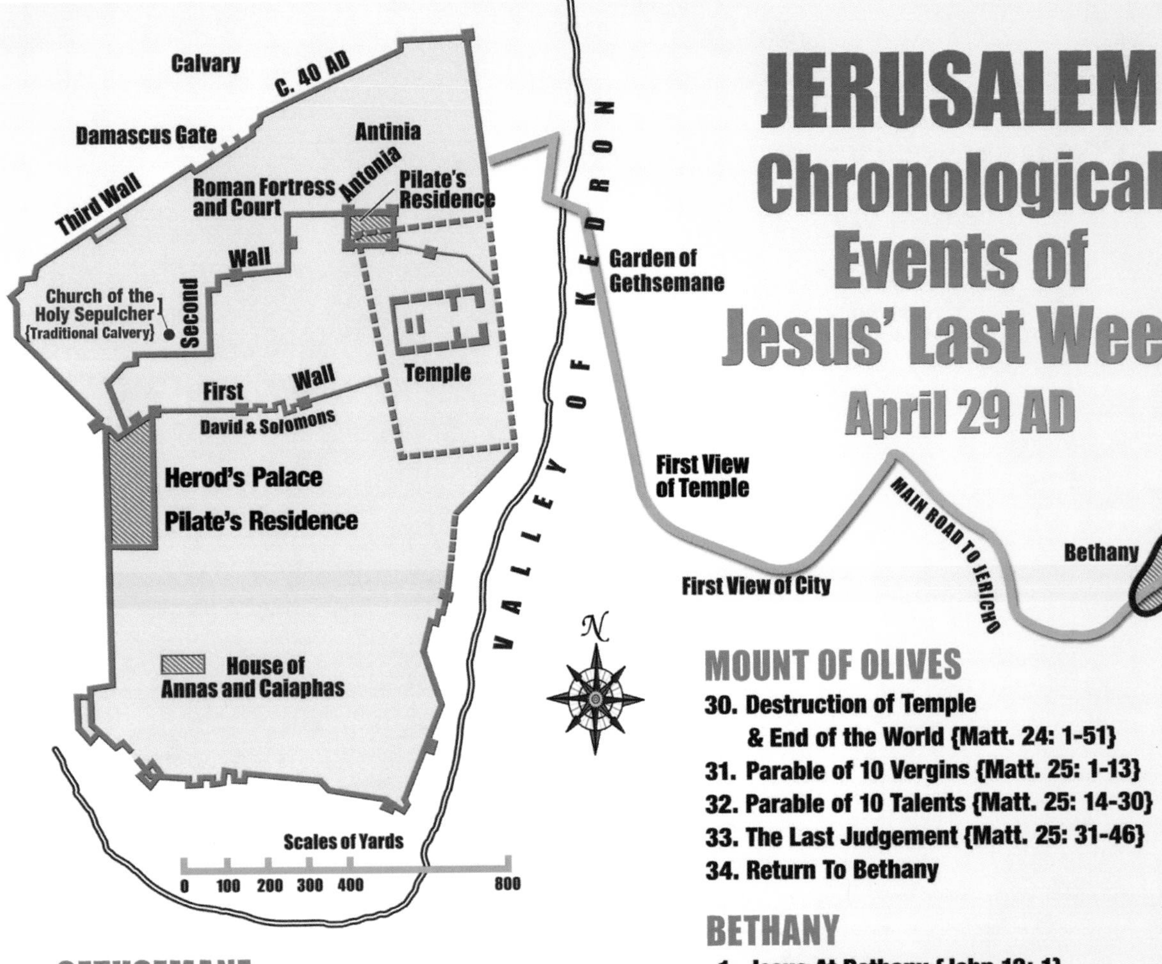

GETHSEMANE

43. Agony {Matt. 26: 36-46}
44. Betrayal {Matt. 26: 47-50}
45. Arrest {Matt. 26: 50-56}

JERUSALEM

5. Triumphal Entry {Mark 11: 8-9}
6. Visited Temple {Mark 11: 11}
7. Returned to Bethany {Mark 11: 11}
11. Cleansed Temple {Mark 11: 15-19}
12. Return to Bethany {Matt. 21: 17}
16. Authority Questioned {Matt. 21: 23-27}
17. Parable of Two Sons {Matt. 21: 28-32}
18. Parable of the Wicked Husbandman {Matt. 21: 33-46}
19. Parable of Marriage of King's Son {Matt. 22: 1-14}
20. Question About Tribute {Matt. 22: 15-22}
21. Question About Resurrection {Matt. 22: 22-23}
22. Question About Great Commandment {Matt. 22: 34-40}
23. Question About Christ {Matt. 22: 41-46}
24. Condemnation of Scribes & Pharesees {Matt. 23: 1-36}
25. Lament Over Jerusalem {Matt. 23: 37-39}
26. Widow's Mite {Mark. 12: 41-44}
27. Greeks Seek Jesus {John 12: 20}
28. Discourse On Light of the World {John 12: 20-50}
29. Consultation of Rulers {Luke 22: 1-6}
38. Pascal Supper {Luke 12: 7-38}
39. Discourse On Way, Vine, Comforter {John 14: 15-16}
40. Prayer of Jesus {John 17}

MOUNT OF OLIVES

30. Destruction of Temple & End of the World {Matt. 24: 1-51}
31. Parable of 10 Vergins {Matt. 25: 1-13}
32. Parable of 10 Talents {Matt. 25: 14-30}
33. The Last Judgement {Matt. 25: 31-46}
34. Return To Bethany

BETHANY

1. Jesus At Bethany {John 12: 1}
2. Annointed By Mary {John 12: 2-11}
3. Sent For Ass {Matt. 21: 1-7}
4. Rode Donkey To Jerusalem
8. Returned To Jerusalem {Mark 11: 11}
9. Journeyed To Jerusalem {Mark 11: 12}
10. Cursed the Fig Tree {Mark 11: 12-14}
13. Returned From Jerusalem {Matt. 21: 17}
14. Fig Tree Withered {Mark 11: 20-26-14}
15. Journeyed To Jerusalem {Mark 11: 20}
35. Returned From Olivet
36. Sent Peter & John To Prepare Passover {Matt. 26: 17-19} Thurs?
37. Went In Evening To Jerusalem To Passover Supper {Mark 14: 16-17}
41. Peter's Boldness {Matt. 26: 33-35}
42. Went To Gethsemane {John 18: 1}
46. Taken Before Annas {John 18: 13-15} Fri? 1-3AM
47. Taken Before Caiaphas {John 18: 19-24}
48. Taken Before Sanhedrin {Matt. 26: 59-66}
49. Denials of Peter {Matt. 26: 69-75}
50. Condemnation By Sanhedrin {Luke 22: 66-71}
51. Taken Before Pontius Pilate {Luke 23: 1-5}
52. Taken Before Herod {Luke 23: 6-12}
53. Condemned & Scourged {Luke 26: 13-25}
54. Crucifixion {Luke 23: 26-38} 9AM
55. Death of Jesus {Luke 23: 45-49} 3PM
56. Jesus Is Burred {Luke 23: 50-56} at 3-6PM

ISRAEL WITH THE WEST BANK, GAZA STRIP, GOLAN HEIGHTS
National capital
District (meḫoz) centre
City, town
Airport
International boundary
Boundary of former Palestine Mandate
Armistice Demarcation Line
District (meḫoz) boundary
Main road
Secondary road
Railroad
Oil pipeline
LEBANON
UNIFIL
UNDOF
SYRIA
Tyre
Qiryat Shemona
Al Qunayṭirah
GOLAN
Nahariyya
'Akko
Lake Tiberias
Tiberias
Haifa
Nazareth
'Afula
HAIFA
Dar'ā
Irbid
Hadera
Netanya
Ṭūlkarm
Jordan
Jarash
Nābulus
Herzliyya
TEL AVIV
Az Zarqā'
Tel Aviv-Yafo
WEST BANK
Bat Yam
Rām Allāh
Amman
Ramla
Jericho
Ashdod
Jerusalem
Mādabā
Ashqelon
JERUSALEM
Bethlehem
MEDITERRANEAN SEA
Qiryat Gat
Dead Sea
Gaza
JORDAN
GAZA
Hebron
Khān Yūnis
Beersheba
Al Qaṭrānah
Al Arīsh
Ak Karak
Zefa'
Bi'r Lahfān
Dimona
Aṣ Ṣāfī
Abū 'Ujaylah
Zin
'Ayn al Quṣaymah
NEGEV
Mizpe Ramon
Bi'r Ḩasanah
Ma'ān
EGYPT
Ra's an Naqb
SINAI
Al Kuntillah
Yotvata
An Nakhl
0 10 20 30 40 50 60 km
0 10 20 30 40 mi
Elat
Ṭābā
Al 'Aqabah

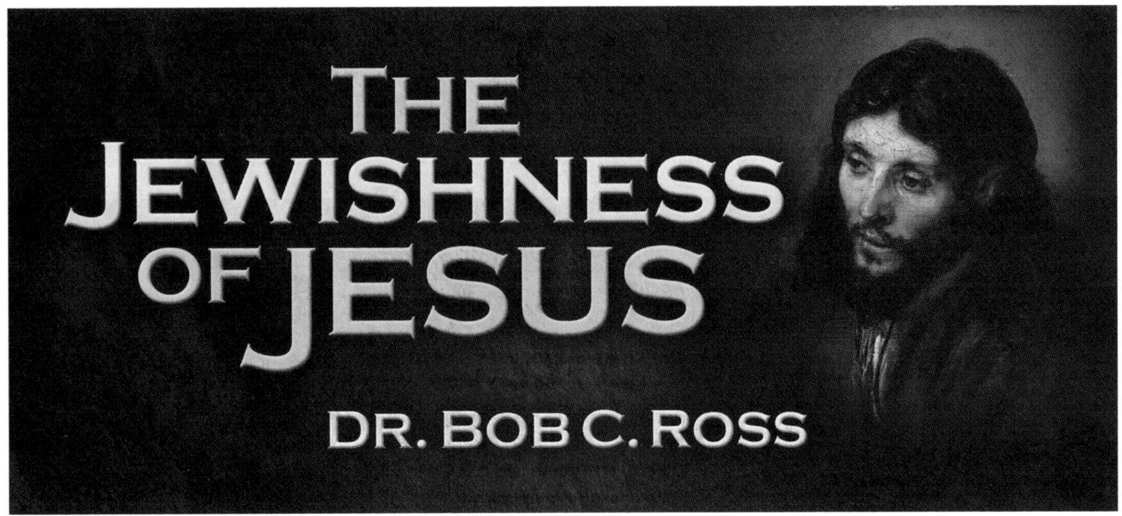

EXPERIENCE THIS INSPIRING BOOK WITH STUNNING PHOTOGRAPHS AS WELL AS THE EBOOK WITH EXCITING VIDEO LINKS.

A comprehensive study of the life and Jewish heritage of Jesus.

The Jewishness of Jesus interprets His life and ministry through the First Century Jewish contextual lens of His heritage and background.

Visit The *Jewishness of Jesus* on Facebook and watch the exciting video! You will get a preview of the book and learn why our refreshing approach and interpretation of Jesus' life and ministry is so important for Christians and Jews.

www.JewishnessofJesus.com

TO BE PUBLISHED IN 2015

PHOTOGRAPHY and MAP ACKNOWLEDGMENTS

Bob Ross' Discover Israel Archives: Front cover; Title page; Dedication page a,b; Pages 6, 9b, 10a, 11a,b, 12, 13a, 14a,b,c,d, 15a,b,c,d,e,f, 16a,b,c,d,e (d,e Citadel Museum), 17a,b (Citadel Museum), 21b, 22a,b,c, 23a,c, 24a,b,c, 25b,26, 27a,b, 28b, 29a,b, 30a,b,c, 31a,b,c, 32a,b, 33b, 34a,b, 35a (Israel Dept. of Tourism sign), 37a,b,c, 38a, 39a,b, 40a,b (b, Megiddo Museum), 41b, 42a,b, 43a,b, 44a,b,c,d, 46b, 47a, 48a,b, 49b,c, 50a,b,c, 51a,b, 52b, 54b, 55b, 56, 57a, 58a,b, 59a,b, 60a,b,c, 61a,b,c, 62b, 63a, 64a, 65, 66, 67b, 68b, 70a, 71a,b,c, 72a,b, 73a,b, c (picture of back cover, *Will the Real Jesus Please Stand by Vendyl Jones),* 74a, 75a, 76a,b,c, 77a (unknown)b,c, 78a,b, 80a, 81a,b,c (Citadel Museum), 82a (Davidson Excavations) b, 84b,c, 86a,b, 87a,b, 88a,b, 89a (King David's City), b,c, 90a (Citadel Museum) b,c, 91, 92a, 93a, 94c, 95a,b, 96b, 97a,b,c,d,e, 98a,b, 99a,b, 100c, 101a,b, 102c (Citadel Museum), 103a,b,c, 104a,b,c, 105a, 106c, 107a,b (Topographical map of Jerusalem, Vendyl Jones), 108b, 109a, 110b,c, 111b,c, 112a, 113a, 114a,b,c, 115a,b, 116a,b, 117a,b, 118b, 119a, 120a, 121a,b, 122a,b, 123a, 124a, 128a,b,c,d,e,f,g,h, 130a,b,c, 131a, 132b,d, 133a,b,c,d, 134b,c,d (unknown source), 135a,b,c, 136a,b,c,d, 137a/b,d,e,f, 138a,b,c, 140b, 141b, 142b, 147b (unknown), 150b, 152a,b (unknown), 155a, 156a (unknown), 164b, 165, 170b,d,e, 171a,b,c, 172a,b,c,d, 173a,b,c,d, 174a,b,c, 175c, 177a, 178b,d, 182, 183, 184 (information and layout), 186 (unknown), 188 (National Newspaper Snapshot Contest Award, 1960), 189, Back cover b,c.

We thank Wikipedia for numerous photographs and accompanying sub-title information. These have greatly enhanced the production of ***Discover Israel***.

Wikipedia: Pages 7, 8, 9a, 10b, 13b, 17c, 18a,b,c,d,e,f,g,h, 20, 23b, 24b, 33a, 36a, 41a, 45, 46, 49a, 53a,b,c, 55a, 63b,c, 67a, 68a, 69, 79, 83a,b, 84a, 85a,b, 92b, 93b, 94a,b,d, 95b,c, 96a, 98c, 100a,b, 101c, 102a,b, 103d, 105b, 106a,b, 108a, 109b, 110a, 111a, 112b, 113b, 118b, 119b, 120b, 121c, 123b, 125a,b, 127, 128i, 129, 130d, 131b, 132a,c, 134a, 135d, 137c, 139, 140a, 141b, 142a,c, 143a,b,c, 144a,b, 145a,b, 146a,b,c, 147a, 149a,b, 150a, 151a, 154a, 155c, 156b, 157, 158a,b, 159a,b,c,160a,b,c, 161a,b, 162a,b, 163a,b, 164a, 166, 167a,b, 168, 169 map, 176a,b, 179 map, 187, Back cover a.

Map Imaging and Digital Illustrations – Craig Lundie - Adquest Creative: 18 (7 image montage), 19, 20 (modified), 21a, 25a, 28a, 36b, 38b, 46a, 47b, 52a, 54a, 57b, 64b, 70b, 74b, 75b, 80b, 119b, 121c, 126, 131c, 134b (design), 135a (design), 146b,c, 154b, (design), 169 (modified), 175b, 177c, 179 (modified), 180–181 (Moody Atlas, modified), 182, 183, 184, 185, 186 (*An Atlas of the Life of Christ*, John Stirling, Revell Co.), 187, 190 (montage with Michael Angelo's Image of Jesus), Back cover c (imaging and design).

Norma Parrish Archbold, *The Mountains of Israel:* 144a, 144c, 148a
Moshe Atiya: 57a (Atiya Productions at Holyland Christian Maps)
Dr. Ian Barnes, *The Historical Atlas of The Bible:* 121c
Barry Beitzel, *Moody Atlas of the Bible Lands:* 180, 181
Dr. Richard Cleave: 30b,d, 124, 155b (modified)
Dr. Gary Crossland, *Merged Gospels*: 170a,c, 175a, 177b
Frontpagemagazine.com, by **Citizen's Warrior**, June 6, 2011: 148b
Vendyl Jones, *Will the Real Jesus Please Stand*–back cover, 73c; Jerusalem Topo Map–107b
Mendel Nun, *The Sea of Galilee and Its Fishermen in the New Testament:* 30c
Dr. Randy Ross, *Remarkable – the Book*: 178c
John Stirling, *An Atlas of the Life of Christ:* 186
Ed and Norma Leavitt, *Bronze of Samson:* 118

Fish nets drying after a storm at the Sea of Galilee

Front & Back Cover Photograph: Bob Ross
Spine Photography: Bob Ross
Cover Art: Craig Lundie

PHOTOGRAPHY CREDITS

Many of the photographs in this book are from the photographic archives of Bob C. Ross, Discover Israel Ministries, P.O. Box 866022, Plano, TX 75086
Great care has been taken to cite all sources whenever known.
If we have inadvertently failed to mention a source please call it to our attention, and amendments will be made in the following edition.
We shall also be grateful for pointing out any errors, omissions or incomplete information.
Please address comments to:

DISCOVER ISRAEL MINISTRIES
PO BOX 866022 • Plano, TX 75086

www.discoverisraelministries.com

INDEX OF PLACE NAMES

Geographic Areas in Blue • Maps and Events in Brown

"TOUR" OF JERUSALEM BY SECTORS

Sectors in Blue

JERUSALEM OVERVIEW 80-82

CPSIA information can be obtained
at www.ICGtesting.com
Printed in the USA
LVIC04n1743220215
427539LV00001BI/1